Life Transitions in America

Life Transitions in America

FRANCESCO DUINA

polity

First published in 2014 by Polity Press

Polity Press
65 Bridge Street
Cambridge CB2 1UR, UK

Polity Press
350 Main Street
Malden, MA 02148, USA

ISBN-13: 978-0-7456-7061-4
ISBN-13: 978-0-7456-7062-1(pb)

A catalogue record for this book is available from the British Library.

Typeset in 11 on 13 pt Scala by
Servis Filmsetting Ltd, Stockport, Cheshire
Printed and bound in Great Britain by Clays Ltd, St Ives plc

For further information on Polity, visit our website: www.politybooks.com

Contents

Figures and Tables

Figures

Tables

Acknowledgments

This book benefited greatly from the suggestions of a number of academics and experts in various fields of sociology, including the life course, culture, demography, gender, and health. Jonathan Eastwood (Washington and Lee University), Liah Greenfeld (Boston University), Roberta Strippoli (SUNY Binghamton), Tim Marjoribanks (LaTrobe University, Australia), and John Glenn (US Global Leadership Coalition) shared with me valuable ideas about the overall direction of this project, the text, and life transitions in different countries. My comparative perspective was further enhanced in 2012 when I visited McGill University in Montreal, Canada, to discuss this book with leading sociologists and demographers. There, Professors Shelley Clark, John Hall, Céline Le Bourdais, Michael Smith, and Elaine Weiner offered substantive and methodological insights. My time at the McGill Community for Lifelong Learning with former president Pat Steele and current president Colin Hudson also proved very fruitful.

I wrote several of this book's chapters while on sabbatical from Bates College (an American small Liberal arts college in Maine, where I taught from 2000 to 2013) in 2012. The College also supported me with funding for research, which allowed me to hire Kevin Regan during his senior year at Bates: his help was invaluable, and this book owes much to him. My departmental colleagues – Professors Emily Kane, Heidi Taylor, and Sawyer Sylvester – proved themselves, as always, unfailingly supportive and helpful. I was able to present my research on this project at two departmental research lunches in 2011 and 2012, where many of our majors were present. Bates, and its Sociology Department in particular, is lucky to have such inquisitive and intelligent undergraduates on campus. Their questions and reflections helped me refine several of my claims. I joined the University of British Columbia in 2013. Immediately upon my arrival, I received generous financial support to review the proofs of the book and benefited from a supportive intellectual environment.

At Polity Press, Jonathan Skerrett once again embodied all the qualities that authors wish all editors could have: a keen intellect, a deep understanding of the material at hand, vision and the ability to offer constructive criticisms, and total reliability and clarity. Ian Tuttle copy-edited the manuscript with attention and precision. Four anonymous reviewers, in turn, greatly helped me improve the book. They were at once supportive and able to offer profoundly useful suggestions for changes. What follows owes much to them as well.

Finally, I would like to thank my wife Angela and our two children Sofia and Luca. In many ways, I wrote this book with them in mind: life is full of transitions, and many of these have to do with family. Yet, writing this book meant spending endless hours away from them. They never objected and instead supported me with a positive and loving spirit throughout.

Part I
Introduction

1 Discourse and Transitions in Life

Transitions are an important part of life. We start experiencing them at a very early age – we begin kindergarten, or join and then leave a summer camp – and continue to do so as we grow into adults and old age. Transitions provide texture to our lives. They are also moments of potentiality and definition. Something comes to an end, and something new presents itself to us. In some cases, the "new" is already somewhat defined or will give us only a few chances to pause and think: we have gotten a new job or our first child is born, for example. In other cases, the "new" is rather fuzzy at best and quite often allows us time for reflection. Something that took up much of our energy and attention is suddenly over. We have purchased our first home, obtained our divorce, run the marathon, or finished our college thesis.

In all of these moments, an apparently innocuous but in fact challenging and often frightening question presents itself to us: *What's next?* With the force and logic that propelled us forward to this point now less relevant, we stare at what is in front of us and wonder what, exactly, should happen now. We sense the infinity before us. Some of us decide that we cannot afford to think for too long and are eager to come to some sort of resolution. Others begin to feel depressed. And still others rejoice and savor the opportunity to craft their future. Reflecting on the past, we wonder about its possible connections to whatever our next steps might be. Are we progressing toward something? Are we leaving the past behind once and for all? Are we alone? We feel time going by, the pulse of life itself. These are some of the most defining moments in our lives.

This book explores the *dominant discourse* on life transitions in America: the "ensemble of ideas" and "concepts," to use the words of prominent Dutch political scientist Maarten Hajier, which are constantly articulated in the media, the statements of leading figures, the majority opinions in survey polls, the stances found in the policies and programs of powerful organizations, movies, leading websites and blogs, greeting cards, and other elements of what we may call public culture, and which give "meaning"[1] to those transitions and, in fact, as social theorist Anthony Giddens sees it, help us make sense of and organize in practice those transitions.[2] What common language and themes do we encounter? What interpretations and recommendations are consistently being put forth? How are we told to think about and make use of transitions?

The analysis will reveal that there are two primary approaches to transitions in the American dominant discourse – what I call *New Beginnings* and *Continuity with Others*. The first approach emphasizes newness, openness, and personal recreation. Transitions are depicted as opportunities for self-improvement and self-transformation, as points of departure and instances where we should capitalize on the change before us to create something new. Even negative transitions are cast in this light. This is an optimistic, energizing, almost aggressive interpretation of transitions. The second approach emphasizes the cycle of life, our connection to others, and predictability. The emphasis here is on the natural order of things, tranquility, even inevitability. It is a more accepting interpretation. Both approaches have deep roots in American history and culture. They stand, as well, in sharp contrast to each other, but are also complementary. The logic and flavor of one helps us appreciate the logic and flavor of the other. Both deserve careful unpacking and understanding.

A major impetus for writing this book was how prominently transitions figure in the lives of many Americans. Americans think about them a lot and conceptualize many moments in life as transitions. Transitions are at the *forefront* of our collective preoccupations: they are a constant subject of conversation among friends, family members, and colleagues. We worry about them, take them very seriously, and subject them to consideration and analysis. We can see clear signs of this preoccupation by browsing through the sections and books of American traditional and virtual bookstores. If we look at the Self-Help or Self-Improvement sections – themselves typically very large relative to the rest of the holdings – we quickly notice that a great number of books are related to managing specific life transitions: the teenage years, young adulthood, getting married, becoming fit, becoming parents, addiction and recovery, surviving break-ups of personal relationships, aging, retiring, and so on. Entire sub-sections of barnesandnoble.com are devoted to these transitions.

Under "Aging" alone we find over 4,500 books. "Divorce" has over 1,500 titles, and "Addictions & Recovery" has around 2,900 books. On amazon.com, we find an entire sub-section labeled "Personal Transformation," with a total of 35,521 books.[3]

These are impressive numbers, and they become all the more so when we consider the categorizations and books found in book-stores in other countries. amazon.com has over the years built major sites dedicated to the Italian, French, and Spanish markets. What do we find there? On the Italian site, there is no dedicated section for Self-Help or Self-Improvement. Under the many sections that do exist, none is devoted to any major transition. The same applies to the French site. Only under the Spanish site do we find, under the section *Salud, familia y desarrollo personal* (Health, family, and personal development) a sub-section called *Desarrollo personal y autoayuda* (Personal development and self-help). No further categorization is given, however, and the viewer has to search by typing keywords for specific transitions. Even then, the number of results is quite small, with *Divorcio* (Divorce), for instance, generating only 343 titles (as compared to 17,950 on the American site), and *Jubilación* (Retirement) yielding only 100 titles (against 15,712 available on the American site).[4]

Tellingly, some of these differences in categorization can also be seen on the amazon.com site dedicated to the United Kingdom market, even though here one presumably can find most of the books that are available on the American site. Specifically, there is no section for Self-Help or Self-Improvement. "Self-Help" appears only as a sub-section of Health, Family & Lifestyle, but under its space we find no sub-sub-sections for life transitions (we do find, by contrast, books under "Memory Improvement," "Stress Management," and other such topics).[5] Sub-sub-sections on topics such as divorce or father-hood do exist, but, interestingly, are found in a different sub-section of Health, Family & Lifestyle that is less directly related to change and transformation in one's life ("Families & Parents"). All this strongly suggests that Americans are interested in, and devour a huge number of, books on how to manage their lives and change.[6]

Evidence of our preoccupation with transitions is found, as well, in the thriving industry of personal coaching. According to a 2007 PricewaterhouseCoopers study, the United States accounts for 50 percent of the US$1.5 billion global coaching industry. Of those US$750 million, a third is directly generated by "life coaches," many of whom can be assumed to focus on transitions.[7] In the United

States, a huge number of organizations and companies offer workshops, seminars, and speakers specifically on managing transitions
in life – from overcoming grief from personal losses to coming back
to civilian life after military service. One can hire specialized personal
coaches to deal with particular transitions: "certified career coaches,"[8]
"divorce coaches,"[9] "family transition coaches," "empty nest transition
coaches,"[10] "retirement coaches," and more. And, to match the need
for coaches, a whole other set of companies produces those coaches
with certificate-awarding programs, training kits, seminars, and so
on.[11] There is nothing to parallel this sort of activity in European or
Asian countries. As two scholars of the life course put it,

> contemporary U.S. society is replete with organizations and bureaucra-
> cies devoted to telling people how to *do* biography . . . Mass-market books
> and magazines provide instructions on the pace and timing of falling in
> love, finding a mate, ending a relationship, kicking a habit, downsizing an
> addiction, preparing to retire, and getting ready to die.[12]

Survey data from the General Social Survey[13] makes clear, as well,
how much Americans value certain transitions as important for the
proper unfolding of one's life. The majority of Americans believe
strongly, for instance, that young people should move out of their
parents' homes if they are to function as adults,[14] and nearly all
Americans believe that those same people should obtain a full-time
job.[15] A strong majority believes, in turn, in the continuing importance of having children for a life well lived,[16] while, according to the
World Values Survey,[17] Americans are almost unique in the developed world for their widespread belief that getting married remains
a valuable thing to do.[18] At the same time, many Americans also find
themselves worried about experiencing unpleasant transitions, with
almost half of all Americans, for instance, fearing to one extent or
another losing their job,[19] while many find themselves experiencing
major transitions in their lives, such as moving home.[20] All this suggests that transitions are squarely on the minds of many Americans.
We worry about them and spend considerable resources going
through them and thinking about how to manage them best.

   In light of this, this book examines the dominant discourse in
America on life transitions. In the next section, I situate the book in
the existing scholarly literature, specify its methodology, and offer
a synopsis of the findings. Before proceeding, however, two important clarifications are in order. First, the dominant discourse on any
given transition at times exhibits major variations that reflect the

existence of different age, gender, religious, class, and other factors in American society. There surely exists, for instance, a clear dominant discourse on having the first child; at the same time, that discourse takes on at least two variations, depending on whether the perceived audience is women or men. Whenever possible, I take time to highlight and examine those variations.

Second, nowhere in this book do I assume that the presence of a dominant discourse defines how every individual feels about transitions in life. Race, class, educational level, religion, gender, and occupation, among other variables, affect how each person interacts with transitions and the dominant discourse itself. Individuals know (consciously and subconsciously) and actively relate to the broader culture surrounding them, as Giddens and other theorists such as Karen Cerulo and Ann Swidler have argued, and such "agency" is indeed a key characteristic of modernity.[21] I acknowledge this important fact at various points in the book, and discuss existing alternative perspectives when particularly interesting (for instance, when they are embraced by significant numbers of individuals or have received considerable attention by the public media; the recent countermovement rejecting altogether the widely promoted idea that young persons should go to college offers an example). At the same time, it is worth remembering that the dominant discourse on transitions – like the dominant discourse on any subject matter – reaches millions of Americans every day and, in one way or another, is something that either shapes and informs their thinking or, at the very least, must be contended with. The dominant discourse is powerful, and thus needs to be analyzed and understood.

The Scholarly Context, Methodology, and Findings of this Book

How much do we know about transitions? What has recent research revealed about the nature of transitions? Sociologists and psychologists have devoted considerable attention to what they call "life transitions." The sociology of life transitions is an established field of study, falling within the larger subject area known as "life course" sociology. Its main approach may be defined as *structural*. Recognizing that individuals face multiple major transitions in life, sociologists shed light on two related dynamics. First, transitions do not happen in a vacuum but are "embedded in," or belong to, larger systems or processes: they are products of social structures.[22] We retire, for instance, because social security regulations entitle us to funds once we reach a certain age and because we are now labeled as "senior citizens" by local and state laws, associations, retailers, and others. Second, individuals in society belong to different groups or sections of society – ethnic, economic, educational, gender, generational, and so on. These differences, which are also structural, shape in profound ways the sorts of transitions individuals face.[23] Children of wealthy or well-educated parents, for instance, are more likely to go to college than children of poorer or less educated parents; this also means that the empty nest syndrome, which is typically brought about by children heading off to college, is more likely to be experienced by wealthier parents.

Psychologists, in turn, have tended to focus on the mind at the *individual* level as the unit of analysis: how does the mind work when faced with transitions? What steps does a person take, for example, when thinking about the future? What sorts of emotions do individuals feel when thinking about the past and contemplating what lies ahead?[24] Here, the underlying assumption is that our minds are essentially biological or physical entities, physiologically wired to operate in certain ways. The objective of the psychologist is to discover how the "mind" – that of mothers after they give birth, for instance, or of soldiers coming back from war – operates when facing particular challenges or situations associated with transitions. Psychologists look for patterns, to be sure, but only as reflective of the workings of the human mind as a thing in itself, as operating according to its own internal logic and rules.[25]

These are all praiseworthy investigations. Yet, in most cases they fail to consider one of the most salient aspects of transitions: how do we, as *cultural beings*, make sense of transitions? I am not referring here to any one transition (giving birth, for instance, or retiring), since there certainly exist sociological (and some psychological) studies on culture and our approach to particular transitions and, indeed, I will leverage those studies throughout this book.[26] I am instead referring to most, if not all, transitions. What basic, shared perspectives and values do we use to approach transitions, whatever those happen to be? How do we, as members of our society, tend to conceive of the possibilities and challenges that transitions present to us? How are we inclined to describe that which has ended, closure and completion, and our relationship to what "has been"? How do we relate to the future, potentialities, responsibilities, fulfillment, and direction, as they present themselves in transitions? What is our fundamental approach to transitions? We still need to unveil the cultural material that is available to us as individuals to conceptualize and make sense of "what is next?" – whatever the transition might be.

Anthropologist Clifford Geertz famously defined culture as something that can "communicate, perpetuate, and develop . . . knowledge about and attitudes towards life."[27] A more specific definition may make reference to widely shared cognitive paradigms, assumptions and belief systems, structures of thoughts, values, and ways in which we almost automatically make connections between observations and experiences.[28] For the purposes of this book, we can think of culture as commonly available, partial or complete, answers to life's various questions, challenges, and puzzles. Culture offers members of society tools for making sense of the world around them, for interpreting and ordering it. In this book, I want to understand the cultural material that is available in American society to make sense of transitions in life. As already noted, I am not aiming for an exhaustive and comprehensive understanding of all relevant cultural material. This would be an impossible task: there exist too many threads, variations, and perspectives. I therefore have a more targeted objective: to identify the *most common and mainstream viewpoints about transitions that we, as members of our society, are routinely exposed to and which inform to varying degrees and in various ways our outlooks.*

There is no single guidebook for readily identifying dominant discourses in any given society, and indeed the issue is subject to considerable academic debate.[29] My approach in this book is to identify and then examine (in light of the eight transitions and five guiding questions which I specify below) a wide variety of sources and data points which at once reflect and contribute to the making of our most common and mainstream viewpoints – our dominant discourse about transitions. Those sources and data points include:

- popular books (self-help, religious, etc.) on transitions
- statements and written comments made by prominent individuals in society such as business leaders, politicians, professional athletes, coaches, etc.
- materials (guides, brochures, etc.) that schools, hospitals, insurance and financial companies, and other organizations make available to their audiences and customers
- religious materials (brochures, sermons, etc.)
- popular movies and television and radio shows
- government laws and policies (and the related debates) about a great variety of issues (such as parenting or marriage)

- the policies, statements, and programs of organizations such as colleges, hospitals, and professional associations
- advertisements and marketing materials (for college degrees, for instance, or retirement)
- popular websites and blogs
- majority opinions in national surveys such as the General Social Survey, the World Values Survey, and the United States Census
- reports from representative focus groups, personal interviews, and surveys conducted by academic researchers and think tanks.

To the extent that existing academic works analyze any of these sources and data points, and explore how they relate to the dominant discourse on any given transition, I incorporate those works into my account.[30]

Importantly, throughout, I also consider data on large- and small-scale trends in our society (such as marriage rates, unemployment figures, or college attendance rates) to provide more context for the findings that emerge from the analysis. That data will come from many research and policy organizations such as the Pew Research Center, the Organization for Economic Co-operation and Development, various United States government agencies and organizations (for instance, the National Center for Health Statistics), and specialized research centers (such as the Higher Education Institute at UCLA). For reference purposes, I identify in the Appendix the major sources I consulted for each transition.

Our attention will go to eight major transitions in life. I selected these transitions for a number of related reasons. First, most of us are likely to experience most of these transitions and to be familiar with all of them. Indeed, all of the transitions are prominent in American society: many of them are considered milestones, most of them preoccupy us intensely at one point or another, virtually all of them are the subject of many self-help books and visits to counselors and psychologists, most are the primary concern of entire organizations and associations, and at least a few appear in one form or another in popular movies, folk tales, and religious stories and rituals. All this makes the selected transitions inherently important and therefore interesting.

Second, these transitions by and large happen at different points in our lifetime (the exceptions are surviving a life-threatening disease, which can happen at any time, and losing a job, though this can only happen in adulthood): they are "spread out" and thus "belong" in our minds to different phases of life. If we are looking for patterns in our discourse about life transitions, it seems wise to consider the entire life course.

Third, the eight transitions are quite different from each other – something that will make the analysis challenging but also more convincing in terms of overall conclusions. Some of the transitions are clearly positive (getting married, for example), while others are typically seen as negative or, at the very least, problematic in the first instance (losing a job, for example, or the death of our parents). The transitions also concern very different, and perhaps the most important, areas of our lives, with some of the transitions touching on more than one of these areas at once: family, work, and health.

These are the eight transitions, presented and examined in the book in approximate chronological order:

1. Starting college
2. Getting married
3. The first child
4. Losing a job
5. Surviving a life-threatening disease
6. Divorce
7. Parents' death
8. Retirement

Of course, other major transitions could have certainly been considered: graduating from college, menopause, the empty-nest phase, and the death of a close relative other than parents come especially to mind. Limitations of space and of resources available for research made a full consideration of these transitions impossible. I will turn to them, however, in more succinct fashion in the last chapter of the book.

To structure the investigation, I propose that most, if not all, transitions in life (including the eight selected transitions) present us with five basic questions and that, for each transition, the dominant discourse in our society is likely to articulate one primary answer for each of those questions. When we look at those answers across all transitions – as we find them expressed repeatedly and consistently in the sources and data points mentioned above – we observe a certain pattern which is likely to be unique to our cultural context.

Here are the five questions:

1. Origins: Who initiates the transition?
2. The self: What opportunities does the transition give to us for our personal development?

3. The past: What are we leaving behind?
4. The future: What will the future bring to us?
5. The actors: Whom does the transition concern?

Let us reflect for a moment on each of these five questions.

The first question that all transitions present to us concerns the **origins** of what is about to happen. Does the transition reflect our internal volition and desires, or is it, by contrast, the product of greater forces that are beyond our control? In popular books, the claims of public leaders, popular movies and songs, and so on, we may be depicted as the initial cause of the transition: we may be seen as responsible for bringing about the changes before us. Something that we did or have omitted to do has brought the transition about. On the other hand, the transition may be described as something that is happening to us – as an occurrence in which we find ourselves – because of the nature of human life, society, the unfolding of things, and so on. We can distinguish here between the *internal and external origins* of any given transition. Each perspective comes with potential implications for our perceived responsibilities and duties toward the transition, our place in the world, and how life unfolds. It also has implications for how the other dimensions of the transition (the self or the future, for instance) are interpreted.

As to the **self**, transitions inevitably involve the introduction of change into our personal lives. The question is how those changes are portrayed in the dominant discourse. One critical dimension is whether transitions are presented as opportunities for *the reinvention or the refining of our selves*. Are transitions described as chances to bring about a new "self" or the solidification of the current "self"? Is the survival of a life-threatening disease, for instance, or the changing of careers seen as an opportunity to usher in a rather different self? Is getting married perceived to be the chance to solidify our personas as the committed lovers of our partners? Each option – "reinvention" or "refinement" – demands further specification. How, exactly, are cancer survivors, for instance, to reinvent themselves, if that is indeed the vision in our discourse? Throughout, as with all other aspects of the discourse, we must be sensitive to the fact that the discourse may be multifaceted – that it may vary in some regards as it applies to individuals of different ages, genders, classes, or races.

As to the **past**, transitions necessarily involve time and, in particular, a movement away from things that have already happened. Transitions relegate something to the past; something is indeed forever gone. When we transition from childhood to adolescence, we leave childhood behind. When our parents pass away, they and the time we had with them are no longer there. In life there is always a past, of course. But this relegation may take different forms. One critical difference is between the *dismissal versus incorporation of the past into our lives*. So, to return to our parents dying, for instance, are we to keep them with us in our memory and spirits as we transition to a life without them in a physical sense? If so, how exactly should this be accomplished? Or are we simply to turn away from them and forge ahead in our lives as if they had not existed or have become completely irrelevant? If so, how is that dismissal conceptualized, exactly? When we retire, should we think of the past (our workplace, our former colleagues, etc.) as something that we should not dwell on any longer or as something of importance for our future? We are interested in what our dominant discourse has to say about the past.

Transitions naturally involve the **future**. In some ways, they are foremost about the road ahead of us. But how is that future conceptualized? One critical question is whether in our dominant discourse the future is depicted as a *tabula rasa*, an empty canvas, or, by contrast, as something that is fundamentally bounded and limited. Is the new phase in our life presenting us with multiple potential outcomes, catapulting us into an amorphous space that will demand from us active shaping? Will we have choices before us? Conceiving of ourselves for a moment as sculptors, will the future come to us as a block of marble that contains nearly infinite possibilities? Career changes come to mind here. Or, by contrast, will transitions present to us a future that is already confined and defined, in such a way perhaps that its contours are precisely what is interesting and exciting? Here the question is about an *open-ended versus a well-defined future*.

The fifth question concerns the **actors** involved in the transition. Whom is the transition about? The key issue here is whether in our dominant discourse a single, individual person is portrayed as the central protagonist of the transition, or whether more persons – family members, the broader community, the world as a whole – are perceived to be integral parts. In some societies, for example, retirement is seen as affecting not only the concerned individual but also their children and extended families; in other societies, it is primarily seen as a personal matter involving one single individual. In almost all cases, the actor or actors are given roles. The transition takes on the flavor of a ritual or a rite of passage: the actor or actors have an audience – often an active one. The transition is a dynamic, social occurrence. It is also typically steeped in tradition and established understandings: it belongs clearly to a larger context of symbols and meanings. What does our discourse say on this front? Who is involved, and in what roles? The question here is about transitions being about us *as individuals or us as parts of a larger whole.*

What will our analysis reveal about our dominant discourse on transitions? Two caveats are in order before we review the findings. First, as already noted, the dominant discourse itself, though in most cases very cohesive, is often complex and comes with important sub-themes (the discourse on having the first child, for instance, varies when it comes to men and women; the same can be said for the discourse on losing a job for persons in different age groups). I acknowledge and indeed devote considerable energy to understanding such complexity.

Second, the identification, analysis, and synthesis of sources and data points about transitions are not easy tasks. There is also no established scientific procedure for conducting such an analysis. Indeed, this book constitutes the first attempt, to my knowledge, to offer a portrait of the American discourse on transitions. Given all this, readers will not always agree with the picture that I put forth. I wish to be explicit about the fact that I am presenting a well-informed but also initial portrayal – one that should be further refined and improved – of our discourse on transitions.

We can now preview the findings from our analysis in the coming chapters. Table 1.1 maps the eight transitions, the five questions, and the answers that we find in the dominant discourse in American society. The table highlights the fact that those answers, when taken together, reveal two fundamental approaches to transitions – and ultimately time, change, and life itself. Both approaches reflect values and tendencies that have deep roots in American culture and its history.

As we shall see, with *New Beginnings*, transitions are depicted as either being forced upon us by the outside world or as coming from within us. But in all cases they are viewed, to varying extents, as exciting opportunities for the reinvention of the self. Transitions offer us chances to foster a new "us." The past is left behind: it does not concern us any longer, for it does not inform or shape in any meaningful manner our new phase in life. The old self is accordingly left behind and a new self has the opportunity to come forward. In all cases, in turn, the future is depicted as being open: that is, the transition in itself does not come with instructions for what we should be

Table 1.1: Transitions in American Discourse

| | Group I: New Beginnings | | | | | Group II: Continuity with Others | | |
	Starting College	Losing a Job	Divorce	Retiring	Surviving Disease	Getting Married	First Child	Parents' Death
Origins	External	External	External/Internal	Internal	Internal	Internal	Internal	External
Past	Dismissed	Dismissed	Dismissed	Dismissed	Dismissed	Incorporated	Incorporated	Incorporated
Self	Reinvention	Reinvention	Reinvention	Reinvention	Reinvention	Refinement	Refinement	Refinement
Future	Open	Open	Open	Open	Open	Defined	Defined	Open
Actors	Individual	Individual	Individual	Individual	Individual	Collective	Collective	Collective

doing going forward. The slate is blank, and one of the most exciting aspects of the days, months, and years ahead is that they require definition. We are like painters facing an empty canvas: all is in principle possible, and the very act of shaping what is to come will imply the first imposition of limits and a defining expression of our selves. Thus, it is also the case that these are going to be transitions of the individual above all: they do not really involve others, either as protagonists or partners in the transition. The actor in the show is the single person going through the transition. Others may be present, but as spectators, helpers, witnesses, or playing some other secondary role. The analysis suggests that under *New Beginnings* we find transitions that deal with work, health, and certain aspects of family life (separation or severing of some sort). It is also important to underscore here that the discourse around each specific transition has its unique nuances and articulations. Hence, for instance, the openness of the future when it comes to retirement has much to do with enjoyment and the relaxed exploration of one's self and the world after decades of hard work. This is different from the openness teenagers are described as facing when leaving home for college, which, with one's identity at stake for the first time and much of one's personal and professional life still ahead, comes with higher stakes.

The discourse of *New Beginnings* resonates well, or is reflected in, other aspects of our cultural system – such as an appreciation for individualism, originality, and novelty, coupled with a dissatisfaction with the status quo or, at the very least, a desire to always improve one's situation. We will have many occasions to examine this connection through this book. For the moment we can note here that, when we consider the major advanced industrial countries of the world, according to the World Values Survey, Americans are more likely than the French, British, Germans, and Japanese to think of themselves as valuing creativity and thinking up new ideas.[32] Our everyday language is accordingly rich with commonplace expressions such as "It's a new me," "Tomorrow is a new day," "There is always tomorrow," "Makeover," "The first step is always the hardest," "No pain, no gain," "Nothing ventured, nothing gained," "Variety is the spice of life," and "You are never too old to learn" – expressions that we do not find in the same quantity in everyday French, for instance, or Spanish.[33] "We Americans," Mitt Romney stated in his acceptance speech for nomination for President of the United States at the Republican National Convention in August 2012, "have always felt a special kinship with the future."[34] At the same time, Americans are neither particularly satisfied with their lives nor especially happy. On either front, if we consider the percentage of the overall population in a country that reports itself to be satisfied or happy, the United States does not show up on the list of the top ten countries.[34] A longing for change and novelty seems to have a place in the American collective psyche.

Things are quite different under the second group of transitions that appear under *Continuity with Others*. Here, too, in our dominant discourse, the change is depicted as either internally or externally caused. But what really matters is that these transitions are seen as opportunities to refine our selves: rather than recreate those selves, we are called to build on, add on, or further delineate what we already are. This may happen in a variety of ways, such as expressing existing qualities and talents in new ways, or tapping into potentialities that have so far been neglected. The arrival of a first child, for instance, means that we are going to take on the mother or father roles and, in so doing, express our nurturing sides, as well as our skills as mentors, role models, more experienced beings, and so on. All these activities do not amount to a negation or forgetting of our existing selves but rather imply adjustments and growth. It is then also the case that the past is not seen as something that should be dismissed as irrelevant but, instead, as integral to the transitions as they are happening. The past will be taken into account. And while the future is likely to be constrained (but may not be, depending on the transition), it is also clear that "others" play a central role in these sorts of transitions. What is happening to us is not solely about us as single persons but, rather, as integral parts of something bigger. It seems important to note that the transitions which appear in this group in this book are concerned with family life: with the making (getting married, first child) of such life or its unwanted breakdown (death of parents). Transitions in other areas of life are also surely part of this discourse. But what we observe here suggests that the family may be a critical place where our discourse points us toward continuity and our connection to others. And here, too, we notice important variations of this discourse when it comes to specific transitions.

Though this view of transitions is probably less prevalent than the one found in *New Beginnings*, it has nonetheless a place in the broader American cultural system, as we shall see in the coming chapters. We value order and predictability: rules, procedures, steps, and sequences with expected outcomes in fact pretty much guide most of our daily lives. We derive comfort from the absence of risk and the presence of its counterpart, safety, in everything ranging from food to entertainment to where we live.[35] We thus have an appreciation for phases and the fact that life can, in fact, be seen as a series of linked events and even cycles. We are born, grow up, play certain sports in the fall and others in winter and spring, get married and get "settled," buy a house and have kids, work hard and get promoted, see our children leave our homes, downsize, retire, and so on. We share what one might call a "lockstep" mentality that can often provide us with a sense of security. Interestingly, when compared to other countries, including older European and Asian ones, we feel the importance of traditions to a much greater extent.[36] And this appreciation of predictability seems to apply to us as individuals and as a country. Consider for a moment the popular notion that America is somehow destined to be an exceptional country or the world leader, or the earlier concept of Manifest Destiny – all ideas pregnant with determinism and which in so many ways inform our policies and attitudes as a country in the world.

Now, while these two approaches found in our dominant discourse may seem solely contradictory, they are actually quite complementary: precisely because a significant part of our collective psyche is so restless, other elements in us find special pleasure in the reassurance that life, in fact, is going to unfold in a certain way and that we, in the process, are not alone but in fact intimately linked to others. We may also appreciate that such predictability will generate a certain amount of efficiency: for if reinvention comes with risks and probably false starts and errors, time-tested continuity is built in part on having done away with things that do not work.

Thus, ultimately, we will see that the dominant discourse in our society about transitions in life reflects a multiplicity of concerns and tendencies that, together, can be viewed *as an embrace of openness, reinvention, and potentiality coupled with a more subtle appreciation for boundaries, order, and predictability*. In that space we are told to situate our selves, our becoming, and our unfolding. Most of us are surely not aware of this mindset or its internal tensions. But this does not in any way diminish the impact it has on us or the extent to which it guides us. Indeed, in many ways, it functions best when operating without our conscious awareness. We are presented with different pulls, and each approach is made all the more meaningful because it stands in contrast to the other.

These are important reflections, and they acquire even more salience when we think comparatively. Every culture is different.

What would Table 1.1 look like for a European or Asian country? What would it show? We will discuss data from other countries at various turns, but the two most important differences can already be stated here. First, in European and Asian countries, there is a lesser tendency to view transitions as *New Beginnings*. The perspective of continuity with others is more prevalent, albeit certainly for different reasons and with different cultural underpinnings than in the United States. Second, in other cultures there appears to be less of an interest in objectifying transitions as something to be highly conscious of in the first instance. As a result of this, the boundaries between transitions are often less pronounced. There are fewer categorizations and therefore also fewer formal occasions to celebrate transitions: fewer graduation ceremonies, fewer "over the hill" parties, fewer retirement parties, fewer greeting cards for every transition, and so on. Taken together, these differences suggest that the making of the self is less closely wound into conscious participation in numerous, publicly demarcated and discussed transitions than in the United States. This also means, in turn, that transitions preoccupy Americans a great deal because of how they define themselves by them – that they are a cause of much reflection and worry.

The Pages Ahead

Each of the eight chapters ahead focuses on one transition. We will consider each transition in light of the five questions identified earlier in this chapter. How are the origins of the transition, the past, our selves, the future, and the relevant actors depicted in our dominant discourse? As already noted, each chapter draws from a rich variety of sources and data points. Each of the eight chapters on transitions ends with selected information on other countries to put the American mindset in comparative perspective. These brief comparative assessments also rely on a mixture of quantitative and qualitative data sources, academic studies, reports by independent research organizations, and other relevant data.

The major finding will be clear: in the dominant discourse in American society, transitions are portrayed as either moments *of openness, reinvention, and potentiality* or as occasions for the reaffirmation of *boundaries, order, and predictability*. The two approaches have deep cultural roots in our society and ultimately represent one way of dealing with the most difficult puzzles and challenges that life presents to us. The last chapter will revisit these ideas, consider briefly how they may apply to other major transitions not examined in this book, and conclude by reflecting on the possible drivers – including commodification – of the dominant discourse on transitions in the United States.

Part II
Eight Transitions

2 Starting College

Most students in the United States head for college in the fall after graduating from high school. According to the National Center for Education Statistics, in 2009 the figure was 70 percent – a significant increase from 51 percent in 1975.[1] Though there are important differences in rates across categories of Americans (whites or Asians, for instance, or children from wealthier families are more likely to go to college than students from different backgrounds), attending college is a transition that affects well over 50 percent of students in any given major category (race, class, sex, etc.), and one that most parents, regardless of socioeconomic status, want for their children, regardless of their academic performance.[2] For the majority of these students, the transition involves attending a four-year college and moving out of their parents' homes and living on their own – increasingly out of their own state – for the first time.[3] This is by all means a major change in a young person's life.

What is the dominant discourse in American society about going to college? How do teachers, high school and college counselors, and coaches describe it? How do popular books on going to college talk about the transition? What do colleges assert on their websites and in their publicity? How do the majority of students and parents describe the transition when asked in polls and surveys? The focus in this chapter is on students headed to four-year colleges, though many of the observations apply to those students who attend two-year colleges. The discourse is multifaceted, of course, and does not capture accurately the experience of all students. Indeed, as we shall see, some young students altogether reject the idea of going to college. Yet, if we consider our five key questions about origins, self, past, future, and actors, one clear primary narrative emerges.

By and large, in our dominant discourse, going to college is understood to be a socially-imposed coming-of-age transition that involves a major break from what has come before (home life, teenage years, parental influence, established routines, etc.) and the first real opportunity for the self to craft itself in what is an utterly open future (of usually four years). *Indeed, starting college is broadly presented as the first, most explicit and public, opportunity for self definition in one's life.* As such, it is perhaps the primary coming-of-age transition, the chance given to adolescents to create for themselves, with considerable freedom and without obligation toward the past, their identity as adults. Starting college, therefore, illustrates rather well the idea of transitions as *New Beginnings*. At the end of this chapter, we will see that this perspective – which is ultimately an element of a broader cultural context – is quite different from those found in other countries.

The Making of an Adult

The scene takes place millions of times every late summer. With the help of the parents, the child carefully selects some clothes and personal items for the year ahead to make his future home (in most cases a dormitory room) more comfortable. The car will be packed with boxes and suitcases for a one-way trip and the parents will come back home to a much different place. This is a moment that is symbolically rich with meaning, and that is full of projections and visions for the years ahead. How does our dominant discourse make sense of this dramatic change in a young person's life? Let us consider it from the five angles proposed earlier in this book: origins, past, self, future, and actors.

Origins

Most commentators and experts, and much of the public, believe in the importance of going to college. "In the 21st century," President Barack Obama noted in May 2012 when giving a speech at a high school in Virginia, "higher education cannot be a luxury – it is an . . . imperative that every American should be able to afford."[4] In a highly publicized 2011 survey of the United States population by the Pew Research Center, the vast majority of respondents reported thinking that college is either extremely or very important in helping a young person succeed in the world.[5] Ninety-four percent of parents (with virtually no variation across racial, income, or educational groups) expected that at least one of their children will go to college,[6] with most wanting their children to attend a four-year institution.[7] Why such belief in the value of college? What logic is put forth for the necessity of this transition? Two primary reasons are often given: college is a good financial investment, and college fuels the intellectual development of young minds. Both the nature of our economic system and the logic of human development make college a near imperative. In our discourse, then, college is depicted as essentially a must imposed by the outside world and the requirements of healthy personal development. We do not choose to go, but instead recognize the necessity of going.

Importantly, we can state right away that a counter-discourse is currently emerging. Due to the increasing costs of tuition, some economists and others doubt whether the investment is worthwhile in financial terms.[8] With the advent of powerful communications technologies that allow for distance learning and informal sharing of valuable information, some question the intellectual advantages of a college education. A recent posting on a *New York Times* blog,[9] for instance, was dedicated to the ideas of Dale J. Stephens, founder of *UnCollege*. *UnCollege* urges students to "hack" their education and learn via online resources and other venues,[10] and thus promotes a manifesto titled *Replacing College with Self-Directed Learning*.[11] Stephens' ideas are echoed by prominent business and thought leaders such as PayPal co-founder Peter Thiel.[12]

But these dissenting voices surely remain a minority. In the eyes of most commentators, analysts, students, and parents, financial and personal development reasons make going to college a must. On the financial front, as the Higher Education Institute at UCLA and the *Wall Street Journal* respectively report, over 70 percent of all incoming students at four-year institutions[13] and over 60 percent of Americans[14] prize and believe in the financial rewards of attending college. The Pew Research Center survey reported career development as the primary reason for going to college.[15] The logic has multiple dimensions. The most obvious are the widespread notions that jobs require formal training,[16] that education is vital for getting ahead,[17] and that well-paying jobs (usually professional ones) require a college (and usually a graduate) degree of some kind. "More kids than ever are applying to college," writes best-selling author Harry H. Harrison in his popular book on going to college, "because they know that in this computerized, global economy, a bachelor's degree holds the keys to the kingdom."[18] Employers looking for new hires, the logic states, simply do not consider applicants without a degree. A second dimension has to do with building a useful network of friends and acquaintances. That network, the logic goes, can give students the information and resources they will need to find good jobs, provided, of course, that students take steps to cultivate that network with some care.[19] Such thinking gives the transition of going to college a clear meaning: it is a necessary step toward a more successful financial future.

As one would expect, the financial logic can come with variations. For instance, according to a survey of freshmen administered by the Higher Education Institute, first-generation students (who are more likely to be Latinos than any other ethnicity) are more likely to see college as a great opportunity to jump to another level of economic comfort than second- and third-generation college students,[20] many of whom are accustomed to a higher standard of living and are looking to college as one way (among many) to ensure continuity in their situation. Making money, in other words, means something different to different people. The same can undoubtedly be said about networking, with students' wealth levels, family backgrounds, and previous educational experience (elite boarding schools, for instance, versus underfunded large public schools) surely making a difference for how, exactly, such networking can be advantageous.

The developmental logic focuses more on the perceived intellectual potential of the human mind and the need for cultivation and refinement in young adults. College is viewed as the necessary last step for the proper formation of the mind and, ultimately, personality (graduate school in this regard is more about professional formation than intellectual fulfillment; it is not a must for personal completion). Thus, the person who fails to attend college in a sense remains "under-developed:" more could have come from that person. In college we learn to reason, make sense of the world, and speak in an articulate and informed manner. We acquire both analytical and substantive sophistication, and what we learn is intended to serve us for a lifetime. College completes us. Hence, as results from the Pew Research Center survey show, while professional formation remains the top cited reason for going to college, the second reason is "personal" and "intellectual" growth. Among college graduates themselves, the order reverses, with 74 percent saying that their college education was very useful in helping them grow intellectually, 69 percent saying it was very useful in helping them grow as a person, and 55 percent stating that it helped them prepare for a job or career.[21]

The logic is clear: going to college is a transition that we must undertake. We do not initiate it but, rather, the transition presents itself to us as we finish high school. One must go to college, and is to be praised for understanding and acting on this imperative.

Past

Plenty of books seek to advise incoming freshmen on how to navigate through and survive their college years. Virtually all share the same premise: college constitutes a major break from the past. It's about leaving childhood, adolescence, and family life behind, and beginning a radically different phase of life. The rules, logic, expectations, and objectives of this phase are new: they do not grow out of what came before in the students' lives. Consider the opening passages of *The Naked Roommate*, the top-selling book on college life in recent years, a 2011 *New York Times Best Seller*, and now the basis of an entire online community of college students:[22]

> Welcome to the first page, the first day of college, and my tip. There are a lot of firsts happening here – first time away from home, first time living with a stranger, first college class, first college professors, first pages of textbooks, first college hookup, first love, first loss, first time possibly having sex (or not having it), maybe your first pregnancy scare, first sexually transmitted infection (also called sexually transmitted disease), first time seeing people use drugs, first time borrowing thousands of dollars, and first time spending thousands of dollars, first time managing your money, first time having to make choices on your own, first time staying out all night, first time having to make a new life for yourself, and the first time when you can do as much as you want or as little as you want and have no one to answer but you (assuming you don't answer the phone).[23]

The message is clear: students are embarking on a new world that offers very little continuity from what came before. Though many students will of course bring with themselves their attachments and connections from home, the past is not to be folded into the college experience.

Another popular book, *Navigating Your Freshman Year* – a compilation of chapters written by a group of students from a number of very different colleges and universities across the country – delivers a very similar message, this time with the focus on the instructors and relatives that used to populate the students' previous world:

> Everyone has some kind of advice for you as you leave for college. Your parents want to relate their experiences, your grandparents would like to tell you what the real world is like, and your teachers want to talk about

how wonderful higher education is. But your decision about going to college is not about them or their past – it's about you and your future.[24]

College students, this passage asserts, can dismiss what the most important people in their lives until now have to tell them: theirs is old news, they belong to the past. The transition is a break from what has come before.

Thus, with this in mind, many colleges have organized drop-off day for freshmen in ways that sternly communicate to parents and children the clarity of the break from the past. Revealing, in this regard, is a 2010 *New York Times* article about the activities and symbolic steps that happen on that day. At Grinnell College, for example, the farewell ceremony for parents sees everyone in the gymnasium, with students on one side of the bleachers, parents on the other. The "president welcoming the class of 2014 had his back to the parents – a symbolic staging meant to inspire 'an aha! moment,' said Houston Dougharty, vice president of student affairs." Parents describe the day as one in which "you have to just allow yourself to experience the loss and grieve over what's gone," as "dreading" the moment since the "umbilical cord fell off."[25] Other colleges explicitly bar parents from attending the first gathering of the freshman class, while others go a long distance to tell parents that they must now turn around and leave: their kids are moving on to a new, very different phase of their lives, one that represents a new beginning.

At the same time, and not coincidentally, colleges every year in the United States spend enormous resources on "orientation" programs, social networking events with faculty and other students, clubs, and counseling staff to address precisely the problems that logically arise from setting up the college experience as a decisive separation from home and what came before: students' uneasiness about their new lives and their related longing for what they have left behind.[26] Psychologists, who have developed a whole sub-field of study to understand the "home loss" and "grief" experienced by students going to college in the United States, recommend a number of steps to help students "heal" from the separation.[27] While some recommend more frequent visits home, the majority offer students coping strategies that can enable them to adjust to their new environments and effectively create a new life for themselves.

Indeed, to this date, the vast majority of these programs explicitly or implicitly subscribe to the view, widely accepted by college administrators and academics, and articulated in what are widely considered to be two classic publications by Syracuse University's education professor Vincent Tinto, that "the first stage of the college career, separation, requires students to disassociate themselves from membership in the past communities" and that, because "for virtually all students the process is stressful," college must create "public rituals," "ceremonies," and extensive orientation programs early in their first years to help them "overcome separational and transitional difficulties" by ensuring that they find their place in their new communities.[28]

Now, it is interesting to note that, in practice, going to college does not necessarily mean for all students a quick dismissal of the past. Studies show that the sense of separation, and the ensuing anxiety it might cause, are typically stronger for those who move further away from home, for instance. Students living closer to home seem to suffer from fewer problems. Minorities, in turn, report feeling the disconnect between home and college more forcefully. Women as a whole appear less likely to reject their previous communities.[29] But what is interesting about these studies is that they are themselves premised on the belief that a separation is bound to happen, and are designed to document how, in actual life, some students are having difficulties conforming to expectations. The studies themselves echo the vision put forth in the dominant discourse.

Self

What happens to the "self" when we transition to college? Here, two conflicting narratives seem to be at work. On the one hand, the transition is often depicted as being about gradual personal "development." College "fine-tunes" our minds, polishes the way we speak and act, instills in us important knowledge and information that "completes" our intellectual education as competent human beings who are ready to engage in the world as intelligent citizens. In his 2004 Convocation Address welcoming the incoming freshmen, Stanford University President John Hennessy, for instance, reminded his audience of the goals that Leland and Jane Stanford had when establishing the institution: to produce "cultured and useful citizens" – an objective, he added, that Stanford still strives for "more than a century later."[30] From this perspective, becoming cultured does not entail a repudiation of one's past self but, rather, a refinement. We can see the idea of refinement articulated in the mission statements of many colleges. Here are some examples from three very different schools (a small college, a national private university, and a national public university):

> As a teaching and learning community, the College holds that knowledge is a good to be pursued both for its own sake and for the intellectual, moral, and physical well-being of individuals and of society at large. The College aims to graduate women and men who can think clearly, who can speak and write persuasively and even eloquently, who can evaluate critically both their own and others' ideas, who can acquire new knowledge, and who are prepared in life and work to use their knowledge and their abilities to serve the common good.
>
> *– Grinnell College*[31]

> A liberal arts education can give you the capacity to make well-reasoned ethical and aesthetic judgments. It can help you to develop the qualities you need to be an informed and responsible citizen. And most important, through a liberal arts education, you learn how to acquire knowledge and to expand your understanding.
>
> *– Northwestern University (Weinberg College of Arts & Sciences)*[32]

> Our students learn to think rationally, creatively and critically; to communicate clearly, correctly, and persuasively; to gather and interpret data; and to engage the arguments of others with understanding and respect. These skills and intellectual attributes form the foundation for a lifetime of learning and a thriving democracy.
>
> *– University of Washington, Seattle (College of Arts & Sciences)*[33]

These statements point to a gradual change, consistent with the findings from the Pew Research Center's survey of recent graduates, in which the majority described their education as valuable because it helped them "mature."[34] This is a view that at least in part has its roots in the function of universities in Europe in the nineteenth and part of the twentieth century, which was to complete the upbringing of members – men especially – of the upper classes of society.[35]

On the other hand, we are exposed to a very different, and in fact more prominent, view of the self in this transition: college is a time of discovery, of taking "risks" (intellectual but also emotional and psychological ones), of challenging our assumptions, conclusions, prejudices, and beliefs. A key function of college is to transform students from adolescents with limited and often prejudiced worldviews into sophisticated adults with far more expansive horizons: the sign of a successful education is that the person graduating is dramatically different from the person that matriculated years before. On spark notes.com, the educational support website popular among college students for its short study guides on books (started by Harvard students and now owned by Barnes & Noble), we thus read the following in a section explicitly titled *College Identity*. "The first year of college," it states, "is your big chance to focus on those personal qualities you've always wanted to refine," but, in sharp contrast to that, also "to give yourself a whole new identity." It then continues:

> Challenging your thinking is what college is all about. No matter where you're enrolled or what you major in, college will challenge your worldview and personal values on every level, thus transforming your identity.[36]

The idea "identity transformation" is echoed on the website of the University of North Carolina's Campus Health Services and many other virtual spaces like it. A whole section is called *Developing Your College Identity*, and its introduction states that:

> College is an exciting time in a new setting where you can make new friends, learn new things, develop new skills – and create a new identity. While it's important to maintain a sense of consistency with your old self, college is a time when you can also explore which parts of your younger self you want to keep and which parts you want to leave behind. The resources on the right include thoughts on how to do this well.[37]

Going to college, it seems, is almost akin to a shopping experience designed to remake one's wardrobe: students are given a fantastic opportunity to rebuild themselves, this time in the mold of an adult. With this in mind, developmental researchers often argue that college students are "emerging adults" forming a "new and separate" identity.[38] High school seniors themselves anticipate "identity changes," and social scientists talk about the "reconstruction of self" as an integral part of this transition.[39] Psychologists, in turn, talk of college as providing "youth with an institutionalized moratorium, relatively free from adult responsibilities, where they can experiment with various roles, values, and identity images before constructing a stable sense of identity formation."[40]

In, then, comes a child and out goes a complete, freshly constructed human being. Interestingly, this phase of intense change concerns all aspects of the self – from sexual orientation to perceived levels of moral worth to professional identity. As we learn on sparknotes.com:

> A lot of college students don't really know who they are or what they like when they get to college . . . Experimenting with sexuality is common in college. Straight kids of the same sex may get together and gay kids may hook up with the opposite sex, to see what it's like. People figure out who they are regardless of their experiences. You don't have to label yourself.[41]

Research on ethnic identity, in turn, points to students thinking of college as a profound time of discovery and change. One set of scholars writes that "our findings suggest that the transition to college may serve as a consciousness-raising experience that triggers exploration," with the nature of the "changes" being "dramatic" and unprecedented in one's life.[42]

Consistent with this, many colleges make it a policy to force students to take a broader variety of courses than they are inclined to take (through what have traditionally been called "General Education" requirements), and a good percentage do not allow students to declare their majors until their sophomore years, so that they may explore and run into the unexpected. Faculty and administrators consider their mission partly accomplished when students change their course of study from their original intended major to another one. Such events constitute "good" stories – proofs of the effectiveness of a school's program. An integral part of many college programs are thus study abroad semesters and service-oriented activities and trips, which college officials and students like to define as great opportunities for "self-transformation" and "identity change," as, for instance, was done in a 2012 report by two Northwestern University academics reflecting on a service trip to Nicaragua.[43] We should add here that the dismissal of one's old self seems to take place not only among "traditional" (i.e., very recent high school graduates) college students but also for adults who return to college much later in life and even attend local community colleges. This was the finding, for instance, of a recent study of 70 such adults in two New England community colleges.[44]

Importantly, while college provides the tools and environment for transformation, the expectation is that ultimately students themselves must direct the crafting of their new identities. The stimulus for change may come from the outside, but ultimately students must put the tools and information available to them to good use. Indeed, this is precisely part of the transformative process: an externally supported, but ultimately self-directed and introspective, process of change. Hence, as Stanford President Hennessy put it in the same speech where he talked about refinement, a Stanford education is "a once-in-a-lifetime journey," a time of experimenting and taking "intellectual risks," something that has "transformed the lives of so many alumni," but also something that the students themselves must claim and direct: turning to the parents present at the convocation, he reminded them that "it is your children, as individuals, who will choose what excites them, what generates intellectual passion, and what engages their very able minds. I hope that you will support their choices."[45]

Future

College student Katherine Jackson's opening note to the book *Navigating Your Freshman Year* unequivocally states: "We invite you to open your mind, quell your fears, quiet your insecurities, strengthen your heart, and jump off the high dive."[46] Some transitions – starting a new job, for instance, or having a child – usher in new limitations and boundaries, along with very clear obligations and mandates. Indeed, that is precisely an essential aspect of those transitions. This is not so with going to college. While certainly an incoming freshman knows that there will be classes and exams in the future, there is also a clear understanding that much of what lies ahead is remarkably undefined – and that it will require significant customization.

College is in fact intentionally designed to be at once quite lightly structured (in terms of what one must do and where one must physically be throughout the years, in order to graduate) and, at the same time, tremendously rich with activities and things that one can choose to do. Academically, students must only be in class a few hours a day at most. A comprehensive analysis of the weekday activities of students at North Carolina State University shows, for instance, that students spend less than 25 percent of their waking time at school or in the classroom – much less than in high school. Personal activities, social and recreational activities, meals, and studying fill up much of the rest of the day.[47] In most schools, students enjoy enormous latitude in selecting their courses. They can pick from an often very large number of majors, since each school, even small liberal arts colleges, offer programs in a full range of disciplines from the natural sciences to the arts and humanities.

Completion of a major requires taking certain courses, but elective and especially non-major courses are numerous and varied. The first two years of a college education are in any event most often not focused on a major. Students are told that they need to "craft" their education – a freedom and responsibility that can be traced all the way back to Thomas Jefferson, his beliefs in the purposes of a university education, and his curricular reform of the University of Virginia and its new "free election" system of courses, which broke the rigid standards of the time.[48] If unsatisfied with the existing choices, self-designed majors (which colleges began to offer in the 1960s and 1970s) are now a possibility in over 100 colleges (an increasing trend marked by Indiana University at Bloomington holding in 2009 the first national conference on best practices for individualized majors) including major institutions such as Duke University and New York University (which in fact has an experimental college called Gallatin School of Individualized Study).[49]

On the personal and recreational front, colleges offer more clubs, associations, and even "affinity" groups than a person could ever join in a lifetime. Colleges boast about this in their recruiting materials, and students and their parents know that a universe of possibilities awaits them. At the University of Colorado at Boulder, students are informed that they can choose from over 300 options, from the typical to the rather eclectic, such as the Underwater Hockey Association, Vegan Justice League, and Value Your Future Association (which, quite appropriately, helps students think about their future in college and beyond).[50] Even more specialized colleges sport impressive numbers, and, should the available options not be enough, starting a new organization is often easy. The College of Engineering at the University of Wisconsin at Madison offers an example. Its website of registered organizations states: "There are over 50 engineering affiliated student organizations on campus, so there is bound to be a group that speaks to your interests and passions. If not, start your own."[51] Students can join the Human Powered Vehicle Team or, if that is not to their liking, the local chapter of Engineers without Borders, the Badger Amateur Radio Society, or the Hmong Association of Engineers – which, tellingly, is open to anyone, regardless of ethnic background.[52]

All this makes the transition to college a leap into a time filled with possibilities and potentialities that will require our active oversight and steering. And, importantly, all these potentialities and choices are seen as creating certain challenges, too, which have become the subject of much discussion. In college, note the authors – two college professors – of *The Secrets of College Success*, a popular book on college life, "there's no one there to hold your hand," while, at the same time, there is so much on hand that one should try and "squeeze all the juice out of it and drink it all up."[53] This creates tensions. Students find themselves engaged in far too many things, and "time management" logically becomes a problem. This is not because too many things are imposed on the students but because students quickly take on far more than they can handle. "Time management," states the

Personal Counseling Program at Brooklyn College, means "asserting greater control over the use of one's time and energy." "There are a million things to do," and one must choose and then execute with care.[54]

Actors

All transitions have protagonists. When it comes to our discourse on going to college, the center of attention, the object of change, and the person who is ultimately in control of the transition is the student. On moving-in day, colleges are waiting for the students, not the parents. Going to college is a rite of passage for the student involved: it is a transition of that individual. Parents will experience change in their own lives as a result of this, but in our minds this is an effect of their child going to college (i.e., of their child experiencing the transition) and not a result of the fact that the transition is about them. Thus, the majority of popular books written on going to college are for students, not parents: What are admissions officers looking for? What makes for a strong application essay? How to best study for the SAT? How to navigate the first weeks of college? How to deal with alcohol and sex on campus? What should freshmen do if they find their roommates unpleasant? What are the best strategies for dealing with learning disabilities? The list goes on.

The academic literature on the transition, in turn, zeroes in on the students – their experiences, mental and sometimes physical well-being, expectations, likely challenges, etc. – and not on their parents, relatives, or friends. Researchers investigate a variety of topics, from differences in experiences across ethnic lines to how effective orientation programs are for students, the type of stressors and mental health issues that arise in the first year, the variables that affect how easily students form new relationships, and even changes in students' drinking patterns.[55] Psychologists, education experts, and sociologists report a variety of experiences and patterns on all those fronts.

In turn, the books and materials that do address parents are, for the most part, intended to help them deal with the financial strains that college creates or, alternatively, with coming to accept that they must "let go" of their kids while at the same time continue to be there to help them as needed. With titles like *You Are on Your Own [But I Am Here if You Need Me]*[56] and *Letting Go: A Parents' Guide to Understanding the College Years*,[57] these books are premised on the fact that the students are experiencing the transition: they offer strategies for how parents can best prepare things and themselves *for* their kids. Those resources that do focus on parents as their child leaves for college tend to incorporate their experience into what is likely to be a broader transition in their own lives, such as the empty nest syndrome (discussed in chapter 10 of this book) or life as a couple after the kids leave home. "Much has been written about getting into college," notes a mother, Connie Jones, author of what she calls her own personal memoir about the experience, "and plenty more has been written about how to succeed in college once there. But there is very little to console us parents for our grief, or to tell the story of *our* rite to passage, our letting go . . . the parents I know . . . want to hear stories . . . I have written this book for them."[58]

At the same time, what is remarkable about this transition is the work and energy that others are expected to devote to the necessary preparations and its execution. For it to happen, in other words, the transition is understood to need others and is therefore not a solitary affair: a cast of supporting characters is required. Parents, recommenders, college admissions officers, counselors, deans, older fellow students, grandparents, and friends at various points in time support the student as she goes through the transition. Social scientists define a ritual as "a pattern of prescribed formal behavior, pertaining to some specific event, occasion, or situation, which tends to be repeated over again."[59] College is a ritual, and to take place it relies on a number of helpers and aids. Their roles are quite varied. They can provide money, for instance. Many parents begin saving for the college education of their children years ahead of time. In the 2011 Pew Research Center survey mentioned earlier in this chapter, 80 percent of parents reported that being able to pay for their children's college education is either very or extremely important to them; this was the same percentage stating that a comfortable retirement or owning a home are either very or extremely important to them.[60] Emotional support, guidance, and advice are also given to the student. Together, all these supporting characters function as valuable witnesses to the transition: they are an important audience for the student. The ritual can only work if an audience is present, after all.

Indeed, the audience is critical to the transition and extends beyond those closely connected to the student: ultimately, if we look closely at our discourse, society as a whole is in a sense watching. Having an educated workforce is essential for the country's productivity and progress, and the function of college – as we learned earlier in this chapter – is to transform adolescents into competent, capable, and professional adults ready to make a contribution to society. Thus, the experience is happening at least in part in the public sphere: the student, along with everyone else, knows that they are taking the steps that society requires of them to become model members of society: they are aware – and not without some trepidation – of what is expected of them, as a survey of high school seniors showed.[61] Society, then, is witnessing the student's entry into college. The transition is happening because of society and for society – recall, after all, that the origins of the transition are external, not internal. Going to college is ultimately the initiation of the individual into adult society, and it therefore happens before the eyes of everyone.

College as a New Beginning

We now have a better grasp of our discourse on going to college and the basic stance it promotes toward time and change. Going to college is depicted as an opportunity for re-invention – in this case, perhaps, invention, since it is the first real crafting of the self. What might otherwise be a closed and predictable transition to adulthood – a set of steps and changes that lead to a pre-established outcome – is instead intentionally described and practically crafted to be very flexible and open-ended. College offers students this incredibly important opportunity and charges them, after ensuring that the supporting stage is properly set, with the mandate of creating for themselves a new, adult persona – new selves with new statuses.[62]

We should approach going to college, then, with a certain degree of *aggressiveness* and *openness*, and a sense of *agency* and *independence*. Rather than letting the onset of adulthood constrain our lives, we are urged to seize control over it and, in the process, feel empowered. The students are in the driver's seat and must decide what and who they wish to become. "What do you want to make of yourself?," we – college officials, relatives, former teachers, friends – ask our students. In so doing, students hear what supposedly is a valuable lesson: that time belongs to them, that self-definition is an important part of life, that life *is* in a sense purposeful becoming and transformation, that to be alive means to change in a self-directed fashion rather than to stay static or be driven by others. These ideas, of course, resonate well with many of us because they have roots in some of the deeper values we, as a society, believe in and celebrate: individualism, independence, change, and potentiality. For this very reason, it seems appropriate to note that, despite the new counter-discourse against attending college already noted earlier in this chapter and the research that has started to document it, little about the transition or our discourse is likely to change rapidly in any fundamental sense; the transition is entrenched in our society.

Things could therefore certainly be different. We could use other occasions to mark the transition to adulthood. If fewer students went to college after high school (recall that 70 percent of all high school graduates plan an immediate entry into college), our tendency to mark the transition as *the* entry into adulthood would probably be much less prevalent. The same could be said if the percentage of adults who have completed tertiary education were lower. In the United States, according to the Organization for Economic Co-operation and Development, that figure (for people aged 25–64) was 41 percent in 2009: the average for all the rich countries in the world (a total of 34, including the United States) is much lower – around 30 percent in 2009. In Germany, that figure was 26 percent and in France 29 percent, in the United Kingdom 37 percent, and in Australia 37 percent.[63] College is something that many Americans experience in full.

In most other countries, in turn, college students tend to continue living at home with their parents. According to the US Department of Education, only 31 percent of undergraduate students in the United States lived at home with their parents or guardians in 2008 (though that number probably increased a bit as a result of harsh economic conditions since then).[64] The situation is practically the reverse in many other countries. In France, for example, nearly 40 percent of students live at home. Of the remaining 60 percent, however, the majority lives away from home only during the week and then returns during the weekend and, of course, for holidays and summers; this pattern is typical for those who live far away from urban centers where universities are frequently located. Thus, note, two researchers, "the relocating of provincial students is therefore only partial and may be only temporary. Most often it does not signify full independence from parents, which is usually only attained after the age of 24."[65] In Italy, moving out of the parents' home simply happens with the greatest frequency upon marrying; when students go to college, they continue to live with their parents.[66] And in Germany, most college students live at home and find themselves moving out only after their education is complete and they are able to maintain themselves financially. Indeed, researchers report that attending college is one of the primary reasons for German students to continue living at home.[67]

In many European countries, therefore, the discourse on going to college is not about starting over or becoming adults for the first time. There are not going to be a new home or new roommates. There is no "drop-off" by parents with boxes and suitcases. University life by and large means continuity and the extension of their stay with their parents. All this has led many observers to note that Americans expect their children to transition to adulthood at a relatively early age. Indeed, the fact that many expect it to happen with the move to college is, according to researchers, uniquely American in character, since high school adolescents in many other cultures are not expected to leave home after graduation, regardless of whether they are headed for college or not.[68] In the European context, markers of adulthood are found significantly later in life, even in the late 20s or early 30s.[69]

If we consider the college curricula in other countries, we see that students are presented with far fewer options than in the United States. Most majors require extensive, sequential coursework in a particular discipline and offer little chance for exploration in other disciplines. Majors must also be declared upon entering college, without the luxury of having one or two years to decide. College is not a time of intellectual and personal transformation, but of specialization and technical refinement. A math major in most European universities will be expected to take almost exclusively math classes from the very start; the same applies to any other discipline. The same can be said of Japan.[70] The liberal arts model has caught the attention of some education officials in The Netherlands in particular, with a few universities setting up colleges and curricula that allow for many electives and customization. Officials in England, Germany, Belgium, and Slovakia have also expressed interest.[71] While there may be some change in the future, the current dominant model is one of disciplinary focus and rigidity.

To complement this, nowhere in the world do colleges offer the same number and variety of student clubs, groups, and other sorts of organizations as in the United States. There are several reasons for this, including the lack of financial support by universities, unsupportive campus regulations, low interest on the part of students, and the relatively low number of students living on campus. The result is consistent with the underlying ideas about the function and nature of higher education in those countries: students do not attend college to explore, "test out" new identities and affinities, branch out personally, and ultimately craft new identities for themselves. The stated purpose of higher education, instead, is to acquire specific disciplinary training and thus professionalize students. Hence, the most prevalent types of associations in many European countries are focused on academic disciplines or student representation in campus-wide decision-making processes. The picture on American campuses is remarkably different. Alexis de Tocqueville, in his classic book *Democracy in America*, noted almost 200 years ago how intensely Americans like to form all kinds of associations, so as to connect with others, explore, share ideas, and ultimately cultivate a broader mindset.[72] College campuses are no exception to the rule and are, in this regard as in many others, unique institutions in the world.

In the American dominant discourse, going to college represents a remarkable new beginning. It is a ritual infused with coming-of-age significance: it is a rite of passage with public qualities designed to send off students to four years of personal discovery and transformation. While a supporting cast of characters – from parents to campus counselors – makes the transition possible, students are ultimately expected to take charge of their journey. This, too, is part of the transformative experience of college.

3 Getting Married

Marriage, according to many anthropologists, "is almost universally regarded as the definitive transition to adulthood in traditional cultures worldwide."[1] It retains that function in many contemporary societies. Things are quite different in the United States: our culture favors individualistic markers of self-sufficiency and independence as signals of the achievement of adulthood. While we view going to college, as discussed in chapter 2, as such a marker, we certainly do not think of marriage in the same way.[2] Yet this does not mean that we do not value it; on the contrary, Americans are outliers relative to virtually all European countries and Japan in the extent to which they get married,[3] with educated Americans especially showing high marriage rates.[4] An entire industry thrives in helping those without partners find their ideal match for marriage, while the number of certified therapy counselors – many represented by the American Association of Family and Marriage Therapists – has grown multifold since the 1960s to help millions of couples save their marriages from falling apart.[5] Marriage continues to be a very important institution in American society. What, then, is the dominant discourse on getting married in the United States?

Given the size of the country and the many ethnicities and cultures that make it up, there are perhaps more interpretations of the purposes and meaning of getting married in the United States than in many other countries in the world. And those interpretations are often contentious. The issue shapes social and political debates in a real way, with social conservatives viewing it as exclusively the union between a man and a woman (with the purpose of promoting procreation), and liberals supporting the rights of same-sex couples to marry but also questioning the usefulness of marriage as an institution and thus, in that context, supporting cohabitation and single parents as perfectly fine ways of raising children. The debate is played out in state-level courts, legislatures, and referendums.[6]

Yet, these important differences about *who* should marry and to *what end* have not prevented Americans from developing a rather cohesive discourse on what marriage is *as a transition*. Getting married has to do with the inevitable passing of time and with change. In the face of both, we enter into an agreement with another person that, no matter what, some things will stay the same: that we will love and be with that person for as long as we live. Marriage thus introduces some degree of defiance and control over the very nature of human existence itself. Despite life's unstoppable movement and fluctuations, by marrying we enter into something that is explicitly designed to last for as long as we live. The American dominant discourse depicts getting married *as something that reduces uncertainty in our lives via the permanent embrace of continuity through bondage to another soul.* In a society that celebrates innovation, restlessness, and the constant testing of boundaries, marriage becomes a valuable statement of our often neglected desire for calm and permanence. Getting married, then, becomes a statement – or protestation of sorts – made against life's inevitability and our otherwise strong tendency to pursue movement and change. Let us examine this vision of getting married – this piece of American culture – in some detail.

Bonding for Eternity

Two people stand next to each other and, in either a religious or civil ceremony, they exchange vows and often rings and, in one way or another, promise to love one another forever and to spend the rest of their lives together. Decades ago, the couple was almost certainly made up of a man and a woman, and was very likely to share the same racial, ethnic, and religious backgrounds. Today, we see much more variety in all those dimensions. For instance, according to a 2012 Pew Research Center report, inter-racial marriages in the United States accounted for only around 3 percent in 1980; the figure had shot up to 8.5 percent in 2010. Of couples getting married in the year 2010, 15 percent were inter-racial, as opposed to 6.7 percent in 1980. Over 40 percent of Americans today think that inter-racial marriages are good for society.[7]

Regardless of such diversity, the American discourse on getting married is quite clear: we (and not outside forces) decide that we should get married, at least part of our past is at the heart of the transition, the partners understand that they are taking on a revised role for their selves, the partners are embracing a future with new boundaries, and this major moment of change involves not one but two individuals. Our popular movies, best-selling books, wedding ceremonies, and answers to polls and surveys affirm this story: getting married is ultimately about willful continuity and connection with another person, and thus, in a subtle way, about introducing an element of security and predictability into our lives. Let us examine this element of American culture in some detail.

Origins

For a very long time, Americans understood marriage to be something that, in the normal unfolding of a good life, would happen to them. It existed outside of them, and the task for most young adults was to find "that one" person who could help them step into their expected roles as husbands and wives. Until the middle of the twentieth century, marriage was not a choice, but an integral part of one's life trajectory.[8] Congratulations to newly wedded couples were in order then because the two persons involved had fulfilled a key social mandate in their lives. Marriage rates among adults were accordingly very high – in 1960, according to a 2011 Pew Research Center report, 72 percent of US adults aged 18 and older were married[9] – and single adults were viewed with at least some degree of suspicion.

During the last few decades, however, things have changed significantly. By 2010, the proportion of adults who were married was 51 percent, and projections for the future are pointing to further decreases. Among African Americans, fewer than 50 percent of adults are married. The figure for Caucasians and Hispanics is around 60 percent.[10] Being single, cohabiting, or single-parenting are increasingly common arrangements.[11] "Americans are marrying less now," wrote two family researchers in 2010, "than at any point in the recorded demographic history of the country."[12] These trends signal that getting married in the United States, however prevalent when compared to other countries in the world, has now become optional. To be sure, for certain groups – such as some social conservatives or religious segments of the population – marriage remains the only acceptable form for couples to live together and procreate. And for these groups, outside forces – God, the needs of children to have parents who are permanently committed to each other, the expectations of their family members and communities, even human nature

– often make marriage imperative. Researchers report, as well, that other segments of the population – such as certain individuals in the gay and lesbian community – may actually feel inordinate social and family pressure to enter into heterosexual marriages.[13] But for most Americans – as surveys, talk shows, movies, and popular books all indicate – getting married is now a choice and not an essential component of a successful or well-lived life. Marriage has become "optional," write two experts on the topic, a question of "private taste rather than a matter of shared concern."[14] A small but not significant percentage of Americans (17 percent) even rejects the idea that a couple wanting children ought to get married.[15]

Why, then, do we get married? How do counselors, lawmakers, parents, and journalists account for this transition? We get married because we *want to*. "Why do we do it? Nobody needs to get married, not anymore, and nobody needs to stay married," author Chris Jones wrote recently in an issue of *Esquire*, one of the best-selling men's magazines, that was partly dedicated to exploring the logic behind our continued appetite for marriage.[16] Marrying someone is an act of volition, not inescapable custom. Virtually every popular book on the subject does not instruct readers to get married, but instead helps them think whether marriage is for them, and, if it is, how it can be secured and made successful. Those who are almost ready but still harboring doubt can, for example, turn to *Don't You Dare Get Married Until You Read This!*,[17] those needing guidance on how to make the best decision can benefit from the insights found in 51 *Things You Should Know Before Getting Engaged*,[18] and uncertain Christians can consult the pages of *Should I Get Married?*[19] Many of these books are written by presumed experts on the subject, and many emphasize that marriage has become almost like a good that we can decide to purchase or not, much like a car or a house.

What considerations, we must then ask, lie behind the choice to get married? What are put forth as powerful motivations for getting married in our books, movies, popular stories, and national surveys? Commitment is among the most important drivers: marriage is depicted as something that can increase the commitment of each partner to each other, and people are seen as longing for that commitment – something that appears to be reflective of a number of fears and emotions, including our deep love for a person, our insecurity in an increasingly fluid and unpredictable world, and a related desire for a concrete and publicly institutionalized sign that we are loved. Thus Andrew Cherlin, a leading marriage scholar at

Johns Hopkins University, describes marriage in America as a public institution centered on the notion of "enforceable trust," as something that "allows individuals to invest in the partnership with less fear of abandonment." The commitment is accordingly "usually expressed in front of relatives, friends, and religious congregations. Cohabitation, in contrast, requires only a private commitment, which is easier to break. Therefore, marriage, more so than cohabitation, lowers the risk that one's partner will renege on agreements that have been made."[20] In the words of Deborah Carr, a sociologist at Rutgers University, marriage "marks the completion of a quest for one's intended other."[21]

A second purported reason has to do with settling the romantic side of our lives. Modern life, the logic goes, is compartmentalized into fairly separate spheres: getting educated, having a satisfying job, attaining a certain level of financial wellbeing, having a network of friends, and romance. Getting married constitutes the finalization of our romantic lives: by getting married, we take care in a permanent fashion of that dimension of our lives. When young adults are asked about their motivations for wanting to get married, this idea of "settling down" appears especially widespread.[22] Interestingly, such a step is increasingly seen as something that can take place only once other aspects of our lives (such as having a good and permanent job or having completed college) are properly in place (a line of reasoning that may explain the large numbers of cohabiting couples who plan on getting married at some point in the future).

Financial considerations are also, of course, of much importance. Getting married should, in principle, move us toward a more stable and predictable lifestyle, especially because the partners' resources are pooled together and utilized more efficiently. In cases where a person "marries up," the transition is even more beneficial. Articulated most eloquently by economist Gary Becker in the 1970s, this perspective continues to be voiced in popular books, sermons by famous preachers, and political leaders. But here it is worth noting that the discourse may be reaching a fairly selected audience only: those with some resources on hand already. Evidence indicates that relatively well-off and educated persons are today more likely to marry than poorer, less-educated ones. In the case of women especially, the latter appear to marry much less often and, when they do, to marry someone who belongs to the same educational and economic group.[23] All are likely to list financial considerations as important motivators. Those with no resources may be aware of this logic but, it seems, are more hesitant to follow it in practice.

Finally, of course, emotional and romantic reasons are also put squarely on the list of reasons for getting married. We get married, the narrative goes, because we are in love, and that means wanting somehow to "merge" our lives with someone else's life. Getting married completes us – two candles become one. We find our soul mate, and we wish to institutionalize this match in some permanent fashion. Hence, in a 2007 Pew Research Center survey on marriage, "mutual happiness and fulfillment," and not "bearing and raising children," was the primary reason given for getting married by the majority of respondents regardless of race, age, or church attendance rates.[24] In a 2010 survey by the same organization, "love" topped the reasons couples give for getting married.[25] Telling, in this regard, is also a recent survey of over 1,000 Catholics conducted by the Center for Applied Research in the Apostolate at Georgetown University. Few of today's young Catholics believe that marriage is a "calling from God" (i.e., something with external origins); the vast majority report instead that their spouse must be their "soul mate." At the same time, and quite importantly, a majority of those respondents also believe very strongly in marriage as a lifetime commitment (older Catholics believe more readily that they must marry because of God and the Church, but are also less committed to marriage). The result is an intriguing picture. As University of Notre Dame researcher Christian Smith puts it, "most younger Catholics have defined their inner self as the authority, and many freely distance themselves from church practices they don't believe in." At the same time, with personal love as their main driver, they approach marriage with a powerful sense that it will be an everlasting merging of two lives.[26]

All these reasons seem rather different. Yet, in fact, they are all similar in one fundamental regard: they are internally-driven efforts toward stability and predictability. Our dominant discourse sees us choosing, for a variety of reasons, to get married. Marriage no longer happens to us: we make it happen.

Past

The voluntaristic flavor in our discourse about marriage could easily be accompanied by views of the past as something that should be dismissed. The logic of "choice" could apply to the past: getting married could be seen as an opportunity to leave the past behind – to sever our ties with what has come before. In fact, marriage is depicted as quite the opposite of that, though of course not all our past is necessarily involved. The act of getting married is understood to be the symbolic incorporation and crystallization of the past into something more permanent, official, and often public. In light of what came before we choose to get married. The resulting celebration is therefore a culmination and often coronation of the past. What, exactly, about the past is very much at the center of getting married? Upon a closer look, we see a number of distinct threads.

The most obvious is the relationship between the two partners. Couples take what they have experienced together, pause before it, and embrace it. Getting married becomes the transformation of what was until now a relationship that was informal and in principle always at risk of dissolution into something more formal, permanent, and institutionalized.[27] It is conceived, as a recent study by Cornell University and University of Central Oklahoma researchers found, as a logical "next step" in a relationship, especially in the eyes of middle-class Americans.[28] We find this view present in both secular and religious weddings. In the latter, for instance, whether Jewish, Christian, Muslim, or another religious denomination, the couple or religious figure leading the ceremony regularly asks God to bless or consecrate, once and forever, the partners' love for each other – a request that obviously assumes the existence of that love prior to the ceremony. No one therefore marries a complete stranger, and even those guides and partner searchers that promise their readers and customers the fastest path to finding a mate for marriage recognize the necessity of at least a few months of courtship for building a proper relationship. We are to marry the person that we have found and that we have come to know, or think we have come to know, as many leading marriage counselors, such as *New York Times* bestseller author Gary Chapman, point out.[29]

Interestingly, we should note that the idea of marriage happening because of the romantic love that exists between two individuals is relatively novel. As sociologist Liah Greenfeld has argued, it is premised on the idea of individualism (or the inherent worth of every individual), the possibility and in fact necessity of realizing one's personal aspirations and dreams, and the elimination (or at least reduction) of a rigid social system (with impenetrable sets of classes, castes, power elites, and so on) that might otherwise dictate who should marry whom. These developments took place first in sixteenth-century Europe (England especially) and today are everywhere but probably reach their strongest expression precisely in the United States.[30] Thus it was in the United States in particular that love became the primary criterion for the selection of a wedding mate as early as the nine-teenth century, as Carol Wallace has written in her impressive history of weddings in the United States.[31]

At another level, however, getting married is also often described as representing both a personal and a shared accomplishment. At a time in the United States when marriage is optional (with some of the characteristics, for some of us at least, of a purchase) and when, should one want to marry, one is encouraged to engage in a process of introspection (should I, in fact, get married?), articulation of goals and preferences (what am I looking for in a partner?), search and selec-tion of a "good" mate (where should I look for that person, and will I be able to find him or her?), and then begin and nurture a relation-ship, the act of marrying stands out as a finish-line of sorts. We have worked hard and asked ourselves many difficult questions – 1,001, if we follow the advice of Monica Leahy, another prominent marriage counselor.[32] After many deliberations, beautiful moments but also challenges, and efforts, we can happily say that we have "made it." We have reached an important milestone in our lives.

The logic of accomplishment extends beyond the final seizing of an objective. The age at which we get married for the first time has steadily increased over the last few decades (from the early to the late twenties)[33] and for more and more Americans marriage can only happen once they feel comfortable in other areas of their lives. One gets married, therefore, once other things have been "achieved." Increasingly, as noted already, it is therefore the highly educated – in fact, those with the most wealth above any other predictor, as an analy-sis of large-scale data from the National Longitudinal Survey of Youth shows[34] – that are more likely to get married. Thus, as Andrew Cherlin has observed, marriage is increasingly understood to be a status symbol: something that we can aspire to, and can only afford, when we have done well in other spheres of our adult lives, and something that we can then showcase along with our other successes.[35] In the words of University of Pennsylvania sociologist Frank Furstenberg, "marriage has become a luxury good."[36] This is consistent with the fact that, as we already discussed, marriage in the United States does not represent the transition to adulthood but, rather, typically con-cerns to adults already: marriage is now part of the evolution of adult life.

Because getting married is in most cases a public occurrence, others also participate. And, according to the dominant discourse, what they bring, in many regards, is also the past. Now, in some respects, the transition actually represents a letting go of the past. The traditional dance of the bride with her father is emotionally moving (and more bitter than sweet) precisely because it represents the break from the past. In the last few years, one of the most popular songs played for the occasion has been *I Loved Her First*, by the group *Heartland*.[37] The lyrics are the words of a father who reminds the new husband that, indeed, he loved the bride first, but acknowledges that "time changes everything, life must go on, and I am not going to stand in your way." Maids of honor and best men, in turn, stand witness to their friends moving on, and for this reason organize bachelor and bachelorette parties that signal the end of life as single, "free" individuals, as research shows.[38]

But it is also true that, in our discourse, the past, as it concerns others, is something that becomes integrated into the transition in very important ways. Parents may be letting go of their children in one sense, but many claim that they are making room for a new person in the evolution of their own lives: at the heart of many a toast by fathers and mothers is the welcoming of their new daughter- or son-in-law to their family and its history. The same can be said of the siblings of the bride or groom: families are evolving, not breaking apart. Thus, according to a recent study by sociologist Medora Barnes, Americans are more and more aware of the role that weddings play in bringing two families together and, because of this, the participation of family members in the marriage ceremony has only been increasing in recent decades.[39] To this we can add that friends and other witnesses are not disappearing, but allowing their relationship with the bride and groom to adjust in light of the new arrangements.

In a more subtle fashion, getting married is also understood to be about cyclicality and the reproduction of a particular societal order. Marriage is an old and generally revered institution. Couples are participating in a centuries-old ritual and, as research shows, a growing majority of Americans are choosing to celebrate this very fact by opting for traditional weddings – i.e., those done in religious settings with the bride dressed in a long white gown, a multi-layer cake, ample flowers, a reception, and a honeymoon.[40] There is little that is revolutionary about getting married – and indeed many researchers of the wedding ritual point, critically, to its frequently conservative, heterosexual, and patriarchical qualities and the fact that the participants are consciously or unconsciously choosing to affirm the established view of the world as they get married, as recent analyses of books giving advice to brides on wedding preparations[41] and homosexuals' perspectives of the typical ceremony clearly show.[42]

Of course, other parts of the past may in fact be left behind because of the transition. Our discourse allows for this. A bitter relationship with a previous spouse or partner may finally be relegated to irrelevance, as may happen with painful memories of an unhappy childhood or something else. Not the whole past is incorporated into the act of getting married. But there is no doubt that much of the past is, indeed, an integral and central part of the transition: getting married is, fundamentally, about the past as much as it is about the future. "I loved her first," *Heartland*'s song goes, after all, "I held her first, and a place in my heart will always be hers."

Self

Just as in our discourse the past is not dismissed in the act of getting married (and is instead incorporated into the transition), our old selves are not rejected in favor of new ones but are instead carefully brought into the transition. Weddings are not supposed to produce, wholesale, new identities. Instead, they bring about a *refinement* of our selves. Social psychologists talk about "identity shifts" because of marriage.[43] The transition gives us further definition and instructions, and this may very well be one of its attractive qualities. The exact nature of that refinement varies greatly depending on a number of variables: conservative Catholics or Protestants, for instance, are exposed to different views of how getting married will change them than non-religious liberals. But when we consider the relevant logic across different categories of individuals, we can see that the refinement concerns at least two aspects of one's sense of self.

First, our position relative to our partner is seen as undergoing an adjustment. Married people remain committed, in love, and kindly disposed toward each other, but they now can refer to themselves with new labels: wife, husband, spouse, partner, and so on. They do not make up those labels on their own – they already exist in society, and find specific articulations as we move across religious, educational, economic, and other sorts of groups. The labels come with particular responsibilities, expectations, and rights; they "carry with them a recognition, of the legal, moral, and emotional relationship between the partners," as Linda Waite and Maggie Gallagher note in their book *The Case for Marriage*.[44] The two individuals are accordingly expected to sense a change in who they are: the "other" will now figure more prominently in their own definition of self. Consider, in this regard, the fact that the vast majority of women in the United States continue the practice of changing their last names upon marrying when there are no legal or formal reasons for doing so,[45] or the fact that partners often report taking on personality traits from each other.[46] Boundaries are in principle and practice altered to a certain degree by the presence of a spouse.

Political, religious, and other orientations support different variations of these dynamics. The conservative version sees the couple as stepping into traditional roles where the man and the woman complement each other. "Complementarity" was very much at the heart of the proposed Federal Marriage Amendment of 2006, for example, which would have limited marriage in the United States to unions between a man and a woman. Those who spoke in favor of it included Congresswoman Marilyn Musgrave, notable university professors, and representatives of the Alliance for Marriage, the American Center for Law and Justice, and the Family Research Council, among others. All subscribed to a view of man and woman as different from each other – emotionally, psychologically, physically – and of marriage as a way to bring those beings together in harmony and balance.[47] Tellingly, in the House of Representatives, the votes in favor were 236 and those against 187, not enough to pass the amendment but an impressive showing of what many Americans think.

For rather large numbers of conservative Protestant Christians, the adjustment has to do with accepting one's position in a hierarchy: the woman becomes the submissive follower of the man, who takes on a leading role, as recent scholarship and in-depth interviews show.[48] The words of Joshua Harris, Senior Pastor of Covenant Life Church in Gaithersburg, Maryland (a church with nearly 20 pastors and thousands of members), in a recent article in the *Journal for Biblical Manhood & Womanhood* are in this sense representative. "Women are not told [by God] to submit to all men," he notes; "they are only called to submit to their own husband. So this isn't a statement of male superiority. It's God's direction on the ordering of a marriage. It's also a reminder to single ladies to be very careful when choosing a husband. After you marry this man, God's Word directs you to be submissive. Don't marry a man whose leadership you can't follow."[49]

The more liberal interpretation of getting married begins with a stronger assertion of equality between the two persons involved and describes the required adjustment as one of supporting one another's personal and professional ambitions. Marriage fosters a stable and mutually reinforcing relationship where each person is able to choose his or her own next steps but is also mindful of the needs of the other partner: these are marriages where, in the words of one prominent marriage counselor and author, "power is shared" and which require "intentional cultivation of the individual" so that each partner can flourish in line with his or her vision of what is good.[50] "Mutuality" is a key word in these marriages.[51] These are "peer marriages," as Pepper Schwartz – a relationship expert with multiple contributions to the *New York Times*, *Glamour Magazine*, numerous blogs, TV shows such as *Good Morning America* and *Oprah*, and other outlets – puts it.[52] The country as a whole, large-scale statistical analyses show, has increasingly subscribed to this more egalitarian interpretation since the late 1970s, with variables such as education and employment positively predicting who is more likely to adopt this perspective.[53] However different, then, these perspectives – conservative, religious, liberal, and others – in many cases are similar in one regard: they do not see getting married as occasioning a major overhaul of one's self, but a modification or refinement as the partners enter into a new arrangement with each other.

Second, our discourse sees getting married as modifying our position in society. In many respects (our job, our professional quali-fications, etc.) we will stay the same. But a married person is, as a member of society, rather different from a single person. "Marriage," note Waite and Gallagher, "changes not only the couple's relationship with each other, it changes the couple's relationship to the outside world. By choosing to marry, couples are entering a social institution that changes the way they will be treated by others, including, in many cases, the government, business, and religious communities."[54] By and large, the changes include an increased external appreciation of who we are. Simply put, getting married should improve our posi-tion in society because it elicits a certain respect for various reasons, including the recognition that a person must have earned someone's love and respect, and that he or she has proven willing to commit to something. A married adult often, to this day, comes across as more "complete" or "wholesome" than a person who has never married, especially if the latter does not have a partner.

We can see this quite clearly when we consider public atti-tudes toward never-married adults. "The overriding public sentiment toward never-married men is disapproval," writes Charles Waehler in his groundbreaking study of bachelors in the United States. Even most of the positive images that we have of bachelors (such as the young man who loves his independence or wishes to be professionally secure prior to marrying), Waehler notes, come with negative undertones, such as selfish, narcissistic, and immature.[55] Attitudes are even worse toward never-married women. Many Americans feel that there is something potentially troubling about being single, though interesting exceptions of course exist.[56] Government policies (such as those found in the 1996 Personal Responsibility and Work Opportunity Reconciliation Act and subsequent legislation) promoting marriage (for the purposes of reducing poverty rates, among other reasons) fuel the public perception of the desirability of being married. And continuous reports, based on nationwide polls and other data, showing that married people in the United States seem consistently happier (as well as less likely to live in poverty) than singles probably add to that perception,[57] though in fact recent academic research seriously questions this idea.[58]

Thus, a slew of books are available to either help singles resolve their perceived problem by taking control of the situation or, if that is not possible, accept their condition as a positive thing (which means, in fact, to acknowledge that it is normally seen as *not* a positive thing). In this vein, Susan Page opens her wildly successful book *If I Am So Wonderful, Why Am I Still Single?* (translated into 20 foreign languages) in this fashion: "So why are you still single anyway? Just unlucky?"[59] And virtually all books on the topic evoke in their very titles the feeling of inadequacy that we equate with being single, as the examples of three of the most popular books make clear:

- *Seeking Happily Ever After: Navigating the Ups and Downs of Being Single without Losing Your Mind (and Finding Lasting Love along the Way)*[60]
- *Being Single in a Couples' World: How to Be Happy Single while Looking for Love*[61]
- *Revelations of a Single Woman: Loving the Life I Didn't Expect*[62]

Getting married means taking on a new, publicly-approved, role that endows us with a new sense of legitimacy and adequacy, and of course considerable expectations. This is not so much about transformation and reinvention as it is about stepping into a position that society as a whole sees as natural and logical for an adult.

Future

By and large, our discourse sees marriage as putting limits on the future: it is an act of mutual constraining in a society that otherwise values movement and change. "The marriage contract," write Waite and Gallagher, "is in one sense liberating: the security of a contract frees individuals to make long-term exchanges that leave each person better off. But any contract also necessarily constrains the parties involved . . . As part of this new bond, they have less freedom to act unilaterally than unmarried people – almost by definition – if they are going to live up to the promises they've exchanged."[63] Indeed, it can be easily argued that marriage *is* presented as the way to make the future more orderly and bounded. In this and many other regards, marriage is a conservative, not revolutionary, social institution: its primary purpose is to introduce predictability into our lives.

Order and boundaries are introduced precisely into those areas otherwise marked by a fair amount of unpredictability. Table 3.1 identifies the more important areas.

Marriage "settles" one of the most intimate aspects of our lives: going forward we will have one committed sexual and romantic companion. Let us observe here that Americans are very active sexually prior to marriage, especially at a young age, though in terms of attitudes they tend to disapprove of adolescent sexual intercourse more so than in many other countries.[64] A 2004 World Health Organization study of 27 European nations, for instance, reported the percentage of 15-year-olds who have had sexual intercourse. All nations averaged well below 40 percent.[65] A study for the United States set the figure at 41 percent.[66] Other studies show that "nearly 65% of American

Table 3.1: Marriage, Order, and Boundaries

Area	Introduction of Order and Boundaries
Sex and romance	Sex, and romance more generally, shall be limited to the two partners only
Living arrangements	Partners will live together, without non-family members or extended family members
Daily events	Waking up, breakfast, dinners, exercising, and entertainment will involve at least to some extent the partner
Children	Partners will be present to help and raise children
Aging	Partners will age (i.e., experience life) together; each will have a companion

teenagers have had sexual intercourse by the time they graduate from high school" and, importantly, "most with more than one partner." To that, we can add that 10 percent of adolescent girls (around 800,000 teens) become pregnant prior to age 19.[67] Researchers analyzing data from the National Survey of Family Growth and other sources for the period 1954–2002 came to the simple conclusion that "almost all Americans have sex before marrying,"[68] while other researchers report that 90 percent of young adults become sexually active during adolescence and prior to marriage.[69] By all accounts, Americans have rather active sexual lives, often with more than one partner, well before marriage.

Getting married brings order and boundaries, at least in principle, to our sexual and romantic lives. The transition is understood to eliminate in principle the possibility of any other sexual or romantic partner and, in turn, involves the expectation that we will have sex and romance with our chosen partner. As Steven and Sue Simring, self-described as "America's foremost husband-and-wife marriage-counseling team," put it in *Making Marriage Work for Dummies*, marriage means that you "declare to the world that you are making a lifetime pledge to another human being."[70] The vast majority of Americans expect partners to be faithful to each other and not have sex with others, though we should note that differences exist across racial and class groups in the acceptability of extramarital affairs.[71]

Getting married is also seen as settling our living arrangements and daily routines. We already noted that most Americans leave their parental homes at a young age, and that this is quite different from what happens in many other advanced industrialized countries, where young adults tend to live with their parents well into college and beyond.[72] A long unmarried period thus begins. A vast majority will have multiple roommates over time, often starting with college and continuing after graduation. Millions will at some point cohabit with a partner for a relatively short period of time (and then either marry or separate).[73] An increasing percentage (over 20 percent by 2000) will live alone for some time.[74] The number of persons under 35 living alone, according to a 2012 report, exceeds 5 million.[75] Most will change dwellings more than once, and many will change cities. According to figures released by the US Census Bureau, for instance, nearly 25 percent of 25–29-year-olds moved homes in the one-year time period between 2010 and 2011.[76] For almost everyone, this will be a time characterized by fluidity and movement, regardless of class, racial, or other factors, with employment, educational, personal, and other reasons driving the change. Daily life, in turn, typically unfolds in a fairly independent fashion: waking up, grocery shopping, having meals, going to the gym, doing laundry, and leaving and coming back from work are often carried out individually.

Getting married supposedly changes all this: the partners will only have one roommate (each other), friends and relatives will not live with them, changing homes will happen less frequently, and everyday living will be coordinated and shared in various ways. If we take the period between 2010 and 2011 again, for instance, according to the US Census Bureau, only 7 percent of married individuals (living together) changed homes. The figure was half the rate for never-married persons and almost a third of the rate for separated individuals.[77] Marrying is a major step toward "settling down." Alternative perspectives – for instance, where the married couple shares their home with a roommate – are problematic. Humorous and illustrative in this respect is an episode of CBS's hit sitcom *How I Met Your Mother*, where cohabitation in a New York apartment among three of the main characters (Ted, Marshall, and Lily) is acceptable until Marshall and Lily get married. Then, after a short period of continued habitation among the three, Marshall can no longer contain his discontent and explodes at Ted, equating their current situation to the Real World House – the home at the heart of the famous MTV reality TV show *The Real World*, which sees strangers living together under the same roof for several months: "[You] make me feel like I'm living in the Real World House . . . I cannot take this anymore! Ted, Lily and I are married, now. It is time; we are getting our own place!"[78]

Marriage is described as introducing order and boundaries in another crucial area: having children. In our discourse, by and large, marriage is the proper gateway to having children – with all the constraints that this generates. According to the General Social Survey, over 70 percent of Americans either "strongly agree" or "agree" with the idea that "people who want children ought to get married."[79] Single parenting, while more accepted than decades ago, is far from being widely embraced: according to the World Values Survey, nearly 48 percent disapprove of women being single parents (by contrast, the corresponding figures in France, Great Britain, Germany, and Japan are 26, 35, 36, and 35 percent, respectively).[80] This strong link between marriage and children in our discourse is explained by different factors, such as the absence of a strong safety net for single parents who may lose their job or develop serious illnesses, and the high number of single mothers who are poor and unable (partly due to limited social services, such as inexpensive daycare facilities) to take good care of their children. But for some interesting exceptions (such as large numbers of successful African American women who rather remain single), getting married offers the partners reciprocal insurance about childrearing.

Finally, getting married is about dealing with one of the most troubling aspects of life itself: getting old. Marriage allows two persons to live together *through* time, providing a constant (a partner) throughout all that life brings to a person, including inevitable decline and eventual death. Marriage is about cyclicality, moving through time, and ultimately life (in the form of procreation) and death. We get married to experience and live life with a partner. Consider the most recommended vows one finds on the most popular wedding and gift registry website in the United States – weddingchannel.com – which has more than 1.5 million unique visitors per month. These can be non-religious, Jewish, Christian, Muslim, or of other kinds, but they all commit partners to be together for the long haul: the spouses promise to cherish each other throughout life,[81] take care of each other for as long as they live, honor each other until death does them part, and honor each other all the days of their lives.[82]

Actors

As noted, in our discourse, getting married is in good part an individualistic act, consistent with how we approach other aspects of our lives: we enter, as Cherlin puts it, into "individualized" marriages.[83] It is a personal choice made out of a desire to have a particular kind of future. On the other hand, and inevitably, in our discourse getting married, in its essence, involves someone else: the "other" is a vital component of the transition. The transition *has to do* with someone else and indeed each partner (and society as a whole) understands that the "other," the partner, is also a protagonist. What role, then, does the "other" play in this transition? We should reflect on this, for it is both particular and quite different from what we find in chapters 4 and 8, when we examine the arrival of the first child and the death of one's parents.

To begin, the "other" is a willing partner – that is, someone who is interested in taking on this important step in life with us. There is a volitional quality to his or her role. The pronouncement of "I do" signifies precisely willfulness and the fact that matters could be otherwise. "Consent" is a legal requirement for getting married in virtually all state constitutions in the United States. In California, for instance, the Family Code portion on marriage (Section 300) opens by stating "Marriage is a personal relation arising out of a civil contract between a man and a woman, to which the consent of the parties capable of making that contract is necessary."[84] A number of resources are accordingly available to the American public to offer advice on how an aspiring spouse can lure his or her partner into agreeing to get married. How, asks, for example, Dr. Patricia Allen, television personality, seminar leader, and best-selling author of *Getting to "I do"* (now in its 32nd printing), do we convince the other that marriage is in order? The book is for women readers especially and answers one key question: "how to get him to ask you to marry him in one year ... I will show you the clues you have been missing and why. I will tell you ten secrets that will allow you to meet the man you want to and become engaged, very likely in the first year."[85] The individualistic qualities of life in the United States, coupled with the fact that marriage is increasingly optional for couples, makes the choice to get married particularly willful for *both* partners.

At the same time, the "other" is someone who is intimately connected to us. It is someone who has expressed his or her desire to love and take care of us, to share much of life with us. The other is also the person toward whom we have powerful feelings (attraction, admiration, etc.), and whom we wish to hold on to for the rest of our lives. This applies to couples of all types – across religious affiliations, economic classes, political orientations, and so on. We sense mutuality, reciprocity, and, very importantly, exclusivity in our love for each other: getting married happens (as of the last century or so) in the United States (and much of the Western world) between two "love" protagonists, as Stephanie Coontz, a historian of marriage, notes in her study of marriage.[86] Reciprocal and exclusive love is thus at the heart of partner-matching sites, personal ads sections, and countless songs.

With the above said, it is also clear that getting married is understood to be a public and visible transition in various respects. Virtually every state in the United States requires the physical presence of the couple within its territory in order to authorize the marriage – a testament to the fact that the partners must be "seen" and their union be made "solemn" by a state-authorized person.[87] Society must approve the step, and often religious figures are also involved. In the most typical format, guests and relatives are present to witness and (for some) directly participate in the ceremony. All have expectations of what should happen during the wedding and for years afterwards:

getting married, note researchers Waite and Gallagher, comes with "a very public package of expectations about how two people should behave."[88] The ritual is complex and well-scripted, with variations available for secular and religious weddings. The coordination and planning often involves parents, relatives, and friends. Yet, even with all of this in place, it is important to stress that the public nature of the transition does *not* mean that these "others" are an integral, core element of getting married. As Coontz states, others – parents and siblings included – are in the last analysis not included in the transformation that takes place: the dominant view is that "parents and in-laws should not be allowed to interfere in the marriage."[89] Even children who may already be around from a previous marriage are not protagonists. If they are still young, their lives are likely to change significantly because of the marriage. But the act of getting married is not about them; they will witness the moment and feel its effects thereafter. The real actors are the two partners, with others playing a supporting role above all.

Moving through Time Together

In our dominant discourse, getting married is not about reinventing the self by catapulting it into an open-ended future that has little to do with the past. It is instead about growth, continuity, and our relationship with one other person. It represents a volitional move on the part of two people, who choose each other, to celebrate and cement their past together into a more official and durable form – one that involves the witnessing and sanctioning of society. One of its core functions is to introduce order and boundaries into the partners' lives. It generates a sense of permanence and predictability. How, exactly, this is accomplished can vary a great deal. As we saw, for instance, conservative or religious couples may put more emphasis on complementarity, or the idea that the union of the two partners receives its strength from the fact that each person is different and endowed with a constitution that "fits" the other well. More liberal partners may instead point to the power of "mutual" support that the partners offer each other. However different, all these represent different venues that bring the partners to the same endpoint: a certain degree of control over the future.

We live in a society that in so many other respects celebrates movement and change with significant passion. We are constantly running from task to task, place to place, mission to mission: in the

American mythology, as sociologist Liah Greenfeld puts it, "the sky is the limit."[90] Getting married stands in sharp *contrast* to life in other regards and acquires a good deal of its significance because of this. We may say that getting married, with its promise for a more orderly future, generates a certain degree of welcome dissonance with the rest of our lives. Perhaps this accounts in part for the relatively high interest in marriage in the United States when compared to other advanced industrialized countries, and for why Americans are almost unique among developed countries in their widespread belief that getting married remains a valuable thing to do.[91] This might be worthy of note for those sociologists and other researchers of the family interested in explaining the differences in marriage trends between the United States and other countries.

Our discourse could paint a different picture of this important transition. In many European and other economically advanced countries, there exists an appreciation for the stability that getting married offers. But life is fairly stable and predictable in most other respects as well: less geographical movement, more permanent jobs, a more substantial safety net, and so on. In those societal contexts, getting married can easily be seen as one of many steps in a calmer, fairly set life (in Southern European countries, for instance, individuals live in their parents' homes until marriage causes them to move out; until then, they have had a pretty quiet existence[92]), one that can bring together not only two isolated individuals looking to join together, but entire families.[93] Thus, in Japan for instance, the tradition of having elderly parents live with their married children has only partly abated with time (with the interesting result that the wife, typically in charge of the household finances, controls not only her husband's money but also that of her parents or in-laws, depending on who might live in the household).[94] In 2002, 30 percent of Japanese aged 65 and older lived with their married children (the equivalent figure in the United States is less than 5 percent). Similar arrangements are observable throughout East Asia.[95] In-laws and other family members live on or near the premises of married couples in Southern and Eastern European countries with noteworthy frequency.[96]

Infidelity, in turn, which goes so directly against the dominant understanding in the United States of marriage and the stability it can bring to the two individuals involved (so much so that discoveries regularly cost political leaders and others their careers), is in some countries tolerated with much more ease. We need only think here of the funeral of French President François Mitterand in 1996, where his wife and his long-term mistress stood side-by-side at the grave accompanied by their respective legitimate and illegitimate children, or by the public claims of another French President, Giscard d'Estaing, that he had as many mistresses as the salons of Paris. These differences point to a rather different understanding of the nature of marriage.

In the mainstream American discourse, getting married is the willful assertion of permanence and order by two persons entering into an exclusive union that sets them apart from a world that is otherwise fast-changing and unstable. It is the celebration of a personal love story, and the shift of the two partners into new roles (husband, wife, etc.) that does not reinvent but refine them. Continuity and connection are at the heart of this transition.

4 The First Child

Having the first child is one of the most complex and intense transitions in life. It is long and contains very diverse phases: planning, the pregnancy, and the arrival of the baby. It brings profound change to our understanding of life itself, most of our daily routines, and many of our priorities. It also alters our relationship to our partners, our selves, and others. How do most prospective and actual parents, health organizations and doctors, our movies and songs, government agencies, religious organizations, and popular and children's books talk about having a first child? Like all major transitions, including those involving concrete physical changes, having a first child is subject to intense cultural interpretation. What does the dominant American discourse say about this transition?

Despite government policies that are often deemed family unfriendly by the standards of the developed world, the fertility rate in the United States is quite high: the National Center for Health Statistics puts it at 2.1 children per woman.[1] Given that most of these children are from wanted pregnancies,[2] we can infer that Americans like having children – with the ideal number, according to the General Social Survey, actually being two for over 50 percent of Americans (only 2 percent of Americans believe the ideal number is one).[3] At the same time, the once powerful expectation that all women should give birth to at least one child – by way of a heterosexual marriage typically between partners of the same race and with a clearly gendered division of labor – is becoming weaker. Many women are not having children, the numbers of homosexual and inter-racial couples are growing (the US Census Bureau reports a 62 percent increase in the number of same-sex unmarried partner households between 2000 and 2010, for instance, and a 28 percent increase in inter-racial or inter-ethnic heterosexual married couples[4]), fathers actively participate in childrearing and many mothers work,[5] around

40 percent of children are now born to unwed parents (40 percent of whom are cohabiting),[6] and reproductive technologies make it possible for greater and greater numbers of single adults and same-sex couples to have children. Having a child is no longer a pre-set, nearly mandatory transition that is bound to happen in a remarkably predictable family setting.

Yet, such flexibility in whether and how we become parents has not led to a proliferation of mainstream interpretations of what it means to have a first child. The dominant discourse – which, it turns out, is adopted by many heterosexual as well as same-sex couples[7] – builds on the perceived stability and unity that marriage or long-term cohabitation create. While the number of single women without a permanent partner having a child has increased, having a first child remains, in the mainstream perspective, a way to "complete" or "grow" a couple's intimate union and in so doing an important step in one's personal development – a way to participate in the life cycle of birth, development, and death. The child comes from a willful decision made by the parents, represents a logical step that builds from the past (the past of each parent and of the two parents as a couple), involves a refinement of the parents' sense of self, ushers in a future that comes with serious responsibilities and duties, and is about more than the parents' individual selves. Much like getting married, this transition is therefore about *Continuity with Others* and *is part of what we mean by "getting settled," but comes with a special appreciation for completion, life's cycle, and inevitability.* The discourse hence belongs to a broader cultural context – one that deserves analysis and should be kept in mind by scholars of marriage in America.

Becoming Parents

"In the United States," write LaRossa and Sinha, two experts on parenthood, "thousands of books on fatherhood and motherhood are published each year, while classes for expectant and new parents have proliferated." The transition, they argue, has become a major object of public attention and social construction. "It is difficult," they continue, "to envision a parent in this country who has not been touched, at least in some way, by these therapeutic vocabularies and programs."[8] Moreover, the vocabularies and programs come from more than books and preparatory classes: they also come, as those researchers themselves note, from a great number of "organizations and bureaucracies," such as government offices, churches, and healthcare providers.[9] What, then, is the primary discourse that emerges from these sources and that informs the perspectives and viewpoints of parents and others around them?

Origins

What drives prospective parents to have their first child? More precisely, when we consider the dominant discourse – what those parents, our popular books, professional family experts, and others say – about becoming parents, does it present an internal or external logic for having a child? Is the first child reflective of a choice on the part of the parents or is it something that, for one or more external reasons, the parents know that they must do? We can begin by observing two important empirical trends. First, the age at which adults become parents has been steadily increasing over time. According to the National Center for Health Statistics, the average age of first-time mothers has increased 3.6 years, from 21.4 years in 1970 to 25 years in 2006.[10] In 1970, 1 out of 100 first-time mothers were 35 years or older. By 2006, the figure was 1 out of 12.[11] First-time fathers are similarly waiting longer to have children. Second, the number of adults – married, cohabiting, singles, or in whatever type of household – who do not have children has greatly increased over time, as Figure 4.1 shows.

Households with no children represented almost 70 percent of all households in 2010; they accounted for less than 50 percent in 1975. These trends suggest that having children has increasingly become optional and that societal pressures to have children, while real, are not overwhelming. The dominant discourse on why parents have a first child cannot, therefore, possibly be about conformity with what everyone else is doing. One can easily choose not to have children and this will be accepted; indeed, well over 70 percent of Americans believe that in a married couple the wife can refuse to have children even if the husband wants them.[12] And when a child is wanted, one generally is thoughtful about the timing, most likely with educational, employment, and other considerations in mind.

What about religious pressures? One can easily imagine God figuring prominently in the dominant discourse of American society many decades ago. What about today? Does the discourse point to God and his will? God, the logic could suggest, wants humans to marry and procreate. Some preachers and priests certainly turn to Genesis (1:28) to urge couples to welcome children in their lives: "God said to them,

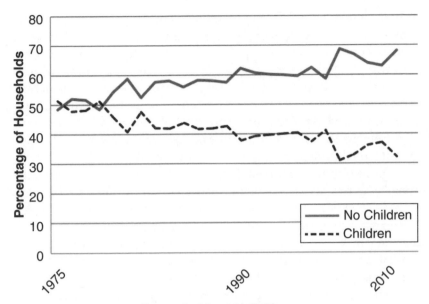

Figure 4.1: Percentage of Households with Children

Source: General Social Survey. Figure derived from cross-tabulation of variables hhtype1 and year.

'Be fruitful and multiply and fill the earth and subdue it and have dominion over the fish of the sea and over the birds of the heavens and over every living thing that moves on the earth.'" Consider the words of project director Aaron Mercer at the National Association of Evangelicals' Generation Forum (the association is headquartered in Washington, DC, and has, as members, over 40 denominations representing approximately 45,000 churches): "Children are a blessing from the Lord, and we should be promoting a culture of life in our nation."[13] Parents should be open to life's conception and welcome it. The perspective of celebrity Pastor Joel Osteen of Lakewood Church, the largest congregation in the United States, sums up this view: "God formed our children with a plan and a purpose, and part of fulfilling that is their unique personality. Part of parenting is simply to unwrap the gift that God has given us."[14]

While certainly present in American society, the religious logic for having a child is actually embraced only by a minority of adults. To begin, only 18 percent of all households in the United States consider themselves to be very religious;[15] most tellingly for our purposes, in turn, only 20 percent of married couples with children consider themselves to be very religious. A good 35 percent of surveyed couples claim that they are either slightly religious or simply not religious; the remaining 45 percent report being moderately religious.[16] The dominant discourse is unlikely to pivot around God. It is also instructive to note that children are increasingly being conceived by adults who are not married, and who are, as one might therefore expect, less inclined to be very religious.[17] In 1975, 95 percent of households with children were headed by married couples; by 2010, the figure was 63 percent.[18] Children are born into significant numbers of non-traditional (single parent, cohabiting partners) types of households.

A more internal, volitional logic actually appears in our discourse about why two adults – whether heterosexual or not – should want to have a child. This is the view of couples wanting to complete and expand their union with a third human being that they wish to love dearly. We encounter this logic in our popular stories, movies, mainstream political rhetoric, and in the results of surveys, polls, and focus groups across different sections of society and over time.[19] The marriage or union of couples reaches a point of maturity and the partners begin looking for a "next step" – something that can expand both their personal and joint boundaries. They desire to broaden their love and emotional reach, and, in a positive and affirmative nod to life itself, decide that the time has come for a third person in their family – a child that is a "part of both of us." "The primary reason to have your first child," Alan Singer tells readers of his popular book *Creating Your Perfect Family Size: How to Make an Informed Decision about Having a Baby*, "is that you and your partner want to raise and love a child." The "desire to be a parent," he stresses, "is not universal or automatic." He then notes that survey after survey of American adults over the last 30 years show that love, companionship, and fun are the primary reasons for parents wanting to have a child.[20]

Singer is indeed correct. A considerable amount of studies based on interviews and focus groups points to a number of closely related reasons for wanting to have a child. At the very top we find a desire to "complete" a couple's marriage,[21] wanting "to give love [to] and receive love" from a child along with an interest in "the emotional benefits of the parent–child bond," and "personal fulfillment."[22] Prospective parents talk about their desire to give birth to a human being that represents their love together: a child fulfills the parents. Indeed, "vicarious fulfillment" – another term for the sense of happiness that parents expect to feel from having a child – appeared as the main driver among a group of young male respondents in a study conducted as early as the 1970s. "Mutual love between mother and child" was in turn the top reason given by young female respondents.[23]

Such logic of completion, growth, and self-fulfillment is prevalent not only among heterosexual couples but also gay and lesbian couples, albeit with some modifications. Results from surveys and interviews show that the reasons gay, lesbian, and heterosexual couples give for having children "converge" around the same "dominant" themes embraced by most parents in society.[24] Hence, a recent carefully designed study of 70, mostly white, gay men interested in adoption shows most respondents believing that having a child is "psychologically and emotionally rewarding" and that "raising children is a natural part of life" which they are eager to pursue. Understandably, those men also list a desire to teach tolerance to others as another reason for a child.[25] Lesbians, too, view parenthood as an important choice they make to enhance their personal development, happiness, and emotional wellbeing.[26]

Couples for the most part choose to create a new human being. External sources of pressure do not figure prominently in how we talk and give meaning to having a first child. We instead adopt the perspective of positive affirmation and the conscious embrace of life. It is a matter of choice.

Past

Our counselors, teachers, parents, and popular movies depict many transitions as opportunities to forget the past – to move on, sever our ties from what has already happened, and pursue something new. Having a first child is, by contrast, portrayed in at least three ways as being about the past. First, and most obviously, the child is the product of, and embodies, the love between the two parents. *Where Did I Come From?*, by best-selling author Peter Mayle, has sold over two million copies since 1977. It is a short book that explains to children where they come from. Its message is as simple as it is revealing of how we talk about couples and the arrival of a child:

> This book is for you . . . we wrote it because we thought you'd like to know exactly where you came from, and how it all happened . . . What happens is this . . . The man loves the woman. So he gives her a kiss. And she gives him a kiss. And they hug each other very tight. And after a while . . ."[27]

A few biological descriptions follow. Mayle has made the order of things clear for many generations of young readers: everything starts from the love between a mommy and a daddy. Indeed, as marriage historian Coontz has shown, our collective imagination (however inaccurate it might be) has told us for decades that parents first meet (ideally as virgins), then fall in love, then marry, and then have a baby.[28]

Second, having the first child is linked to the replication of one of the oldest and most revered institutions in society: the family. "The family," writes University of Chicago sociologist Linda Waite, "is one of the foundational social institutions in all societies."[29] Most Americans accordingly value family enormously: "three-quarters of all adults (76%) say their family is the most important element of their life at this time. An additional 22% say it is one of the most important elements but not the most important."[30] There is little variation in stances across racial, gender, or educational backgrounds,[31] though we note some across political lines (with conservatives being more pro-family than liberals).

Now, for most Americans, starting a family means having a child. According to a major report by the Pew Research Center, when asked what constitutes a family, 99 percent of Americans point to a married couple with children; they have doubts about all other combinations, such as unmarried couples without children.[32] As playwright and author Rachel Shukert put it in a piece in *The Daily Beast* (the online home of *Newsweek* magazine), "in our society, a childless marriage is like the January of the retail season—Christmas is over, Valentine's Day not yet arrived, and no one knows what the hell to sell you. A transitional period, best rushed through as quickly as possible."[33] Despite more tolerance for childless couples (which began in the 1960s and 1970s, with the founding of organizations such as the National Association for Non-Parents), we continue to be, in the words of scholars of the family, a stubbornly "pronatalist" society[34] – that is, perhaps more accepting of those who choose not to reproduce but still certainly very positively inclined toward those who do have children (a stance that has probably intensified with the spread of "family values" ideologies in the 1990s and other related developments in our "cultural discourse"[35]).

The first child is thus understood to be, in the American dominant discourse, not only a matter of physical but also highly valued *institutional reproduction*. New parents recreate the same prized space – the family – that many of us have experienced and that is ultimately a central part of our reality and sense of social order. Parents undertake the task of reproduction knowing that "others" are watching, and those around them express their approval for their contribution to the reproduction of such a fundamental institution. Numerous studies show that Americans thus very much appreciate couples who do have children.[36] Only 20 percent of Americans think by contrast that a family without children is a desirable thing, while over 40 percent think it either undesirable or very undesirable.[37] When asked "What do you think is the ideal number of children for a family to have?," only 1 percent believe the number should be "zero."[38] The majority think it should be "two" – a figure that has been confirmed by Gallup and other sources of data (until the 1960s, according to Gallup, the number was three or greater).[39] Indicative in this regard is an article featured on *WebMD*, one of the most popular American medical websites. It reassures those who prefer not to have kids that they are not alone and support is available: "Today, resources for the voluntarily child-free abound. Support sources include social networking groups, like Childfree Meetup; websites, such as nokidding.net; and books, including *Families of Two: Interviews With Happily Married Couples Without Children by Choice*."[40] Starting a family – that is, having the first child – continues to be a good thing to do, not only for the parents but for the continuation of society, order, and life as we know it.

The third connection to the past has to do with personal memories, older generations, and the desires to provide children with the same loving and caring environment that many of us experienced as children or that we believe we should have experienced. This is the logic of "giving back," of doing for others what others did for us, of families as constituting generations of love. We find this theme regularly in the media, surveys, focus groups, and interviews. We see it, for instance, in how Hallmark, the greeting cards company, helps new parents think about how to celebrate their newborns:

> For many families, the birth of a baby brings a longing for rituals and traditions – ways to affirm the family's history and unique characteristics. Some new parents turn to the family and cultural traditions with which they were raised; others create their own ways that they will pass on to their children. These customs can be something as simple as wrapping your newborn in your old baby blanket or dressing the baby in the same gown that has been used for generations at the christening. Not sure how to create traditions in your growing family? Here are a few ideas to inspire you.[41]

We hear it in the representative words of a 39-year-old white gay physician, interviewed by two researchers, as he explains why he wants to have a child:

I was very close with my brothers and my parents and the whole sort of family atmosphere was so enjoyable and fun and neat. I want to try and recreate something like that, because I think that nothing can really replace the bond you have in a family scenario and there's just so much love and fun and adventure that happens. In a way it's kind of like another extension of being in a relationship; you're just adding more people to your life that you love and care [about].[42]

And we encounter it in the statement by pop star Jay-Z, when he replied in 2012 to questions about how a figure like him would raise his new child with his partner, musician and actress Beyoncé: "I imagine I'll take things I learned from my mom . . . and apply that."[43]

In our dominant discourse, having a first child is ultimately about continuity. It represents a bridge to those who came before us most intimately, to the broader community, and ultimately to the social order in which we find ourselves. It is deeply related to the life cycle, the passing of time, the past, and the future.

Self

An entire industry of consultants, counselors, authors, and health-care providers capitalizes on the transition of adults to "mothers" and "fathers:" it is, without question, one of the most important and symbolically laden transitions in life, as research shows.[44] But does its significance mean that those same voices see it as a major opportunity for the reinvention of the self? Or is this transition depicted as something requiring an adjustment in who we are – perhaps allowing certain aspects of our human nature to come forth? The latter perspective is the most widespread, but with important differences between women and men. Let us consider women first.

Historically, the dominant discourse in the United States (and much of the rest of the world, for that matter) on motherhood saw it as a "natural" dimension in the life of a woman and, as such, constituting a logical step in her evolution. Well into her thirties, a woman was viewed as a potential mother – with her monthly menstruation serving as a reminder of her physiological essence. Pregnancy was therefore the fulfillment or actual materialization of something that could always happen.[45] The gender revolution that began in the 1960s changed many things about both public and private perceptions of women and how they should live. By the late 1970s, as *New York Times* best-selling author Peggy Orenstein writes in her book *Flux: Women on Sex, Work, Kids, Love and Life in a Half-changed World*, women became the "New American Dreamers," and many were "convinced that [they] had no limitations."[46] Women from previous generations were Good Women; the liberated ones were New Women.[47] They could aspire to promising professional careers, play physical sports, refuse to conform to established standards of beauty, and expect their husbands to help with domestic chores and childrearing.

But these powerful changes did not spell out the end of the view of motherhood as natural and, because of that, as a predictable step in a woman's life trajectory. For instance, in her journey through the United States in the 1990s interviewing 200 highly diverse (across racial, class, religious, professional, and geographical lines) women, Orenstein found strong confirmation of this perspective. Reporting her findings in her book, she states that for nearly all the women she met the "childless choice" was simply unimaginable, something that they could not see themselves ever pursuing.[48] Choosing not to have children was what required justification and explanation.[49] Very revealing, in this regard, are federal guidelines issued by the Division of Reproductive Health at the Center for Disease Control and Prevention (CDC) concerning "preconception care." As *Washington Post* staff writer January W. Payne put it:

> New federal guidelines ask all females capable of conceiving a baby to treat themselves – and to be treated by the health care system – as pre-pregnant, regardless of whether they plan to get pregnant anytime soon. Among other things, this means all women between the first menstrual period and menopause should take folic acid supplements, refrain from smoking, maintain a healthy weight and keep chronic conditions such as asthma and diabetes under control.

Payne then notes that "some medical facilities have already found a way to weave preconception care in with regular visits. At Montefiore Medical Center in the Bronx, N.Y., a form that's filled out when check-ing a patient's height, weight, and blood pressure prompts nurses to ask women, 'Do you smoke, and do you plan to become pregnant in the next year? And if not, what birth control are you using?'"[50]

This, however, complicates matters: women now have a multiplic-ity of interests, aspirations, and inclinations. The current discourse on having the first child centers, as a result, on precisely this dilemma: how can a woman successfully "combine" her role as mother with everything else that is now also part of her identity – her profession, her personal interests, being physically fit, and so on? How can a woman be true to her natural calling to be a mother and the other aspects of herself? This is not a matter of crafting a new self, but of dealing with a burgeoning – perhaps too big – sense of self. The potentiality of motherhood, which has always been there, must now express itself in relation to other aspects of the self. In the words of Stanford University psychologist Dr. Laraine Zappert, the key question facing mothers today is no longer one of "competence" but of "process:" "How do I do the things I have been trained to do and still have a life?"[51]

One recommended way is to try and be everything. "It is our vision," write Joelle Jay and Amy Kovarick in their popular book, *Baby on Board: Becoming a Mother without Losing Yourself*, "that women will figure out how to have it all . . . our unique, personal, one-of-a-kind way of living that takes into account everything that matters to us." Their task, upon giving birth, is "to maintain a balance between your career, your baby, your partner and you."[52] Dr. Zappert articulates the same stance when outlining "strategies" for women to "fully engage in [their] careers and still maintain some semblance of balance in [their] lives" in her book *Getting It Right: How Working Mothers Successfully Take Up the Challenge of Life, Family, and Career*.[53] This advice is echoed every month, in different guises, in the national monthly magazine *Working Mother*, which has a circulation of over 800,000 and a dedicated website.[54] It also appears in many other books often written by successful women, many of which, it is worthwhile to note, seem to have educated professional women as their target audience. Their titles alone – *Mothers on the Fast Track: How a New Generation Can Balance Family and Career*,[55] for instance, or *Working Mom's 411: How to Manage Kids, Career and Home*[56] – are quite revealing.

The "have-it-all" approach has had its critics – among them former director of policy planning at the State Department and Princeton University professor Anne-Marie Slaughter, in a compelling cover story in the July 2012 issue of *The Atlantic* magazine[57] – for being inspiring but ultimately unrealistic. A second popular recommended strategy has therefore been to embrace full-time motherhood (i.e., to move out, at least temporarily, of the workforce) *but* to make clear to everyone that this is a deliberate, positive decision made freely – i.e., that the move does not violate women's recently conquered freedom and in fact represents an assertion of that freedom, and therefore maintains continuity with who they have been up until the child's arrival (the other interests are in any event put on hold at the most, and not denied). We see this approach in the language of organizations such as MOMS Club®, a not-for-profit entity started in 1983 by a new mother in California with 2,000 chapters throughout the United States. Its members are full-time mothers, and it has four simple goals and four equally simple guiding principles. These include:

- *Goal #1:* "to provide a support group for mothers who choose to stay at home to raise their children."
- *Principle #1:* "that women must be free to choose their personal path to fulfillment."
- *Principle #2:* "that, for women who choose it, raising children is an important and fulfilling full-time job."
- *Principle #3:* "That a family's decision for a mother to stay at home to raise the children often involves considerable financial sacrifice."[58]

The four statements are remarkable in their preoccupation with declaring that the transition to motherhood does not entail a loss of control or identity. The choice to be a full-time mom is not a return to a world of submission or inequality but the reflection of continued power and freedom. Stay-at-home moms number in the millions, nine-time *New York Times* best-selling author Laura Schlessinger tells her readers in *In Praise of Stay-at-Home Moms*, and this is who they are: they "are women who know in their hearts that staying home to raise children is the right choice for the whole family. Some do it from the outset of their marriage, while others make the difficult transition from career-women to homemakers. Either way, it is a choice . . ."[59]

Fatherhood, too, means adjustment and refinement rather than wholesale reinvention of the self. But the specific nature of this change is different from what is described for women. Let us begin by noting that across all segments of society men have become more intimately involved with their children's lives. Once primarily the family disciplinarians, they are now also caretakers – they change diapers, feed the baby, wake up at night, look over homework, and play with their children. According to the Pew Research Center, in 1965, for instance, married fathers with children younger than age 18 spent an average of 2.6 hours per week caring for those children (provided they lived in the same home). The number rose gradually over the next two decades – to 2.7 hours per week in 1975 and three hours per week in 1985. Then, from 1985 to 2000, the amount of time married fathers spent with their children *more than doubled*. In 2000, the figure became 6.5 hours. "From 1965 to 2000," note researchers at the Pew Research Center, "married mothers consistently logged more time than married fathers caring for their minor children, though the gap between mothers and fathers in time spent on child care narrowed significantly."[60]

The change has not gone unnoticed by counselors, therapists, personal leaders, workplaces, healthcare providers, and others, and has led to a new narrative about becoming a father: men must reach deep within themselves (deeper than is the case for women) to find, and then express, those character traits required to become a true, complete parent. No one doubts that those traits were there decades ago, but nearly everyone agrees that they were essentially dormant. By pausing and getting in touch with this neglected part of themselves, men can now become excellent fathers. The narrative for how this can happen takes on different flavors.

According to one version, the arrival of the first child helps men overcome their immaturities and tame their wilder instincts. "Fatherhood," according to two researchers, "can lead men to become less self-centered, more giving, and achieve a greater sense of direction, responsibility, and maturity. It can also lead men to take fewer risks and temper their lifestyles."[61] By slowing them down, fatherhood allows men to become more balanced and complete adults – much like the women that they married. We can call this the developmental story. A second version – often encountered in training classes for new parents offered by hospitals and counseling services – emphasizes the cultivation of the nurturing figure.[62] Reports from focus groups thus show men embracing more complex roles for themselves: those of "provider, teacher, protector, caretaker" and, when it comes to their spouses, of "supporter" and "co-parent."[63] Men get in touch with their softer, more "feminine" sides.

A third version paints men as almost clueless and helpless but willing and actually capable, if so they desire, to deal with the practical challenges that a new child brings on. Mothers are experts, but fathers are in need of a "survival toolkit" – not unlike the tool boxes they keep at home to fix their homes, lawnmowers, and snowplows – which will instruct them, using language and metaphors they already understand, how to change diapers, put babies to sleep, and prepare meals. The adaptation here is perhaps less than in the previous two cases: it concerns practical preparedness above all. "You are about to become a father," opens *Father's First Steps: 25 Things Every New Dad Should Know*, written by Robert and James Sears, two best-selling authors, brothers, pediatricians, and frequent TV commentators:

Or maybe you have your own bundle of joy already. Maybe you are holding this book because your wife, girlfriend, mother-in-law, or a well-intentioned friend thinks you need it. If so, don't take it personally. Somebody was just probably looking for a cute present and thought you'd be more likely to read a short book than a whole encyclopedia on parenting. Anyway, your wife will read all the important books and fill you in on what you need to know, right?

Maybe. But as a new dad you don't want to risk being left out of the loop, do you? You want to be just as prepared as your baby's mother, but you want the short version, the CliffNotes, the facts you need to know without all the extra stuff. That's what *Father's First Steps* is all about.[64]

Because all these are fairly new visions of fatherhood, the discourse is itself still far from settled. Family researchers point to dilemmas and complex experiences facing fathers. There is a conflict between traditional and more contemporary roles.[65] Yet, what is clear is that our discourse on fatherhood does not see men as facing an opportunity for wholesale self-redefinition. Rather, it presents them as needing to learn how to express hitherto historically neglected qualities. As with women, this task is one of adjustment and modification, and not reinvention.

Future

Prospective parents are told over and over that they cannot imagine how greatly their life will change once their first baby is born. "Having a first child," notes best-selling author John Medina in his 2011 book on how to raise babies and young children, "is like swallowing an intoxicating drink made of equal parts joy and terror."[66] Observers of one education course (stretching from the second trimester to the sixth postpartum month) taught by licensed parent educators for married or cohabiting couples in Minnesota describe the spirit of the course as follows: "Like astronauts who soon will leave earth's atmosphere and go into outer space, the couples were perceived to be in training for what may be the ride of their lives."[67] Terms such as "before," "after," and "on the other side" were routinely used to denote the difference between the normal (pre-child) and the extraordinary (post-child arrival). The transition is often described as exciting, scary, and full of uncertainties. We hear that nothing prepares us for parenthood, that it is new territory and journey: "no matter how much you prepare for it, parenting will blow your mind," writes Rachel Sarah on babycenter.com, a website owned by Johnson & Johnson and winner of the "Best Family and Parenting Site" category in the 2006 and 2011 Webby Awards (which are given annually by The International Academy of Digital Arts and Sciences).[68]

Yet, none of this is intended to mean that the dominant discourse in our society depicts the future as wide open with possibilities and lacking definition. Certainly, the life of the baby itself is indeed full of potential: all is possible and nothing is yet defined. But the life of the parents is seen as heading practically in the opposite direction: it takes on a massive amount of limitations. New parents report feeling highly constrained right after giving birth – a state of mind that researchers call "constrained autonomy."[69] The majority of Americans (52 percent) believe that the arrival of the new baby should translate into mothers staying at home for as long as the child is below school age. Only less than 12 percent believe it is necessary for women to work full-time while the child is under school age.[70] What, then, are the perceived limitations of the future?

In the most practical sense, personal freedom throughout the day is greatly diminished. Consider the language on electronic cards on the popular 123greetings.com website congratulating new parents. One – viewed online more than a quarter of a million times and sent more than 50,000 times – has a drawing of a rocking baby and clock, and states this:

> Now that your baby is here, it's time to brush up on your math . . .
> 1+2+3=24/7
> 1 – "nappy change" (every one hour)
> 2 – "feed" (every two hours)
> 3 – "loud cries" (every three hours)
> 4 – but it all adds up to "happiness unlimited 24/7"![71]

What was once taken for granted – sleep, relaxed meals, time with friends, exercising – now becomes almost a luxury. "Parenthood is the greatest joy you'll ever experience," asserts the authoritative site *WebMD*; "It can also be one of the most exhausting and challenging times in your life. At the end of each weary day, you may wonder, 'What happened to me?' Having a baby can affect your whole life – from your family and friends to work to how you spend your (incredibly rare) 'free time.'"[72] There is a consensus on this front: the transition to parenthood dramatically limits how much free time parents have.

A new child reduces the parents' spending power, and a recurring theme in our dominant discourse is the financial burden associated with parenthood. Certified financial planners, in perhaps too crude a fashion, urge parents to become aware of the "total costs" of having a child in the United States – a cost that needs to take into consideration healthcare coverage and college tuition rates. But they are far from being the only ones. The United States Department of Agriculture (Center for Nutrition Policy and Promotion) has kept track of and publicly released estimates of costs (based on survey data) since 1960, and those figures are then used to establish child support guidelines, determine foster care payments, and more. A report from 2012 puts the total costs of raising a child born in 2011 to the age of 17 (and thus not including college) at around $295,560 for a middle-income family[73] – a figure that in the eyes of experts and commentators alike is actually unrealistically low. These and earlier reports[74] are widely discussed in media outlets such as CNNMoney,[75] *Time Magazine*'s website,[76] and bloomberg.com.[77] Parents worry, and a wide variety of sources address their concern. Telling, in this regard, is how the website babycenter.com provides parents with a "Cost of Raising a Child Calculator"[78] and a "First-Year Baby Cost Calculator."[79]

In a more abstract sense, parents are seen as taking on social and moral responsibilities. New parents constantly hear that they are expected to fulfill their duties as parents. Thus, according to recent research, one "common" and "assumed" reason for "parenting is the fulfillment of social responsibilities associated with conceiving and bearing a child."[80] Fathers and mothers know that they are expected to take care of their children. "In becoming fathers," two scholars note, "men often experience a shift away from their individual concerns and toward family and broader social relationships."[81] Among other things, the image of parents as role models is especially important. Children, the narrative goes, mimic how parents act, interact with others, take care of themselves, react to situations, manage their money, and much more. It is therefore incumbent upon the parents to act as models in all relevant areas of life. "Parents, what kind of role model are you?," asks best-selling author and relationship expert Margaret Paul in one of her regular contributions to the *Huffington Post*. A barrage of familiar questions then follows:

> Do you role model following your passions, or do you spend your spare time watching TV? Do you role model taking good care of your health, or do you smoke cigarettes, eat badly and get little exercise? Do you have a spiritual practice that is meaningful to you and moves you into your heart, or do you stay mostly in your head? Do you have a process for managing

your conflicts with others, or do you tend to withdraw, get angry, resist or comply as a way to control or avoid conflict? Do your children see you avoiding life's difficulties with alcohol, drugs, gambling, spending, TV or other addictive behavior, or practicing learning from life's challenges? Are you boring because you just try to be safe and maintain the status quo, or do you extend yourself and take some risks that result in aliveness and vitality?[82]

The narrative, we should note, has recently become more gender-focused, with a number of resources now explicitly devoted to fathers and how they can serve as role models for their male children. Books such as *Better Dads, Stronger Sons: How Fathers Can Guide Boys to Become Men of Character*[83] (written by Rich Johnson, founder of Better Dads, "a fathering skills program" designed to inspire and equip men to be more engaged in the lives of their children[84]) and *The Next Generation of Dads: A Book About Fathers, Mentors and Male Role Models*[85] communicate to men powerful normative ideas about what they should or should not do as fathers.

Actors

Sociologists and psychologists talk about parenting as being, in significant part, role playing: men and women "act" as parents. "When individuals interact with their children," notes family researcher Barbara Mowder, "they are performing the role of being a parent."[86] Scholars suggest that the concept of "parent" exists independently of any given person having his or her first child. "Parenting," writes Mowder, "in contrast to procreation, therefore, is the performance of the social rather than the biological parent role, requiring that individual parents recognize, assume, and perform the parent role."[87] It is in part an "externally imposed" role, though Mowder also adds that it "is partially an individual creation in that people conceptualize parenting based on their own prior experiences in a parent–child relationship, their thoughts and feelings about being a parent, and their childrearing expertise and understanding."[88] Theories of parenting as role playing, such as Parental Development Theory (PDT), for instance, abound.[89] We have already seen, to some extent, in the "Self" and "Future" sections of this chapter what those roles look like.

Such academic discussions on "parenting" highlight something important about our discourse that is evident already in countless books, websites, and government policies about becoming parents: this is a complicated, symbolically rich transition that involves typically three individuals (two perhaps if a parent relies on reproductive technologies): the baby itself and then the two parents. This is not a transition of the individual but of *multiple protagonists*. How are those actors portrayed, then, in our dominant discourse? We note a few key attributions.

First, the child, who is the core protagonist, arrives onto the scene as an innocent and defenseless being. The child is utterly vulnerable and therefore in immediate need of care and protection: "Babies are helpless," we read in a recent article in *Scientific American* written by Stanford University researcher Melody Dye, "and more to the point, *hopeless*. They could not learn the basic skills necessary to their independent survival even if they tried."[90] But such helplessness is somehow balanced by the perception that the baby "brings joy, wonder and delight" – as one can, for instance, read on howstuffworks.com[91] (a website that has attracted nearly 60 million visitors annually since 2008 and has won multiple awards[92]) – and ultimately embodies enormous potentiality. "A baby's developing brain," states, for example, the website of Early Moments' book clubs for children (which parents can join and have access to classic Disney, Dr. Seuss, and other books), "can be likened to a blank canvas, ready to be painted and shaped by the millions of sensory experiences she'll be presented with during her first year of life. The colors, textures, and sounds in books will help accelerate your baby's mental growth and awareness of her surroundings."[93]

The narrative of potentiality takes on a number of specific forms. A whole industry is dedicated to helping (usually middle- and upper-middle-class) parents raise their newborns into "super-babies," or at the very least strong achievers who can make their parents proud. We see examples in the famous DVDs, toys, and books produced by BabyEinstein™ (now owned by The Walt Disney Company), and in books by best-selling authors such as Dr. Jenn Berman's *SuperBaby: 12 Ways to Give Your Child a Head Start in the First 3 Years*,[94] Dr. Jill Stamm's *Bright from the Start: The Simple, Science-Backed Way to Nurture Your Child's Developing Mind from Birth to Age 3*,[95] and John Medina's *Brain Rules for Baby: How to Raise a Smart and Happy Child from Zero to Five*.[96] Government guidelines on sound nutrition and immunization schedules depict babies as entitled to a safe future where they can flourish and not be harmed by preventable health problems.[97] And life insurance companies focus on the practical necessities of life that every responsible parent must meet to ensure that their children can, in fact, grow and reach their potential. As we read on the website of MassMutual Financial Group®, "Yes, death can be traumatic to think about, but what's worse? Your thinking about it or your children living with the consequences of you not thinking about it and not preparing for it?"[98] Religious, secular, conservative, and liberal variations add further specificity to this narrative.

If the baby is one actor, the parents are the other two actors. In fact, they are actually depicted as forming a single entity: baby is on one side, parents are on the other. Their individual roles may vary, as we noted already earlier in this chapter: the father may be depicted as less competent and knowledgeable, and couples indeed appear to embrace this perception.[99] "Marital couples'" note researchers of the family, "tend to acknowledge a division of labor whereby the wife is recognized as the expert in matters pertaining to parenting."[100] At the same time, increasingly parents are seen as playing an equal role in parenting.[101] But these are differences concerning the internal workings of a new entity: the parents. The arrival of the first child creates that entity, and sets the stage for the relationship between the child *and* the parents. The narrative is typically one of asymmetry, in so far as the parents are depicted as having great power (and responsibility) over their newborn. But the baby, too, appears to have power over the parents: it softens and opens their hearts, making them feel like children again. Thus we read on the website families.com, a major virtual community of parents, that

> children approach the world with such wonder. Everything is new to them. Children allow you to experience some of that wonder . . . having children allows you to do childish things. You don't see many childless couples going to Disneyland or playing at the park. Because these are activities that parents and children do. You can watch your favorite cartoons, play games, and throw around a ball with your child.[102]

And on askmen.com, the largest men's lifestyle website with nearly 20 million readers per month, we learn the top ten benefits of having a child. In the top spot we read that children make parents happier and, in the third spot, that children increase the parents' self-esteem. Children even keep their parents sane while making them thirstier for knowledge.[103]

The actors in this transition are three, then: the baby and then, together, the parents. Others, such as grandparents, may be involved and engaged, to be sure, but not as integral parts of the transition itself. Indeed, they are not needed for the transition to take place – and this can be seen in the number of very limited resources (books, services, government funds, and programs) that are available to them when compared to the parents. Having a first child concerns the nuclear, not extended, family.

Looking for Continuity

We see contradictory tendencies in American society. On the one hand, family life is far less stable than in many other countries: divorce rates are among the highest in the developed world, individuals marry more partners in their lifetime than in other countries, estranged children are numerous and growing, and family members live much further apart than in many other societies. On the other hand, Americans claim to value family greatly – more so, according to many studies, than other, more traditional societies. Their reproductive behavior seems to confirm this latter stance, both when it comes to the higher number of children they have and the relatively younger age of first-time parents.[104]

These contradictory tendencies may in fact complement each other. Precisely because so much of life – including family – is in a state of flux and unpredictability, Americans are particularly keen to look for stability and order in certain spheres of their lives. Having the first child – and therefore starting a family – offers them such an opportunity, and this is reflected in our dominant discourse about the transition. That discourse depicts the newborn as embodying the parents' love and past together, and as ushering in a long period that is seen at once as unknown but also full of new limitations and boundaries. The parents are seen as needing to find ways of adjusting to the new reality: this usually does not call for reinvention of the self, but for managing and juggling successfully multiple tendencies and inclinations. What this means for women and men is different, however: women have to find ways of still asserting their recently acquired freedoms while becoming good mothers, and men have to reach deep into themselves to find their softer sides. The parents are also seen as protagonists in the transition, along with the child, who is seen at once as vulnerable and full of potential. The discourse on having the first child is clear: this is a time of life to build, connect, grow, and, in the process, celebrate continuity.

This is a particular depiction of the transition. Alternative constructions could surely be in place. The discourse could be more monothematic, for instance: in older and more settled societies (many European, African, and Asian countries), having a first child can easily be understood to be an affirmation of continuity in a cultural context that on the whole celebrates continuity itself. A newborn, then, is seen as reaffirming the social order. Thus, "what," exactly, the newborn actually ensures in terms of continuity can vary across cultures. We saw that in the United States the discourse focuses on the child as embodying and expressing the romantic love between the parents. Others – such as the extended family – are not generally part of the picture. The United States is not unique in this regard.[105] But in other contexts, the child may be seen as perpetuating the extended family, the clan, or even the nation. This is the case in Denmark, for example, where the small size of the country (the Danes often refer to themselves as the "tribe") coupled with the historically very high homogeneity of the population (along with a generous welfare system that represents the collectivity and its support for parents) inform the dominant interpretation of starting a family as being a matter of national reproduction. Hence Danes celebrate birthdays by putting Danish flags on cakes, hanging Danish flags from windows, and waving Danish flags when wishing someone happy birthday (and, in fact, marking others' birthdays on calendars with a Danish flag).[106] The birth of a new baby is a collective, not only private, matter.

Attitudes toward gender may in turn translate into a positive discourse about newborns of one sex but not the other. We did not see the American discourse promoting newborns of a particular sex. But, in many societies where continuity – especially of the family line and its wellbeing – is very important and depends on male babies, the image of baby girls comes with serious compromises. India and China are obvious examples. Government policies may intensify those differences. In China, the national one-child policy makes it all the more important that the first child be a boy: parents feel that they do not have a second chance to attain their objectives. Such strong preferences for boys, it is important to note, has had terrible consequences for baby girls with hundreds of thousands missing, sold, or killed. India, according to the United Nations, is now the most dangerous place to be a girl.[107]

The picture of the parents and how they change because of the first child could also be different. Consider the case of mothers. In the United States, the perceived adjustments are premised on the notion that modern mothers have power and autonomy – and that this was only recently won and must therefore be carefully guarded: simply put, their commitment to continuity is an expression of freedom (something that, again, juxtaposes the two themes of openness and continuity). In other societies, the dominant discourse may recognize such power and autonomy to a much more limited extent. The case of China comes to mind again. As Kerry Kennedy (President of the Robert F. Kennedy Center for Justice and Human Rights) put it in the *Huffington Post*, with the imposition of the one-child policy for urban couples, "starting in 1979, the government of China stripped women of their power over their bodies and erased a family's right to make the most cherished, private and fundamental decisions about their future."[108] Public and private pressures not to have children – which can range from shaming to forced abortions – complicate things even further. Women who have their first child in China are therefore doing so in a constrained environment. It is an assertion of freedom, but one that is understood to end with the arrival of the first child. The idea of having two or more children, so common in the United States and other developed countries[109] (including most of Europe[110]), simply cannot be entertained.

In other countries (in Asia, Africa, the Middle East, and parts of Europe), in turn, female participation in the labor force is quite low to begin with,[111] so that the dominant discourse on motherhood there may not include the difficulty of juggling the various priorities that are otherwise prominently discussed in the American discourse. In yet other countries, women, even those enrolled in higher education, are simply not even expected to enter the labor force in any really meaningful way; there, the transition to motherhood is even more linear and coherent. "In some Gulf countries," as Dima Dabbous-Sensenig, Director of the Institute for Women's Studies in the Arab World at the Lebanese American University, notes, "many women go to university to find a better husband or to fill time before they get married."[112] Lack of legal protections at the workplace, harassment, and cultural norms relegating women to the domestic sphere all contribute to keeping women out of the workforce.[113] In those contexts, the discourse on the transition to motherhood is logically quite different than in the United States.

In sum, as is the case with getting married, the arrival of the first child in American discourse is understood to be an affirmation of continuity and connectedness in an otherwise fast-changing world. It is also a shared transition, but only among a very small set of actors – the parents and, when present, the child. It asserts connection, belonging, and a sense of order with important variations for men and women. Such a narrative likely explains, at least in part, why Americans seem quite keen, when compared to adults in other developed countries, to have children – a point of possible relevance for demographers and others interested in fertility rates in the United States. It also contrasts sharply with, and thus counterbalances in a valuable way, how we approach many other important transitions in life, such as going to college. The next chapters shed further light on this contrast.

5 Losing a Job

The financial crisis of 2007–8 and the Great Recession that followed have caused tremendous turmoil in the American labor market. Estimates of total lost jobs exceed 10 million. Blue- and white-collar workers alike, along with their families, have been affected. Even before 2007, however, Americans were no strangers to layoffs. Compared to many other countries in the developed world, job security in the United States since the 1970s has historically been low, partly because dismissing workers in the absence of large-scale collective agreements and protective national laws has been relatively easy: cyclical recessions have led to large-scale terminations of jobs time and time again.[1] Such job insecurity, coupled with limited welfare programs for the unemployed, but also a historically high rate of new job creation and thus the existence of real prospects for finding new employment for those who have lost a job,[2] has made the job loss transition a subject of significant debate and concern in American society. It is a recurring theme in mainstream media, popular books written by career counselors and psychologists, Internet blogs, and even movies and songs. It is the subject of academic and government studies, and has spun an entire industry of "outplacement" service providers – with Right Management, the largest provider, generating over $375 million in revenues in 2010 alone.[3] How, then, is the transition understood and depicted in the dominant discourse?

We can start by noting that the discourse – especially when it comes to recommendations for what a laid-off person should do – primarily focuses on young and middle-aged white-collar workers. This may be a reflection of the fact that, starting in the 1990s, large numbers of workers in the service sector began, for the first time, to feel the effects of economic downturns.[4] The narrative urges workers to distance themselves from the loss and find the strength to turn the problem into a valuable opportunity for exploration and reinvention.

Specifically, the origins of the problem are often depicted as external: the worker is not responsible for (despite what she may be inclined to think), but instead is a victim of, the situation. The past must be let go: a period of real grief or mourning is in order, but this should end fairly soon. What follows is an opportunity for the self to reinvent itself. The future, in turn, is often broken down into two phases. The very immediate future is clearly delineated: one ought to take concrete and timely steps to get over the shock of being dismissed and ensure that the basic necessities of life are met. But the medium- and longer-term futures come as an undefined stretch of time: there will be a job, but what that job will look like is open and undetermined at the start. The laid-off person faces the challenging but also exciting task of contemplating the shape of that future. In all this, the actor – the protagonist – is the worker herself. She is the one who experiences the job loss and, as an individual, must find the strength to begin a new phase in her life. Family members and others are affected by the transition, but this is not about them.

In the job loss transition, we thus see once again elements of American individualism, open-mindedness, and propensity for invention and reinvention. We noticed something similar in chapter 2 with going to college. In the job loss transition, however, the narrative is developed in the context of a negative event. Something undesirable and out of our control happens, and the correct course of action is to turn this into something positive. We sense optimism and resilience: the call for *turning a personal tragedy into a catalyst for potentially exciting and freeing change for the individual* – an approach captured quite well in a great number of books on the subject, personal accounts of painful dismissals followed by powerful self-discovery and recreation, and the recommendations given by public and private employers.

Turning Adversity into Opportunity

In 2006, according to the Bureau of Labor Statistics, the unemployment rate in the United States was 4.6 percent. In 2010, following the financial crisis of 2007–8, it had reached 9.6 percent.[5] In 2008 alone, 2.6 million jobs were lost nationwide – a figure that equaled the number of existing jobs in states such as Wisconsin, Missouri, or Maryland.[6] By 2011, 14 million persons were unemployed – the largest number since the Great Depression.[7] Figure 5.1 shows the changes in national unemployment rates between 2000 and 2012.

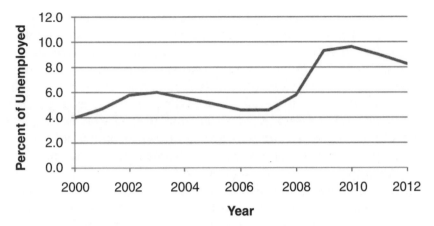

Figure 5.1: Unemployment Rate in the United States

Source: US Bureau of Labor Statistics (http://data.bls.gov/pdq/SurveyOutputServlet)

Most sectors of the economy from finance to manufacturing have been affected. With dwindling savings and resources,[8] workers remain very anxious about losing their job. Data suggests that around three million Americans who have lost their job in recent years have actually stopped looking for a job[9] – a worrisome sign of dejection and renunciation.[10] Labor market researchers have talked about downward spirals, the loss of the American dream, and a widening section of society living with little hope.[11] Ethnographic research reveals American businesses showing little regard for those workers that they are about to dismiss.[12]

It would be reasonable to expect such a crisis to fuel a very negative interpretation of this transition. In several respects, the evidence validates this expectation. But in other regards we encounter a fair amount of positive and hopeful language. The dominant discourse does not portray this transition as an irreversibly painful or undesirable situation: what seems like an unwelcome punishment harbors exciting, even "incredible," possibilities and potential, according to Michael Froehls, author of *The Gift of a Job Loss: A Practical Guide to Realizing the Most Rewarding Time of Your Life*.[13]

Origins

What causes a worker to be laid off? How does someone find himself in such a situation? The discourse on this point is consistent:

affected workers are seen (and are indeed urged to see themselves) as victims of their situation and not responsible for their predicaments. Outplacement firms, researchers, and counselors alike talk about large-scale changes as the causes of a worker's misfortune. The most typical culprits are systematic fluctuations in the economy (cyclical recessions above all), financial crises, and related waves of corporate restructuring. The message, from academics to counselors, is simple: as Katherine Newman (until 2010 a professor of public affairs at Princeton University and now at Johns Hopkins University) puts it, though tempting, "stop blaming yourself."[14]

The University of Southern California has a Center for Work & Family Life, whose mission is to help the university's faculty and staff, and their relatives, deal with the competing demands of work and family. Part of its focus is on job loss, whether at the hands of the university itself or in the broader labor market. On that front, the center makes available for the community a handout titled *Coping with Losing Your Job Employee Handout*. The handout opens by stating that "for some, losing their job is one of the most difficult things that can happen." It then continues:

> If this is true for you, you need to know that:
> 1) It isn't your fault
> 2) It's all right to feel bad about it
> 3) You're not a bad person
> 4) You can survive this, your life isn't over.

"This is something that has happened to you," it then adds, "but it isn't the only thing that is important about you. There's a lot more to you as a person and now is the time to focus on the positive things about you since you may already be feeling negative."[15]

Numerous other universities, from Dartmouth College in New Hampshire to the University of Nevada in Las Vegas,[16] have something very similar available for their respective communities. The phrasing may vary a little, but the content is nearly identical. "Don't get caught in the 'blame syndrome.' Families are not to blame for problems in the economy," we read on the website of the University of Florida.[17] "Don't blame yourself for the cutbacks that left you jobless," states a University of Illinois handout.[18]

Workers should not internalize the loss. A June 2012 article by J. T. O'Donnell, a career and workplace expert who founded the top-ranked career advice site careerrealism.com, in the "Jobs" section of aol.com adopts similar language in the wake of Hewlett-Packard's announcement of an impending 27,000 layoff initiative (the largest in the company's history and amounting to 8 percent of the company's workforce). There we read:

> The reality is that anyone can end up out of work from an unexpected corporate restructuring. It pays to know what immediate steps to take if and when you are faced with being laid off. There are four steps to successfully surviving a RIF (reduction in force).

The first is to "Make Peace with the Separation ASAP." To do this, O'Donnell urges readers to accept that "as painful as it may feel, this was a business decision. We all know corporations don't have feelings. This was not a personal attack or a reflection on you as a worker. It was simply a question of your role no longer being seen as a fit with the financial model of the company."[19]

Outplacement consultants, we learned recently in a *New York Times* article, routinely emphasize that "people are not eliminated, positions are eliminated. (Or, preferably, they are 'made redundant')."[20] In the same vein, Harley Shaiken, a professor at the University of California, Berkeley, an expert on labor and free trade, writes that "many mistakenly blame themselves for losing their jobs. The millions who are suffering the catastrophic consequences, however, didn't make the decisions that got us into this mess."[21] And on job-hunt.org, a leading career search website, we find a section dedicated to "surviving a layoff" that opens in the following fashion:

> People are usually laid off for being in the wrong place at the wrong time in an organization which has decided it needs to cut expenses, specifically the people costs it has. . . . Don't expect logic in who gets laid off and who doesn't, which departments survive and which don't, etc. There is often no discernible logic involved. It's just the luck of the draw, and it is not a personal failure, so don't let it destroy your confidence.[22]

"I lost my job last Friday," wrote TV news anchor and *Huffington Post* contributor Bob Sellers. "I am one of the white collar casualties of a struggling economy and changing industry [television] – and let's be frank – managers looking for a scapegoat to save their own jobs. 'Why?' I asked. 'Ah, it's just the business,' he said. 'That's just the way television is.'"[23] The same manager who recognized his good work, Sellers notes, had nominated him for two Emmy Awards, and who asked him not to take a new job in Washington, DC, a few months before because they were happy with him and wanted him, could only point to the "industry" to explain his termination.

The predominant logic, then, is that workers typically find

themselves in the midst of large-scale structures and places that are undergoing changes that affect workers not as individuals but as cogs or elements of a much bigger system of countless parts. "You have been laid off," we read on the cover of Martha Finney's *Rebound: A Proven Plan for Starting Over After Job Loss*, and "you are not alone. And it's not your fault: you're just one of millions of smart, high-quality people who are being shown the door."[24] "Coast to coast," Finney writes, "– maybe even around the world, given the fact this is one big global economy – people understand that this is an era of no-fault layoffs."[25]

Such reasoning, as we will see in the next pages, has important implications for the way all the other aspects of the transition are understood. A no-fault, no-responsibility mindset allows for a much more energetic and positive interpretation of the situation. Losing a job is not the end of one's career or a sign of inevitable decline. It is the beginning of a transition, as RiseSmart, a leading outplacement firm, makes clear with its trademark approach, Transition Concierge®,[26] designed to help laid-off workers make sense of their experience.

Past

Work is often central to a person's life. Many Americans identify closely with their jobs and derive a sense of purpose from their employment. "Our identities are tied up in what we do for a living," write Dr. Alan Wolfelt (Director of The Center for Loss and Life in Colorado) and Dr. Kirby Duvall (family practice physician) in *Healing After Job Loss*.[27] Psychologists and academics are keenly aware of this fact.[28] National surveys show that career and work are, for Americans, among the most important aspects of life.[29] "Professionals," we read on the website of the Department of Labor of New York State, "identify strongly with their careers."[30] "Without work, who was I? . . . The loss of my job triggered a cascade of self-doubt and depression . . . my nightmare had finally come true . . . I have lost the very thing that defined my days, paced and regulated my life," confides Dominique Browning, former editor-in-chief of *House & Garden* magazine, in her book on suddenly losing her job and having to find a new way of life.[31] "When you lose a job," states Nancy Hunnicutt, career transition counselor in Colorado, "you also lose an important piece of yourself."[32] The loss of a job, especially if not part-time and if held for years, can therefore be traumatic and, in very practical terms, have terrible consequences for the worker and her family. Given this, how is the relationship between a worker and her past depicted in the dominant discourse? How should one deal with the simultaneous feelings of attachment and personal investment in a job *and* the forced severing of ties to that job?

Over and over again, we run into the themes of *grieving, healing,* and *moving on.* First, as to grieving, the laid-off worker is urged not to ignore the sensations of anger, disappointment, and disorientation. The past should not be too readily dismissed: this would be a denial of one's actual and inevitable attachments to the job, and thus carry significant emotional risks and the likely failure to properly reach closure. We must therefore grieve – that is, dwell for some time in mixed, occasionally positive but more often negative, feelings and thoughts. "Feel your grief . . . practice moving through your grief and pain rather than trying to go around it or ignore its presence," write Dr. Wolfelt and Dr. Duvall in their book.[33] And this grieving can contain elements of anger toward those we perceive to be responsible for the turn of events, as Michael Lazarchick, acting president of the National Employment Counseling Association, a division of the American Counseling Association, suggests.[34] Remember, after all, that in most cases we are not to think of ourselves as the cause of our predicaments.

The North Carolina Office of State Personnel, leveraging materials from the National Employee Assistance Services, thus seeks to help the state's workers with a handout titled *Coping with Job Loss: The Grieving Process.* Its message is very representative of what we find in countless books, articles, counseling websites, and other sources,[35] and is at the very heart of the mission of the many One Stop Career Centers set up throughout the nation by the United States Department of Labor, as a recent academic study of staff members at one such center documented.[36] The message equates job loss with the loss of life, wants laid-off workers to acknowledge and accept their emotions and feelings, and offers an objective, almost clinical description of the grieving process:

> The process one goes through during the loss of a job is much like the stages of grief experienced when someone close to us dies. Grief is the healing process we go through after suffering a loss. Grieving involves feelings, attitudes and behaviors that persist over a period of time. Everyone in the person's environment is affected – spouse, children and other family members. It is normal to grieve when you have experienced any devastating loss. The grief process is:

- a set of reactions to loss or the threat of loss, and
- the process of experiencing the psychological, social and physical reactions to your perception of loss.

A person may move back and forth between the different stages of grief – experiencing waves of sadness, anger and fear. Following are the three stages of the grief process and normal reactions during each stage ... Initial Shock and Denial ... Anger/Sadness (acute feelings) ... Acceptance/Resolution.[37]

Such grieving, now a subject of academic research in its own right,[38] has a function. As the Acceptance/Resolution stage above signals, it is never presented as the end or full solution to the problem of being laid off. It is instead an essential step toward "healing," which, upon close analysis, means essentially regaining the wholeness and balance that were compromised by the job loss. Grief is neither an endpoint nor should it last a long time. It is a crucial part of a broader process, as Lazarchick and other experts point out.[39] The University of Illinois' handout *Helpful Tips for Coping with Job Loss* thus offers "Strategies to Help Resolve Grief," emphasizing that grief is normal but the "key is how long they [the emotions of grief] last, and how intense they are, and how much they get in the way of the person's daily functioning."[40] The Christian Networking Group, a Texas-based group of professionals seeking to bring Christian ethics into business, reminds its members that

shock, denial, anger, acceptance, anxiety and embarrassment are all normal feelings. However, the degree of or length of time that those feelings are prolonged can ultimately cause you more harm than release. Your emotions shine through when you communicate with others, including potential employers. Understanding and dealing with the feelings that go along with job loss grief will help you get to the next level in your next endeavor.[41]

Don Straits, CEO of Corporate Warriors, an outplacement service, writes that "by recognizing the different stages [that follow job loss], you are able to move through them quickly, rather than languish in them for weeks."[42] At the University of Washington, employees who have lost their job are advised to "let go of the 'door of the past.'"[43] Something painful happened to us; we were the victims of circumstances beyond our control. We must accordingly lick our wounds and find our center again.

Our grieving and healing therefore help us reach our third and final stage: we are ready to move on. Accepting that the past no longer matters, free from our emotional ties to it, our mission is to move on: that is, *to stop looking back* and start looking forward. "The 'acceptance' stage is the best place to be when starting a job search," we read on New York State's Department of Labor's website.[44] "Spot the horizon, spot the light at the top of the stairs," write Dr. Wolfelt and Dr. Duvall. "If your encounter with job loss has left you emotionally intact," write the authors (two professional counselors and a financial planner) of *The Healing Journey through Job Loss*, "then you are in good shape for the things that are yet to come."[45] Career counselor Estelle Cimino, after recommending to those who have lost their job to grieve and "allow yourself to feel what you feel," reminds the same readers that "when you get knocked down, the sooner you get up, brush yourself off, learn what you can and get back into life the better you will feel. As you rekindle relationships and step more fully into job search mode, the faster you will move beyond the loss. It is not just for you, but is an inspiration for everyone to see and it can make all the difference."[46] We find the same message on monster.com, one of the leading job hunting websites in the country, in a special report on job loss. The first step, again, is to take "grieving time." But this is a step to help one leave the past behind: "When you are ready to pick up the pieces and move on with your life," human resources expert Roberta Chinsky Matuson writes, start thinking about the future, not the past. "Go ahead and mourn, and then prepare yourself for the new life ahead of you . . . develop a plan" and get ready to "bounce back."[47]

Our vision of the world, in other words, should no longer be informed by our past: we have kicked it out of our minds. We will undoubtedly leverage from the past whatever might be useful as we move forward, but this will be an instrumental and very selective relationship to our past: we will use our networks, for instance, or past experience to move forward. But this in no way means that the transition amounts to an incorporation of the past into the present and future. The past is gone, and this very state of mind is what must be embraced and followed for a productive move toward a new future.

Self

The dominant discourse in the United States portrays some transitions – such as going to college – as offering obvious and fantastic opportunities for the transformation and reinvention of the self. Indeed, we sense a general expectation that the self will be changed a great deal by the transition. The narrative around job loss does not immediately focus on such change. In the first instance, the self needs to retreat, regroup, and come to terms with itself: one must take care of one's self. We grieve not only for the job that is gone, but for the part of ourselves that was intimately tied to the job. Sensations of guilt, fear, and disorientation must be dealt with. We need to reflect on what has just happened, and, as Matuson recommends, engage in some self-reflection and introspection.[48] This does not imply drastic change in our selves.

But the narrative on job loss typically moves quickly from the short-term shock to what can happen in the longer term. And here the newly unemployed are seen, in no unequivocal terms, as experiencing unexpected, valuable occasions to rethink who they are, what they can do, and what they want to achieve in life. "As hard as it is to be out of work," the Department of Labor of New York State urges recently unemployed workers to realize, "it also can be a new beginning. A new direction may emerge which will change your life in positive ways. This may be a good time to reevaluate your attitudes and outlook."[49] The National Veterans' Training Institute, the only organization in the nation catering to the employment needs of war veterans (funded by the US Department of Labor), tells veterans that "like any other calamitous event . . . the job loss can present an opportunity for growth . . . this is the time to reassess your strengths, weaknesses, and interests if you are to gain the confidence and optimism necessary for starting over again . . . this may turn out to be a positive turning point."[50]

Indeed, being fired or terminated is often presented as a "gift in disguise," as the forced severing of ourselves from what was most likely anyway a less-than-optimal situation. Now we have the chance to recreate ourselves, and it is incumbent upon us to at least contemplate this unique opportunity. Hence, in Froehls' *The Gift of Job Loss*, we read:

> I call it the "gift of job loss." It is a gift, because this new situation is handed to you . . . because your job loss carries a lot of good things, like an unopened present under the Holiday tree. This great gift is the gift of time. All of a sudden you have time on your hands, time you can use strategically to build your future . . . this is an opportunity for you to reflect, plan, and dream about taking one, two, three, or even six months off to pursue a diverse set of activities that might never occur again in your life – activities that might ultimately make you happier, healthier, and even richer than trying to find a job immediately . . . you only live once. Turn job loss into the most rewarding time of your life . . . my time of job loss brought me incredible happiness . . . I gathered new ideas for my career

ahead, potential investments, and startups. I learned a new language. I increased my knowledge about Latin America.[51]

Randy Siegel, a nationally recognized specialist in professional development, self-branding, communications training, and executive positioning, talks about "an unexpected gift" and the possibility of reinvention:

> Open Yourself to Possibilities. Many recently unemployed people have discovered an unexpected gift in their layoffs: the opportunity to realign their careers and lives with their needs, wants, and values. Just because you've been in the same field for twenty years doesn't mean you have to stay in it. Now may be the time to reinvent yourself and pursue your dream job. What have you always wanted to do, but never did? Your education, experience, and skills may be transferable. The biggest mistake job seekers make is to become desperate and settle for a less than ideal job.[52]

Because of job loss, we can, in other words, *transform* and *reinvent* ourselves – whether on the professional or personal fronts. "Allow for Transformation," write Wolfelt and Duvall.[53] The Colorado Bar Association reminds its members and other interested parties that "nasty calls" telling us we have lost our job may actually generate in us a "resolve to reinvent ourselves in midlife," and to heed a "restless longing" we may have inside "to pursue a dream."[54] On the aol.com Personal Branding Blog, we read that the jobs that "have been washed out of the economy during the four or five years simply are never coming back – ever." The logical thing to do for laid-off workers is "reinventing yourself": acquire new skills, enter new industries, and create a brand new profile.[55] A new self can, and indeed should, emerge from this experience, and with this a new phase of our lives can begin: as one article in the job loss section of cleveland.com puts it, "nobody welcomes the loss of a job, but countless men and women are turning a negative situation into one with a positive outcome. If you can look at your job loss as a chance to start a new phase of your life, you, too, may find that reinventing yourself is an opportunity to live the life you deserve."[56] "Switch careers or industries," we read on about.com's career section, "learn new skills," and perhaps "consider relocating."[57]

All this exudes a remarkable sense of optimism. An objectively undesirable situation is portrayed as a valuable opportunity for positive change. We are invited to rethink in comprehensive fashion who we are, even if in practical terms many of us may continue along the same path we have been on before. And this means that the future, too, is bound to be considerably open and undefined, as the next section shows.

Future

The very immediate future comes with clear instructions: there will be disorientation and anxiety, and one will therefore need to take concrete measures to ensure that the practical needs of everyday life are met. These include meeting short-term financial obligations (such as paying rent and utilities), having enough money to buy food and other basic necessities (by claiming unemployment benefits, for instance), arranging for temporary healthcare insurance (through, for instance, available federal government programs such as the Consolidated Omnibus Budget Reconciliation Act of 1986 and the American Recovery and Reinvestment Act of 2009), informing family members of what has happened, and reaching out to one's personal network with an update on the new situation and to begin looking for employment possibilities. Thus the Financial Planning Association, the largest membership organization for personal financial planning experts in the United States, offers the following insights:

> Job loss is a fact of working life in America, even in the best of times. Take a deep breath. You'll get through this, though it may appear pretty gloomy at the moment . . . In times of such stress, it's easy to make hasty financial decisions that turn out poorly. So in the immediate wake of your job loss, don't cash in your retirement plan, sell off long-term investments or move until you've worked out a realistic plan for dealing with your reduced income . . . Tell any children or other family members who depend on you financially how the job loss will affect family spending. Ask them for budgeting suggestions. This can help ease anxiety they may have, especially if you have to make a major change such as moving.[58]

"Get emotional support," we read on everydayhealth.com, "manage your money . . . create a daily routine . . . learn how to manage stress."[59] The discourse also tells us, as we have already seen, that the short term is also likely to cause emotional and mental disturbances, and inevitably entail the newly unemployed moving through a set of "stages," as Dan Straits of outplacement firm Corporate Warriors writes, that include a combination of denial, disbelief, outward anger, self-criticism, withdrawal, grief and reflection, and finally acceptance.[60]

This is all about the short term, however. The medium- and long-term future is quite different. Simply put, the future is in our hands and awaits definition. A wide array of outcomes is possible, and it falls upon us, as individuals, to decide what specific course things will take. Two general directions seem available. We can be passive and let external circumstances dictate what is going to happen. As Nan Russell, radio host and author on work and career issues, puts it:

> Job loss profoundly affects your future. You can yield to its impact like a bitter tasting elixir, transforming you into a victim whose negative mindset and depressed expectations operate like self-filling prophecies. Or, you can grieve while moving through the stages of job loss, dealing with your anger, bitterness and fears, gaining insights, and turning inaction into action to build a great future.[61]

The first direction, if chosen, certainly comes with particular characteristics – and in this sense we can predict ahead of time what those months and years will look like: we are told, indeed warned, that we will wallow in self-pity, experience depression, and perhaps one day find a dull job that will never truly satisfy us. That route is full of predictable "pitfalls," we learn from the University of Georgia's *Surviving Tough Times* series of handouts for families and individuals experiencing unemployment or under-employment, including isolation from others and even substance abuse.[62] But the predefined qualities of this future do not make it inevitable: it is a path that we can choose or reject, depending on our inclinations and preferences. Typical, in this regard, is the exchange between a reader and career transition counselor Kerry Hannon, who authored an article in forbes.com on the importance of being proactive when searching for a new job after being laid off. "Great article Kerry!" states one reader, "I love the positive tone, and it's a great reminder to be proactive rather than wallow." "Thanks ..." Kerry replies, "Wallowing never helps that's for sure."[63]

The second, and most recommended, direction is to capitalize on the opportunity of openness and freedom that is presented to us. Job loss frees the single individual from the constraints he once knew: nothing for the time being tells him where to be, what to do, or how to spend his time. As Steve Jobs put it in his commencement address delivered at Stanford University in 2005 (watched over 15 million times on YouTube) when describing getting fired from Apple, the company he himself had founded,

> I didn't see it then, but it turned out that getting fired from Apple was the best thing that could have ever happened to me. The heaviness of being successful was replaced by the lightness of being a beginner again,

less sure about everything. It freed me to enter one of the most creative periods of my life.[64]

The future becomes wide open, awaiting our direction, our willful definition and imprint. Hannon thus recognizes that we may not be feeling like "turning on our laptop and setting the stage for what's next," but that is precisely what we must do.[65]

Hence in a recent article in the *Boston Globe*, we learn about professionals whose loss of a job (which did not happen "by choice") is described as a "blessing," allowing those laid-off workers to feel "liberated from the shackles" of their previous jobs and to have a "fresh slate" to pursue "a new passion," start "running their own business," have a "saner schedule," or go after those dreams and aspirations they were unable to contemplate beforehand.[66] With such an open view of the future in mind, Jim Davis, blogger, career counselor, and author of the popular *The Job Loss Survival Guide*, advises his readers to "create a vision of what you want your future to be. Then plan how you can make the vision become real, and work toward it a step at a time. It's best to actually write out your plan so you can make it more definite in your mind. You might consider it your personal 'business plan.'"[67] Because of this very mindset, Andrea McCarren, a journalist with WJLA-TV, the ABC affiliate in Washington, DC, acquired quick fame across the world for embarking with her family on a recreational vehicle trip across the United States after being caught in a mass layoff – only three days after covering President Obama's inauguration in 2009. Using social media, she chronicled her process of exploration and soul-searching. It was seen by many as the prototypical American response to her problem – "I had suddenly become the poster child for the financial crisis in the United States," and she was accordingly invited to write an essay about her time of rediscovery in the *Washington Post*, appeared on CNN, and attracted media interest from Taiwan to the Netherlands.[68]

In this spirit, Dr. Lynn Joseph, psychologist, author, career consultant, and "life transition specialist," urges us to engage in visualization exercises[69] where we contemplate multiple futures and ultimately select the most attractive:

> In this exercise, you'll imagine one of several possible paths for your life. Resist the urge to limit your happiness and accomplishments. Have some fun with the experience, and see what creative ideas begin to surface . . . when you have completed the exercise with one of your imagined future selves, repeat it once or twice with other possible future selves. Imagine

what your future might look like if you took a different career direction
... explore your interests ... [when you select one future], notice how
deep that desire is for that future.[70]

It is as if we are in the position of almost shopping for our future, but
what is especially noteworthy is the fact that we are also the very crea-
tors of the various possible futures we are considering – even those
we end up tossing out. We notice, once again, the individualized
nature of this story.

Now, to be clear, a wide open future does not mean that we will
necessarily choose to fully redesign our lives. One obvious trajectory
is that we are able to "transfer" our skills into a new job that, in fact,
relies on those same skills. In this spirit, the US Department of Labor
sponsors a service, found at myskillsmyfuture.com, where laid-off
workers can specify their "old" professional and related skills and use
the site's database to "build a bridge to your new career" – or, more
simply put, find openings to which they can conceivably apply.[71]
Plenty of career planning resources advise workers to think of how
their existing skills may be used in different industries and careers.
In this sense, the future will offer continuity with the past. Yet, what
really matters is that this is generally understood to be part of a larger
discussion where the future is, indeed, open-ended: it is really up to
us to determine what is next.

Actors

The discourse on job loss focuses squarely on the person experiencing the transition. The grieving process outlined by so many experts
concerns that person only: what is described are her emotions,
thoughts, and reactions. There is much discussion about handling
the past, especially the attachment one may have to one's workplace,
colleagues, and professional identity. But, again, such discussion is
about the worker who just lost her job and not anyone else. The same
can be said about the self and the future: virtually every element of the
dominant discourse centers on the worker, not her family, parents,
friends, former colleagues, neighbors, or anyone else. This is a transition of the individual, and not a collective affair.

With this in mind, it is worth noting that "others" do appear in
the discourse on this transition. References to family members, colleagues, and friends abound. They are not protagonists, to be sure,
but they are someone who the laid-off worker must consider as she

moves along the transition. They appear as supporting characters in the transition, informing or even completing our understanding of the nature of this traumatic event.

One's former managers or employers, for instance, appear in the early phases of the transition. They are the ones who make the decision or at the very least inform the worker that the job has come to an end. They are the messengers delivering the bad news. They are portrayed as suddenly distant, often unpleasant, and sometimes hypocritical, especially if they had praised that person's work and contributions over time. "The folding of our magazine was ruthless," writes Dominique Browning, *House & Garden* former editor-in-chief between 1995 and 2007, in the opening pages of her book *Slow Love: How I Lost My Love, Put on My Pajamas & Found Happiness.* "Without warning, our world collapsed. I came to work on Monday, went to the corporate offices for a meeting, got the news, and was told to have everything packed by Friday . . . security guards were posted."[72]

Managers and employers are also described as the legitimate target of the workers' angst and confusion. It is natural, we are told, to feel strong negative emotions toward those who fired us. The discourse thus focuses on how the laid-off worker should relate to those managers and employers: it is a question of reorientation toward those individuals, and, along with that, toward the company or corporation where the worker likely spent years. It is important, for instance, to acknowledge and then come to terms with that anger, so that we do not do anything harmful with it or carry it with us as we begin the process of looking for our next job. As Dr. Lynn Joseph put it in a "Live Q&A" on the website of the *Washington Post*, in response to a question about anger from someone in Austin, Texas, "recognizing that you are angry and who you are angry with, for example, is the first step toward relief . . . Acknowledge and express your feelings safely. Be sure to do it in a setting that is safe from any kind of reprisal."[73]

Family members also appear regularly in the transition, typically as persons who will feel the effects of the transition, who need to be informed of what has happened, and whom the worker should tap for support. The language used by New York State's Department of Labor (Career Services) is representative in this regard:

> Unemployment is a stressful time for the entire family. Your family may experience adverse reactions to your job loss. For them, your unemployment means the loss of income and the fear of an uncertain future. They are also worried about your happiness. Here are some ways you can interact with your family to get through this tough time:

Do not attempt to "shoulder" your problems alone. Try to be open with family members even though it is hard. Discussions about your job search and the feelings you have allow your family to work as a group and support one another.

Talk to your family. Let them know your plans and activities. Share with them how you will be spending your time. Discuss what additional family responsibilities you can take on when your job search day is complete. Add these new responsibilities to your schedule.

Listen to your family. Find out their concerns and their suggestions. Perhaps there are ways they can assist you.

Build family spirit. You will need a great deal of support from your family in the months ahead, but they will also need yours.[74]

Special attention goes to children – both victims and potential sources of support in this transition. Even if young, they will sense what is happening, as a recent article in the *New York Times* about children from a relatively wealthy community in Ohio and job loss notes: they have "eagle ears" and can hear what parents are talking about, even if they whisper, and they worry about how their own lives will change as a result.[75] "Children may be deeply affected by a parent's unemployment," continues New York State's Department of Labor; "it is important for them to know what has happened and how it will affect the family. However, try not to overburden them with the responsibility of too many of the emotional or financial details . . . Keep an open dialogue with your children . . . make sure your children know it's not anybody's fault." And the laid-off worker is also reminded that "children need to feel they are helping. They want to help and having them do something like taking a cut in allowance, deferring expensive purchases, or getting an after-school job can make them feel as if they are part of the team."[76]

The third set of actors we often see depicted in the transition are those belonging to the worker's network. Here, the relationship is explicitly seen on a utilitarian basis: the network can be very useful in helping one find new opportunities. The worker must therefore tap into this resource without hesitation. At the University of Washington, for instance, employees who have lost their job are offered the following piece of advice:

Job-search experts agree that one of the most effective ways to find a new job is through the people you know. These people can alert you to opportunities that come to their attention. They can also be an advocate for you. Make a list of people you know, and identify those you think will be willing to help with your job search:

- Contact those on the list and let them know that you are looking for employment.
- Be clear about the kind of opportunity you are seeking what you would be willing to take.
- Ask them to contact you if they become aware of an opportunity in which you might be interested.
- Make sure you provide people with contact information by which they can easily reach you.
- Distribute your resume to anyone who is willing to read it.[77]

The network includes close friends as well as past colleagues, acquaintances, and anyone who might indeed be reachable via tools such as LinkedIn, Facebook, and Twitter, as Miriam Salpeter, job search coach, social media coach, and writer for the *US News & World Report's* "On Careers" column, reminds her readers in her popular book *Social Networking for Career Success*.[78] Those in our network are always potential, if not already actual, witnesses to our transitions, and we should strive to reach out to them whenever possible. To return to former ABC journalist Andrea McCarren and her post-layoff trip across the United States, her use of social media meant that "1,000 friends" followed her and her family on her transition. "Strangers" through Facebook and LinkedIn offered her a place to sleep, "the use of their cars, and home-cooked meals." Social media, she adds without hesitation, "provided the majority of our story leads." After the trip, she concluded, she "feels confident and optimistic about the future. But what will I do next? Just check my Facebook status."[79]

Job Loss as an Opportunity

The dominant discourse on job loss depicts the transition as ultimately one of opportunity. The person who loses her job is thrown into momentary and painful confusion. The same person is then expected, as an individual, to turn this adverse situation into a freeing opportunity where one has the chance, if she so desires, to craft a new self and a new future for herself. The origins of the job loss are external: one is normally fired against one's will. But throughout this is a story of the worker: it is an individual transition, and one that emphasizes individual initiatives, openness, possibilities, and optimism. It is a story well aligned with broader notions in American culture about the importance of overcoming adversity. As First Lady Michelle Obama stated in her speech at the Democratic National Convention in Charlotte, North Carolina, in August 2012, "let us never forget that doing the impossible is the history of this nation . . . it's who we are as Americans . . . it's how this country was built . . . Because in the end, more than anything else, that is the story of this country – the story of unwavering hope grounded in unyielding struggle."[80] The dominant discourse on job loss is consistent with this worldview.

As with the other transitions examined in this book, matters could be portrayed quite differently. In particular, the insistence on viewing the individual as in charge of his own future – as holding the key to his potential renaissance, as being responsible for pulling himself up by his bootstraps, as Nancy Hunnicutt, career transition counselor at the Larimer County Workforce Center in Colorado, puts it[81] – may be particular to the United States. A recent comparative study of how career transitions are interpreted in China, Europe, and the United States makes clear that "individualistic" accounts are especially prevalent in the United States. In China especially, researchers found a much greater tendency to attribute career changes (and not only the experience of a lost job) to outside forces, such as the labor market, government policy, and the ideas of friends and families: Chinese workers are much less likely to view themselves, as individuals, as in control of their own future. European countries stand between China and the United States in this regard. "Luck," for instance, along with "unsought opportunities" and other "contingencies" are seen as partly responsible for career changes.[82]

The American discourse is also particular in its depiction of job loss as sudden and unexpected: upon going to the office one morning, one learns that she has but a few days at most to pack and leave all company-sensitive materials behind. Academic research suggests that this depiction is in fact consistent with actual, on the ground experiences.[83] After years of working at a company, one's life is abruptly turned upside down. This sets the stage for the importance of grieving, of soul-searching, of making rapid arrangements for the short term. But in other countries the "reductions in force" so typical of the American marketplace happen much more slowly, are often contested, and may even be reversed. Multinational corporations accordingly report their difficulties when trying to implement reductions in Europe – whether in Great Britain, Spain, France, or Germany – that would otherwise happen much more rapidly in the United States. "Don't expect anything [to happen] under three months," states Thomas Belker, managing director of HR for OBI – one of the world's largest home improvement companies – near Cologne, Germany.[84] The European Union's own legal mandate for companies operating in two or more member states requires consultations with works councils, and thus guarantees a more tortuous process. Many national-level laws require long and difficult processes for purely domestic enterprises. The image of the stunned laid-off worker heading home to lick his wounds is unlikely to resonate in Europe. One may be able to cling onto a job after all, sue the corporation, or avail oneself of a transition plan made available by the company or public services.

It also seems important to recognize the fact that job loss and then the possibility of reinvention of some sort only make sense in a context where workers are first fired but then, in light of historical trends and what they know generally happens to individuals in their situation, expect to find a job fairly soon. Chronic unemployment – a situation in which one is unable to find work despite his best efforts – is, in other words, not typical of the United States, at least not until the financial crisis of 2007–8 came along.[85] Data suggests that until recently "in the United States, unemployment has typically been a relatively brief affair. The vast majority of people who lost jobs soon found new work. That is not the way it has been in many other developed countries."[86] Chronic unemployment has existed in certain European countries, such as Spain and Italy, for some time, where certain segments of the population, such as the young, have been unable to find any sort of meaningful employment for decades, and in many parts of Africa and Asia, including Japan.[87] The language of professional reinvention has a place in a historically dynamic labor market – one, we might add, where the idea of career change in midlife or any other point in life is appreciated even for those who do have a job. Here, again, the case of many European countries comes to mind – for there we also observe, next to the permanently unemployed, large segments of the population that work in very protected professions from which they cannot be fired and which they are very unlikely to leave. And here, as is the case with other life transitions, we see a close connection between discourse (and thus culture) and practical reality – a point worth noting given the tendency (described in the first chapter of this book) of life course sociologists to view transitions in mostly structuralist terms.

The idea of reinvention, as an element of the dominant discourse, is also clearly possible only in a system that does not condone in principle or practice widespread work conditions that are unpleasant, difficult to escape, and quite often illegal (i.e., happening in the informal economy or black market). It can only happen in a labor market that overall offers (or has until recently offered) real opportunities for large numbers of workers. The International Labor Organization reported in June 2012 that forced labor is not a situation many Americans need to contend with, but the same cannot be said of workers elsewhere, especially in Asia-Pacific countries.[88] In countries like Afghanistan or Pakistan, the notion of "self-reinvention" is probably meaningless for the vast majority of the population. Media sources, government organizations, and employment experts are much more likely to talk about survival, improvements in basic conditions, migration to urban centers, and other such things.

The dominant American discourse about job loss promotes a distinctive blend of individualism, openness, and reinvention. It represents a remarkably forward-looking positive response to adversity – a call to assert oneself in the midst of challenges and to turn difficulty into an opportunity for a potential renaissance. At its essence, it is therefore consistent with the discourse we encounter for many other transitions and ultimately a broader cultural context, as the next chapter further confirms.

6 Surviving a Life-Threatening Disease

Millions of Americans survive life-threatening diseases every year. The National Cancer Institute states that 11 million Americans are cancer survivors.[1] The American Cancer Association puts that figure at 12 million.[2] These are impressive numbers and acquire even more relevance when we consider that there are approximately 28 million cancer survivors in the world:[3] the United States accounts, in other words, for over 40 percent of all survivors. Other life-threatening diseases afflict millions of Americans as well, with many also managing to survive. The National Eating Disorders Association estimates that around 30 million Americans suffer from eating disorders such as anorexia and bulimia at some time in their lives;[4] the South Carolina Department of Mental Health reported in 2013 that 8 million Americans currently have an eating disorder.[5] These disorders can be deadly: a recent study published in *The American Journal of Psychiatry* estimates that 5 percent of those suffering from eating disorders such as anorexia and bulimia eventually die,[6] while the National Association of Anorexia Nervosa and Associated Disorders estimates that nearly 20 percent of all anorexic sufferers die within 20 years from the onset of the illness. Yet, full recovery is quite common, with studies showing around 50 percent of persons affected returning to normal health after years of struggles.[7]

These and other statistics suggest that many millions of Americans every year find themselves cured, at least for a time, from a disease that would have otherwise killed them. Survivorship is without question at once a momentous and widespread transition – made all the more relevant by the fact that, according to the General Social Survey, well over 65 percent of Americans have at one point or another known someone close to them, including themselves, that has had to face a life-threatening or terminal disease.[8] It has consequently attracted the attention of a diverse set of governmental institutes, hospital programs, medical schools and professional associations, and other organizations. It is the subject of books and reports by experts and survivors, blogs, and personal memoirs. There are many networks and associations of survivors, and numerous extensive academic studies and reports on the subject. Most of the attention is given to cancer, with a lesser, but still significant, amount going to eating disorders: this chapter will therefore focus on the survival of these two types of diseases.

We will observe the articulation of a rich and rather cohesive, though of course not universally embraced or without variations, discourse on how we should make sense of this transition. The discourse is largely addressed to those who have just recently won their battle against their disease. It stresses that what may seem to be an apparently simple transition back to health is in fact quite surprisingly multifaceted and complicated. The overall image is one *of a delicate crafting of one's new life, one that comes with the imperative but also moral freedom to take advantage of our recovery.* The origins of the transition begin with the defeat of the disease. In this regard, this is primarily an internal matter: medicine and other external factors such as family and friends certainly help but, ultimately, the survivor beats the disease. She had the strength and perseverance to overcome this challenge. It was, above all, a personal battle. Here, the past is certainly to be kept in mind, but this does not mean that it will be necessarily incorporated into one's future life. The point of surviving the disease is that it can be relegated to the past.

Thus, when it comes to the future, the discourse depicts survivors in a position of renewed power. More specifically, their survival almost imposes on them the duty – and in a sense the moral freedom – to craft the life they really want to live. Hence, the self – and this is an individual transition above all – is given a second chance at life and, because of this, the opportunity to assert itself in unprecedented new ways. This is a transition featuring assertion, deliberation, and refreshing discovery – unprecedented authenticity, in one word. At the same time, challenges also lie ahead: the joy of surviving is coupled with disorientation, fear of relapse, personal and relational readjustments, and thus the feeling that one must tread very carefully indeed. Survivors have open futures ahead of them and a new chance to decide who they wish to be, but they must approach both things with attention. Thus, this transition, like many others, is about forward movement, but the uncertainty associated with it calls for caution and care as the survivor takes her next steps into a renewed life.

Restarting Life, Cautiously and Thoughtfully

The National Cancer Institute makes a booklet available to patients who have survived their battle with cancer. It is characteristically titled *Facing Forward: Life after Cancer Treatment,* and the website that hosts it introduces the booklet with a quote from a former patient and a response from the institute's staff:

> "While I was having chemo, I quit doing almost everything. So when treatment ended, the challenge for me was, what am I going to do now with my life? What should I go back to doing?"
> – Len

> Many cancer survivors have told us that while they felt they had lots of information and support during their illness, once treatment stopped, they entered a whole new world – one filled with new questions. This booklet was written to share common feelings and reactions that many people just like you have had after treatment ended.[9]

The title and introductory passages capture rather well the heart of the American dominant discourse on surviving a life-threatening disease. It is a phase of its own – "a phenomenon in itself," to use the words of Dr. Fitzhugh Mullan, a member of the Institute of Medicine, and one of the earliest contributors to the cancer survivor discourse.[10] With that in mind, the transition is perceived as offering remarkable openness and new opportunities, a feeling that we should somehow capitalize on our recovery, and disorientation coupled with a feeling that we should tread very carefully. It is a subtle message that deserves close examination, which we may begin by noting that research suggests that not all survivors unquestionably embrace its content[11] and that subtle but real variations on the dominant themes exist, as a recent study of breast cancer survivors from different ethnic groups in Florida shows.[12]

Origins

What, in our dominant discourse, accounts for a patient's success in overcoming a life-threatening disease? To be sure, medicine is often seen as very important, and medical professionals are inclined to emphasize this.[13] But medicine – much like other resources such as friends and mentors – is often portrayed as a tool and the spotlight is put on the patient: it is the patient who overcomes the disease. The narrative takes on a number of variations. One of the most common is that the patient, by way of determination and courage, beats the disease: there was a fight, and the patient has won it. This is most easily observable in cases where the disease has obvious psychological components, such as alcoholism or eating disorders, but it also appears prominently in the case of primarily physical diseases such as cancer.

Thus, as we read on healthguidance.com, a leading health-focused website, in an article on the "best way to survive" breast cancer, "the most important thing to remember when coming to terms with breast cancer is how important it is to fight the disease. Treatment is a great way to do this, but perhaps the most important way is to adjust your mindset to one which is focused on beating the disease."[14] Similarly, in a video released by the Idaho Department of Health and Welfare in 2008, two colon cancer survivors share their personal stories. One, Karen Echeverria, describes the thoughts that came to her right after the successful operation that removed her cancerous mass (and part of her colon as a result). The removal was certainly done in a hospital by medical staff, but this is not what Echeverria felt upon waking up from the surgery and what she shares with viewers:

> When the doctor came into the hospital room and told me that we got it all, you don't have to do anything else, we are finished . . . I felt the sense of . . . I definitely felt strong . . . that I had won, that I had beat [sic] this battle, and, and I do feel stronger because of that; I thought, if I can go through that, if I can go through that emotionally and physically, I can get through anything, I can get through anything.[15]

The message is clear: patients can, and do, win. The treatment, if anything, is part of the challenge – something that has to be endured and overcome. In the same spirit, MD Anderson Cancer Center, ranked the very top cancer treatment hospital in the nation for six years in a row (between 2007 and 2012) by *US News & World Report*, features on its homepage the story of Katherine Hale, a patient diagnosed with uterine cancer and given only a few weeks to live by her doctors "back home." The story is summed up in these few sentences, and makes quite clear why Hale survived:

> "The most important thing in my life is being a mom," Katherine Hale proudly admits. That's why when Katherine's local doctor diagnosed her with uterine cancer and told her nothing more could be done, she told him "I have three kids. I'm not giving up." It was because of her husband, Paul, and children Heston, Lauren and Pamela that Katherine chose to fight cancer. Now she just had to choose where . . .[16]

Hence the narrative includes an element of choice as well: one has the option to fight or give up. And the choice to fight becomes crucial for survival. "This is why I have come here to meet you," Shannon Cutts tells her readers in *Beating Ana: How to Outsmart Your Eating Disorder and Take Your Life Back,* her book about overcoming eating disorders: "so that I can say to you with pride, humility, and the unshakeable conviction that if I could heal from my eating disorder, *anyone* who wants to heal badly enough *and is willing to do the hard work for recovery* can do so too."[17] Jocelyn Golden, in her award-winning book on beating bulimia, delivers emphatically the same message: "The good news is that the first step is often the hardest step. And that is the decision to *choose recovery* . . . Just choose . . . The only issue is taking that first step."[18]

Choice is similarly at the heart of Anita Moorjani's *Dying to Be Me: My Journey from Cancer, to Near Death, to True Healing.* In the summer of 2012, the book was ranked #3 on amazon.com under the subject of "cancer" and #352 among all books. Her personal story has attracted considerable media attention. The title itself highlights the personal dimension of recovery, and a sentence right below the title reveals the core message of the book: "*I had the choice to come back . . . or not. I chose to return when I realized that 'heaven' is a state, not a place.*" The words echo those of Joyce O'Brien's personal account of her and her husband's victories over cancer, titled *Choose to Live!*:

> *I am sorry. I am just not going to die.* That was it. I didn't care what Dr. Coldheart said; I wasn't going to die. I had a three-year-old . . . I wasn't going to die. I was going to find a way to live. It wasn't a matter of *if* I was going to do it. It was only a matter of *how.*[19]

The idea of the successful patient "taking charge" is therefore also part of this narrative. Rather than being passive and simply accepting conventional wisdom or the recommendations of the first doctor one may meet, those who survive take control of their situation: what are the available drugs and treatment options? What are the best hospitals, and how can we get access to them? How should we deal with our insurance company? To survive, one must find answers to all these questions, as Katherine Hale did. This message is articulated by, among others, Lance Armstrong, who is perhaps the best-known cancer survivor in the nation today. As he put it in 2006:

> Cancer is tough, and it still claims too many lives, but I think that hope is the greatest weapon a person has. Ask the tough questions, get a second opinion, take care of yourself, surround yourself with family and friends,

and do whatever you have to do to keep hope alive. . . . It's really important, and I can't stress that enough. You must be your own best advocate to be sure the treatment you are getting is best for you. . . . At a Lance Armstrong Foundation (LAF) event in Austin last fall, a lung cancer survivor told the audience that she changed doctors because the first one seemed to write her off. . . . She said she fired the doctor because, as she put it, "I can't have more hope than you do. I need someone to believe in me." Maybe that's why she is still here and was able to come to Austin to share her story.[20]

The same idea is repeated by other well-known cancer survivors such as CBS News' Bob Schieffer (in a broadcasted appearance at the Aspen Ideas Festival of 2007, for instance) and Hamilton Jordan, Chief of Staff to President Jimmy Carter.[21]

It appears as well in our newspapers and magazines, such as a recent article in *New York Amsterdam News*. The editor herself, Nayaba Arinde, was diagnosed with breast cancer in 2007. In 2008, she shared her reflections of her journey with the readers of the newspaper in a piece titled "Survive and Thrive." Describing herself as "a natural born fighter," she recounts how she consulted with doctors and alternative medicine practitioners from all over the country. The question of "to chemo or not to chemo" weighed heavily on her shoulders:

> Sure, I'd rather put belief in a leaf than let myself get cut and radiated, but I wanted to survive, too. I had little ones – I needed to get through this. So I decided on the chemo. And decided that I would maintain a healthy and leaf-dominated diet, to keep my rejuvenation and strength up.

Those decisions were followed by other decisions Arinde made: to continue working while on therapy, for instance, and to continue a healthy diet once treatment was over. Arinde controlled the process, chose her path, and ultimately survived. "Fear became hope became acceptance, understanding and gratitude," she states. "This was about prolonging my life – right?! Okay, then. Let's go."[22] "Taking charge" is, of course, also at the core of many recovery programs for those suffering from more behavioral afflictions, such as alcoholics, anorexics, and the severely depressed. The cornerstone of Alcoholics Anonymous and its path to survival is the initial recognition by the alcoholic that he has a problem.[23] According to the National Eating Disorders Association, the "first step" for overcoming eating disorders is by those afflicted to be "reaching out to learn more."[24] Initiative is crucial for survival.

We would do well to note variations in this depiction of individual survival. The most notable are religious voices who view God as the ultimate cause for one's survival.[25] This is certainly an alternative perspective. Yet it is worth noting that in these cases too, in a delicate balancing act, considerable weight is given to the individual: the patient must trust God, pray for help, and conduct a righteous life, as a recent study of African American church women and breast cancer survivors in a metropolitan area in the southwestern United States documented. As one woman stated, "and I thought, I can do this, I can take this with Christ, all day, I can conquer this." And, in the words of a second woman:

> Basically, when it came down to what I was going to do, it kind of was left for my choice. But it wasn't my choice. It was God's choice. And the reason that I can say that is because I got all this material off the internet, in doctor's offices, and what have you. And I came home at the end of that week, and I spread all of this information out on my bed, and I was on my knees, and I just started praying, and asking God to give me the direction, to help me with the choice that I had to make.[26]

In the last analysis, a great deal still depends on the patient.

Past

Survivors of serious diseases, part of our dominant discourse tells us, cannot forget their experiences. The possibility of relapse and the long-term effects of treatment mean that the past remains in one's mind. This is the view, for instance, of Dr. Ann Partridge, Director of the Adult Survivorship Program at the Dana-Farber Cancer Institute in Boston, one of the top cancer treatment centers in the United States. In the introductory video to the program, Dr. Partridge states that we have become "victims of our success:" curing successfully so many patients means "we have created some new problems: patients with long-term late effects – because they are getting there . . . [we are] seeing how difficult it can be for them . . . if they are having side effects and long term risks."[27] Thus the first of six featured "cancer survivor stories" available in audio format is characteristically titled *The Importance of Vigilance* and Kari, a patient who has beaten Hodgkin lymphoma, stresses how she "felt it was very important to do everything I could to reduce all of the risks of getting cancer again."[28]

In the same vein, a highly publicized 2010 national survey conducted by the healthcare site livestrong.com (a follow-up survey was under way in 2012, sponsored by the Lance Armstrong Foundation) identifies practical, physical, and emotional needs of thousands of cancer survivors, and thus underscores the "pain and pitfalls"[29] that survivors face. Indeed, 99 percent of respondents, the authors of the survey report emphasize, "experienced at least one concern after cancer treatment ended."[30] In *The Cancer Survivor's Guide: The Essential Handbook to Life after Cancer*, a book written by two influential academics, one reads that "as survivors we face varied physical, emotional, financial, spiritual, and social challenges. We remain in a period of watching and waiting."[31] Something about the past is always with the survivor.

Yet such statements do not mean that the past constitutes the foundation of what comes next – as we saw for getting married or having a first child. The opposite is actually the case: survival is specifically about distancing ourselves from, and doing everything we can to avoid repeating, the past. Survival entails by definition a rejection of, and a break from, the past: a freedom from it. Thus, to return to *Beating Ana*, we learn that "the eating disorder will not go away until we force it to. And the rest of our life is not free or willing to approach us until the coast is clear. Priorities remind your mind of what you are living and fighting for. Get some. Then watch your eating disorder get gone – for good."[32] On the website of the National Comprehensive Cancer Network (NCCN) – a not-for-profit alliance of 21 of the leading cancer centers in the United States – we read about the Dana-Farber Cancer Institute/NCCN Cancer Survivor Information™ program. The introductory paragraph highlights the break that exists between "before" and "after" cancer:

> Welcome to the DFCI/NCCN Cancer Survivorship Information™. You are one of 12 million cancer survivors currently living in the United States! As a survivor, you have overcome many challenges, and your strength and commitment have been important parts of this experience. Now as you finish treatment, we hope to help you stay healthy, in both body and mind.[33]

> Patients and their family and friends often say that it is after treatment is over that they have time and energy to reflect back on the cancer experience. Now is the time for you and the people in your life to think about what you have been through, take stock of where you are now, and look forward to the future.[34]

To ensure the break from the past, survivors are in turn told to take every possible step to keep the disease away. Their "new normal," a term widely used to describe the post-treatment phase, includes doing everything one should do to stay healthy and avoid repeating the mistakes of the past. The American Cancer Society accordingly urges survivors to:

> Think about your life before cancer. Were there things you did that might have made you less healthy? Maybe you drank too much, ate more than you needed, smoked, or didn't exercise very often. Maybe you kept your feelings bottled up, or maybe you let stressful things go on too long.

> Now is not the time to feel guilty or to blame yourself. You can start making changes today that can have good effects for the rest of your life. You'll feel better and be healthier, too.

"Now," it adds, "you may have time to look at your life in new ways . . . make healthy choices."[35] In the same spirit, in *The Cancer Survivor's Guide* we read that "we must eat healthfully, exercise, reduce stress, and otherwise live as healthfully as possible both to reduce our risk of reoccurrence and of developing such non-cancer related diseases as diabetes, osteoporosis, and heart disease." Survivors are then presented with an ominous question: "do you have a plan for staying healthy . . .?"[36] And DFCI/NCCN Cancer Survivorship Information™ offers recommendations and insights on everything from sexual health to smoking.[37] Tips to never let the past repeat itself abound. Survival means doing our very best to leave the past behind.

Self

A view of illness as a catalyst for self-change, sociologist Arthur Frank has argued, has been in place for over a century in the American mindset.[38] In our dominant discourse, surviving a life-threatening disease is depicted as giving patients the opportunity, for the *first time*, to be their true selves. This in itself represents a major departure from who, in practice and actual everyday life, they were before. They enter a time of unprecedented authenticity. Moreover, as they learn more about their true selves, they develop new priorities and preferences. Accounts of life unfolding in somewhat automatic and unreflective fashion prior to the disease are therefore common. But now the muted and half-conscious self is gone. A new, enlightened person emerges from the process.

A typical example is the website of the National Association of Anorexia Nervosa and Associated Disorders and its section dedicated to "Recovery." We are immediately presented with the words of Jenni Schaefer, an ambassador for the National Eating Disorders

Association, and author of a popular book on recovery, *Goodbye Ed, Hello Me*.[39] She shares her thoughts about overcoming "Ed," or her eating disorder:

> The most amazing part about life after Ed has been finding myself. And I discover more about me everyday [sic]. During my recovery journey, I realized that I love nature, which is why I often sit on my back porch. Writing is one of my favorite pastimes, so I have turned the pen into my career. Unlike when I was lost in my eating disorder, my current life reflects who I am and what I love. My favorite color is pink. Guess what color the dress is that I am wearing right now? (Yes, pink.) I like hanging out with friends and having fun, so I do that often. I no longer feel guilty for enjoying myself. I actually just put my pen down to go on a relaxing walk with a friend in the rain! Recovery has even taught me how to metaphorically dance in the rain.
>
> If your life has been touched by an eating disorder, you, too, can experience this incredible freedom.[40]

Schaefer is finally free to know her real tastes, inclinations, and passions. Indeed, she characteristically titles a chapter of her book "Who Am I without Ed?," and recounts what it feels like to let her self be in the world. In one characteristic passage, she reflects on her relationship to her guitar and, in a sense, every other object and thing in her life: "Back then," she notes, "the guitar felt like a foreign object that was invading my space – as most things did with Ed around. Now I love feeling the guitar next to me. I can actually feel the vibrations resonate throughout my body. I never felt them back then, because I was so disconnected from my body. The guitar is no longer threatening. Instead, it is a part of me. We are connected."[41] Prior to recovery, Schaefer did not know her self. As Jocelyn Golden puts it in her book on bulimia, prior to recovery "[you are] isolated from the person deep inside of you. The real you!"[42]

Self-discovery is often accompanied by the emergence of new priorities and preferences. The reflections of Anita Moorjani in *Dying to Be Me* on her transformation after four years of fighting stage 4 cancer offer an illustration of this perspective:

> Once I was well and back on my feet, everyone resumed their respective roles. Danny returned to work, my mother and brother flew back home, and I was left to figure out what I wanted to do with myself. I couldn't imagine going back to being a relocation officer . . . Thinking about going back to work now felt different, and I realized *I* was different.
>
> I felt as though I couldn't relate to anyone around me – or, more accurately, that others couldn't relate to me. If I thought about going

back to work, I couldn't figure out what I wanted to do. Nothing felt right anymore. I felt as though I didn't fit in with the people of this planet and their values. My priorities had changed . . . I saw divinity everywhere – every animal and insect . . . Each morning, I woke up wanting to explore the world anew. Every day was a fresh adventure . . . the deliciousness of each day made me feel as though I'd just been born . . . It was . . . as if I'd been born for the first time on February 3, 2006.

. . . [I got] a second opportunity to express myself here. I no longer wanted to waste even one minute of the great adventure. I wanted to be as much *me* as I could possibly be and savor and taste every delicious minute of being alive.[43]

Thus, learning who we are makes some things less important and others quite urgent. Our own tastes and behaviors change accordingly. Academic research confirms the theme of "self transformation through adversity" as central to the "dominant societal cancer discourse," with important variations observable across ethnic groups, as they "draw" from that discourse to articulate specific versions.[44] Our existence acquires new meaning, as cancer survivor Joyce O'Brien makes clear when describing her life with her husband prior to, and after, their fight with cancer: "We were going through the motions, without a life purpose. We enjoyed our careers, family and friendships and were just putting one foot in front of the other . . . My husband Kevin and I were living life, working hard, playing hard and having fun just like any other 30-year-old couple." But all that changed with cancer and then survival: "Our lives and perception of life have shifted dramatically and we are continuing on our incredibly exciting path of health and wellness. Our lives are better today because being healthy is more than just the body lacking disease, it's about a vitality, a passion for life."[45]

All this suggests that survival entails finding out who we really are and, for the first time, actually expressing and *being* that person. This amounts to a major departure from who we were before. Moreover, our priorities and preferences change. We experience a new sense of purpose and meaning. Taken together, all this paints a picture of survival as deeply transformative.

Future

Our dominant discourse points to the future of survivors as having two dimensions. The first is fairly well-defined: physical and emotional challenges abound, and one must tread very carefully. "Quite possibly," writes Shannon Cutts on her struggles with anorexia and bulimia, "the only experience tougher on the human body, mind, heart, and spirit than falling ill is getting better."[46] Why? In Cutts' words, one reason is simply that *"relapse happens."*[47] Thus, the Institute of Medicine, in collaboration with the American Society of Clinical Oncology and the National Coalition for Cancer Survivorship, held and then published in 2006 the proceedings from a symposium dedicated to the delicate phase of post-treatment. The impetus behind the symposium was to shed light on the "neglected phase of the cancer care trajectory, the period following first diagnosis and treatment." Those recovering from cancer, the report states, have "unique psychological needs" that must be addressed.[48] The National Cancer Institute emphasizes financial concerns awaiting resolutions as an additional likely burden.[49] Dr. Julia Silver, recipient of the 2006 American Cancer Society Lane Adams Quality of Life Award, adds spiritual needs to the list in a major book on recovery.[50]

With this in mind, Dr. Ann Partridge, Director of the Adult Survivorship Program at the Dana-Farber Cancer Institute, talks about the "emotional" difficulties survivors have with "try[ing] and kind of muddle through and find a new normal for themselves ... both physically and emotionally."[51] She sees the task of her program as "creating that roadmap for them that can help ... at least allay some of the anxiety about 'you have a plan ... stick to the plan, and hopefully you will be OK.'"[52] Subscribing to the same logic, the American Cancer Society stresses the inevitable fear of "living with uncertainty," and therefore makes available resources for survivors about their likely physical, emotional, and psychological challenges.[53] Its experts warn, for instance, that, "for some people, emotions that were put aside during cancer treatment come flooding back all at once, and they feel overwhelmed with sadness, anger, or fear. Maybe you feel emotionally exhausted and tired all the time ... All of these feelings make sense. You have just been through a difficult time. You have had to make some major life decisions."[54]

But such predictable hurdles are only part of the story. A more central dimension of our future is the opportunity to seize this second chance at life and craft *the* future that we want for ourselves. Examples abound. The American Cancer Society simply states that "when treatment ends, people begin a new chapter in their lives."[55] Step #7 in the *Cancer Survivor's Guide* urges survivors to "Create your own future."[56] An analysis by the University of Colorado at Denver of prostate cancer survivors' thoughts over a decade reveals that those men consistently felt that "returning to baseline functioning was no longer possible; rather, a new normal now existed."[57] And in a recent article in *Woman's Day*, a magazine with a circulation of almost 4 million, skin cancer survivor and Texan entrepreneur Cathy Bonner shares with her readers the conviction that "suddenly you are thinking about what to do if your time on this planet is limited." She then outlines the *What I Want Next Process*, a brief exercise intended "to recognize the burning desires hiding in the recesses of your mind and heart. It will assist you in figuring out what you *really* want to do next . . . I believe you can create your own future. It is not something that just happens to you. It can be a place of your own design and your own making."[58] Many medical professionals on their part say that survivors ought to think about that "new normal" and determine what it might be for them. As the National Cancer Institute puts it:

> Those who have gone through cancer treatment describe the first few months as a time of change. It's not so much "getting back to normal" as it is finding out what's normal for you now. People often say that life has new meaning or that they look at things differently now. You can also expect things to keep changing as you begin your recovery. Your new "normal" may include making changes in the way you eat, the things you do, and your sources of support, all of which are discussed in this booklet.[59]

The process is certainly exciting as well. As Anita Moorjani writes in *Dying to Be Me*:

> Previously, I'd also thought that my healing from cancer was the culmination of my journey – it seemed to be the pinnacle of everything that had happened in my life and the end of my story. But I understood in Dubai that my recovery was just the beginning. It was the opening of a new chapter of greater unfolding, and all I had to do was to step into the ambiguity.
>   Again, I knew I wouldn't have to do anything; it would just unfold as long as I *allowed* it to happen. And in that moment, I thought, *Bring it on! Whatever you have in store for me, I'm open to it. Now I understand.*[60]

Lance Armstrong echoed this sentiment when stating, prior to his admission to doping in January 2013, that "I can now say that my life is better because of my cancer experience. Though I wouldn't wish it for anyone, I believe I appreciate my life in a completely new and better way because I faced cancer and was lucky enough to survive."[61]

Importantly, the opportunity to craft a new life comes with an almost moral imperative: having avoided death, survivors *should* make the best of life. "Cancer," we read in *Dancing in Limbo: Making Sense of Life after Cancer*, a book published in the 1990s and thus one of the first to explore the question of purpose and meaning after survival (based on interviews with 18 survivors and the two authors' own battles with the disease), "has forced us to evaluate our lives and understand what is important to us . . . It puts an emphasis on 'doing life right' . . . Once we know what is important, we can begin to do those things that make us feel glad to be alive."[62] We cannot waste this second chance at life. As Joyce O'Brien puts it:

> Wow, so after all that, what's next? Where do you go from here? You live life to the fullest, following your dreams, not settling for less, being excited about the endless possibilities and all that life has to offer. You are grateful. You make sure the gift you are given, this gift more precious than any diamond – the gift of life – does not go to waste. You focus on living and achieving your dreams.[63]

In the same spirit, the National Cancer Institute recommends survivors to take time and think about their new lives:

> The end of treatment can be a time to look forward to the future. New rituals and new beginnings can bring a sense of relief and joy . . . Now that treatment is over, try to take time to get back in tune with yourself. Allow healing time for you and your family members and caregivers. Think about what you can do to begin living without cancer as a main focus.[64]

Survivors have both an obligation and freedom to take advantage of the open road ahead of them.

Actors

As is the case for many transitions in the American discourse, surviving cancer is understood to be something that concerns single individuals. But others figure prominently in the transition as parts of the broader picture. The Institute of Medicine maintains, for instance, that "family members, friends, and caregivers are also impacted by the survivorship experience and are therefore included in this [the cancer survivor] definition."[65] The National Cancer Institute writes that "this booklet uses the term 'cancer survivor' to include anyone who has been diagnosed with cancer, from the time of diagnosis through the rest of his or her life. Family members, friends, and caregivers are also part of the survivorship experience."[66] Mentors as well, we learn in *Beating Ana*, figure in the picture,[67] just as they do during the treatment phase itself, as academic research on survivors' narratives shows.[68] Thus, patients go through the survival phase with others near or around them.

The question becomes, then, what role these "others" may play in the survival experience. We observe two such roles, which stand in some contradiction with each other. First, as we might expect, others are seen as supporters of the survivor in this new phase of life. Their help can be emotional, physical, financial, psychological, or moral. The National Association of Anorexia Nervosa and Associated Disorders cautions survivors, for instance, by reminding them that "recovery is a long road. It is a journey that is best traveled with others. Recovery looks different for each person and every family or support system."[69] In her book on being a bulimia survivor, Jocelyn Golden urges survivors to avoid abusive relationships and nourish supporting ones.[70] With a more upbeat tone, DFCI/NCCN Cancer Survivorship Information™ states that "when treatment ends, you are not alone in celebrating and wondering about the challenges that may come next! Spouses, partners, family members, friends, co-workers . . . may feel joyful that you are doing well."[71] Healthcare professionals offer their own knowledge. Cancer centers, such as MD Anderson, organize clinics to help survivors develop a plan for their healthcare.[72] The Cancer Survivors Network directs survivors to a variety of plans in the country designed by foundations (such as the Lance Armstrong Foundation), nurses and survivor organizations (such as the Prescription for Living program), and organizations such as the American Society of Clinical Oncology.[73]

There is, however, a second and rather opposite way in which others figure in this transition. Recall that the discourse stresses the importance of change: upon winning the battle against the disease, survivors have to reassess their lives thoroughly. This includes their relationship to those around them. According to our discourse, during treatment, many – though by no means all, as we read in a guide to surviving bulimia[74] – were supporters. But after treatment, the discourse underscores the fact that many of these supporters are eager, at least in part, to return to their normal lives. With the worst now over, they are likely to assume that all is well and move on: "Family and friends may expect you to bounce right back to being your old self," we read in the comprehensive *Complete Cancer Survival Guide*, written by Peter Teeley, former press secretary to Vice President George Bush, and co-author Philip Bashe.[75] But this clearly is not going to happen. Thus, survivors are urged to cope and actively manage this delicate question of expectation. With this challenge in mind, the National Cancer Institute states:

> Having cancer can change relationships with the people in your life. It's normal to notice changes in the way you relate to family, friends, and other people that you are around every day – and the way they relate to you.

> When treatment ends, families are often not prepared for the fact that recovery takes time. In general, your recovery will take much longer than your treatment did. Survivors often say that they didn't realize how much time they needed to recover. This can lead to disappointment, worry, and frustration for everyone. Families also may not realize that the way their family works may have changed permanently as a result of cancer. They may need help to deal with the changes and keep the "new" family strong.[76]

And on DFCI/NCCN Cancer Survivorship Information™ we read that the transition of survivorship

> may be a time of managing the expectations of those around you. Your family, friends, and colleagues may expect you to quickly return to your "pre-cancer" self. They may think you can be as physically, emotionally, and mentally active as you were before your diagnosis. You may also feel that you "should" be able to easily pick up any responsibilities you set aside during treatment . . .[77]

But this is more than a matter of being more limited, somehow, for a while at least: one's perspective on life changes as well, as we learned earlier in this chapter. This also means that survivors' priorities and values change too. This inevitably means that their relationship to others is also affected. Survivors, the protagonists of this transition, must adjust how others figure in their lives.

Survivorship as Personal Freedom

The American discourse paints survivorship as a complex transition. It surely belongs to *New Beginnings*: much of the discourse emphasizes – indeed, urges as a moral imperative – that this transition should be about crafting a new, fuller, more meaningful life. The self moves forward: discovered, energized, and changed, the survivor feels truly alive for perhaps the first time. Survivorship offers a fantastic opportunity to seize the future and life itself. This is a positive outlook – one that emphasizes happiness and triumph ("success through optimism and a fighting spirit, the hero-survivor mythology," as one set of researchers describes the "dominant cancer discourse" in the United States)[78] rather than victimhood or other perspectives. Yet, at the same time, we hear powerful voices of caution: this is a delicate phase that must be handled with care, not least because of the possibility of relapse and the practical challenges that recovery entails. Optimism is tempered with some degree of tentativeness. Unlike going to college, for instance, or being fired, one is not expected to jump into the future with great enthusiasm and relatively few concerns. One must remain vigilant. The discourse on survivorship offers a particular rendition of *New Beginnings*.

How unique is such a depiction of survivorship? Comparatively speaking, some elements of the discourse are certainly in place in other cultural contexts. Appreciation of the smaller things in life, a closer connection to life, a sense that one experiences events more intensely – all these themes are surely prevalent in the dominant discourses of many other countries. In a recent study of Norwegian survivors of gynecological cancer, for instance, women are seen as articulating their new appreciation for everyday life. In the voice of one participant, "you are much more aware of what is surrounding you ... things outside yourself. You experience nature, the birds, animals and sounds ... a waterfall and a river!" In the same study we also learn about widespread anxiety about relapse, as is the case for the American discourse, even several years into recovery: "It's always there in the back of your head," one Norwegian woman says.[79] Similar language was reported in a study of Australian adults who had survived cancer as children.[80] Studies of a Danish recovery program for cancer survivors, in turn, emphasize a return to some sort of normality – perhaps not a "new normal" as in the American case but some sort of normality nonetheless – after treatment.[81] Yet, next to these similarities we find important differences too.

The emphasis in the United States on taking control, understanding all choices, determination as key to survival, and the near obligation of recrafting one's life – all these elements of discourse are in line with basic American ideas of individualism, overcoming, and heading for an unchartered future full of possibilities. Studies of survivorship in Scandinavian countries, by contrast, point to a different sort of language. In Denmark, for example, recovery programs are publicly funded and universally available, and considerable emphasis is put on the right of former patients to return to their proper place in a collectively-oriented society that cherishes equality, public well-being, and mutual solidarity: "When the social worker tells Susan," a breast cancer survivor, "that she can continue a normal life, she is articulating this underlying ideal of the Danish welfare policy," note two authors of a medical anthropological study. Terms such as *rehabilitation, restitution,* and *reintegration,* rather than overcoming, are thus much more appropriate for the Danish context.[82] The focus is on bringing the individual back to the group. The same can be said for the other Scandinavian countries.

The American discourse, in other words, is in the last analysis about personal freedom – one of the most cherished concepts in the country's collective psyche. It is not about belonging, as might be the case in Denmark.[83] We can attribute this difference to a number of factors, including the fact that the healthcare system of the United States poses enormous challenges even to those who have health insurance: one must always "navigate" complex policies and stipulations to grasp in the first place what treatment and drug options are available at what costs, which hospitals and doctors may be part of one's covered benefits and which are not, what options are realistic, and what things one should know but is not told. One must become a "self-advocate," and indeed national oncological organizations have developed the Cancer Survival Toolbox®[84] to help patients fight for themselves,[85] and one thus emerges victorious from a personal struggle with the system – a very different perspective than what is taking place in Denmark. Interestingly, we should note here the presence of alternatives to the dominant discourse in the United States itself, such as narratives emphasizing anger, for instance, or continued reflection about death.[86]

There is nothing inevitable, in turn, about the actual existence of a well-developed, cohesive discourse on life after overcoming a major disease. The United States itself is proof of this. Dr. Partridge, Director of the Adult Survivorship Program at the Dana-Farber Cancer Institute, notes how "cancer survivorship is actually a fairly new field, because, appropriately so, we focused our energy as oncology providers, scientists, and researchers on getting more survivors . . . and so only in the last decade or so have significant focus and resources gone toward 'now, how do we care for this growing number of people who are living through and beyond cancer?'"[87] Two or three decades ago, in other words, there was no real discourse on survival in the United States itself or, for that matter, in the Western world.[88] One recent academic study of the concept of cancer "survivor" puts the exact date of the birth of that discourse in the United States at 1985, when Dr. Fitzhugh Mullan described his cancer experience in a *New England*

Journal of Medicine article titled "Seasons of survival" and went on to found the National Coalition for Cancer Survivorship.[89]

If we consider Denmark again, the initial date is later, in the middle of the 1990s, following the publication of an influential report by the Danish Cancer Society and a boom in books and memoirs by survivors.[90] In other instances, the discourse is in its nascent stages, and in yet other contexts – especially those where survival rates are to begin with very low, such as indigenous populations in Australia, New Zealand, Canada, and the United States itself – "few positive stories from cancer survivors are disseminated within communities."[91] In these cases, there is no real discourse on the transition of survival.

7   Divorce

Divorce in the United States is on the decline. Rates in the percentage of marriages ending in divorce peaked in the 1970s and early 1980s, as women entered the labor force (and therefore acquired the means to live independently) and state laws made unilateral, rather than consensual, divorce much easier to obtain. Since then, and particularly in the first decade of the twenty-first century, divorce rates among married couples have decreased.[1] Drawing from perhaps the most comprehensive data on the subject, a 2011 US Census Bureau report documents this trend: the percentages of "ever married men" or "ever married women" which have experienced divorce by a certain age (30 years old, for instance) drop several percentage points (falling well below 35 percent) as we move from older to younger generations of Americans.[2] The number of individuals in the overall adult population who divorce in any given year has also dropped since the 1970s and early 1980s.[3]

Why such decline? A combination of factors appears to have been at work. For one, Americans seem keen on "doing it right." A widely cited 2011 study by researchers at Cornell University and the University of Central Oklahoma surveyed 122 young cohabiting men and women and found that two-thirds cited worries about divorce – its emotional, legal, and financial costs – as influencing their decision not to marry yet.[4] The implication is that those who do end up marrying choose better vetted partners: selectivity, in other words, has increased, with cohabitation often serving as some sort of "test-drive" for marriage. A second, and related, factor is that Americans choose to marry later in life, once they feel more secure in other areas of their lives, such as education and work. We discussed this very trend in chapter 3.[5] The resulting sense of security benefits the longevity of marriage. A third reason, if we specifically consider the number of individuals who divorce as a percentage of the whole population, is simply that marriage (and therefore divorce) is less common.[6]

Despite all this, divorce remains a very important transition in American life. The highly regarded annual report *The State of Our Unions*, released by the National Marriage Project at the University of Virginia in partnership with the Center for Marriage and Families at the Institute for American Values, makes this clear time and time again. The 2011 issue shows, for instance, that the overall number of Americans who have experienced divorce in their lives is, because of cumulative effects, now at a historic high.[7] It also underscores the fact that rates may have declined since their peak in the late 1970s and early 1980s but that they remain nearly twice the rate they were in 1960.[8] A 2012 US Department of Health and Human Services report, based on data from over 22,000 interviews, states that the probability of the first marriage lasting 20 years is 56 percent for men and 52 percent for women.[9] Divorce rates are higher in the United States than in the rest of the advanced industrialized world and in all the rest of the world but for five countries,[10] and historical records show that American culture has supported divorce as a practice more readily than other cultures for nearly four centuries – making it, in the words of one prominent historian, an "'American' tradition."[11] Divorce remains as well very much the subject matter of many popular books, movies, and tabloid stories. "With each passing year," Barbara Dafoe Whitehead, award-winning marriage scholar and former co-director of the National Marriage Project, wrote in the 1990s, "the culture of divorce becomes more deeply entrenched . . . An entire children's literature is devoted to divorce. Family movies and videos for children feature divorced families . . . the culture of divorce has generational momentum."[12]

Divorce, then, is a cultural event. Given this, what is the dominant discourse in the United States on divorce? As is the case with many other transitions, divorce is about *New Beginnings*. As Dafoe Whitehead puts it:

> Nowhere else has divorce been so deeply imbued with the larger themes of a nation's political traditions. Nowhere has divorce so fully reflected the spirit and susceptibilities of a people who share an extravagant faith in the power of the individual and in the power of positive thinking.[13]

Divorce, much like surviving a life-threatening disease or losing a job, is *about the individual unshackling itself from an undesirable situation and using the acquired freedom to willfully pursue its dreams*. It is a story of personal choice and overcoming. More specifically, the origins of the transition can be of two types: the individual is either the initiator of the transition (in light of a marriage gone bad) or the victim of another person's decision (the partner wanting the divorce). In either instance, the individual is facing an unwanted and painful situation. Given this, regardless of who initiates the divorce, the past (the marriage, in particular) must be largely dismissed (usually after an initial period of mourning), the self needs to reinvent itself, the future is open (one's life must be "rebuilt," though what this means varies depending on the age of the person as well as the gender), and the actors involved are ultimately single individuals: this is the opposite of getting married and is thus the triumph of individuality over being connected to others. The relationship is finished, and the transition concerns each spouse individually, even if children and others are affected.

An American Tradition

"Perhaps more than any other national group in history, Americans have long exhibited a willingness to break unsatisfactory bonds and seek potentially more satisfying ties despite the costs," writes Glenda Riley, former president of the Western History Association.[14] "During the formative years of the new nation," she adds, "a growing number of wives and husbands sought divorces. Then, as now, divorce fit well with American democracy and individualism."[15] Riley reports the first legal divorce in the United States as taking place in 1639 in a Puritan court in Massachusetts. Divorce, she asserts, is consistent with "Americans' tendency to solve problems by splitting apart and beginning anew."[16]

Our analysis of the dominant discourse confirms that this interpretation of divorce – as a clear instance of "splitting" and beginning "anew" – is squarely in place in American society. Before we consider that discourse in detail, however, two observations are in order. First, the discourse appears to address those with the social, cultural, or economic means (capital, in the language of sociology) to make something out of this dramatic transition. This may be for a combination of reasons. Books, counseling services, and other resources to cope with divorce cost money and time. In addition, even though poorer Americans are very concerned with divorce and its impact on their wellbeing,[17] value marriage,[18] and have higher rates of divorce[19] – all things that would make them a prime target of the discourse – they also tend to marry less than Americans with more resources.[20] This, coupled with the fact that there are more middle-class than working-class Americans, means that as a group the overall number of divorcees from more limited backgrounds is smaller. The dominant discourse on divorce in the United States is accordingly about individuals with certain amounts of resources.

Second, on several occasions we will see that one important subdiscourse has developed around women. Women have historically suffered the most in financial terms from divorce. This has been the result of various factors, including their higher likelihood of staying at home with children and thus putting their careers on hold, taking on custody of the children, and generally lower income levels (which partly reflect discrimination at the workplace). "The weak position of women – especially 'displaced homemakers' – in the labor market," writes poverty expert Katherine Newman in *Falling from Grace*, "translates divorce into downward mobility for many women." Newman then notes that "they cannot secure jobs that pay well enough to stave off financial hardship."[21] Thus, as one might expect, women are significantly more likely (four times more likely, in fact) than men to worry about becoming financially destitute as a result of divorce.[22] In addition, women have proven more likely to seek external support when going through divorce, and to be the ones who initiate the divorce (crucially, because of perceived abuses or injustices)[23]. The dominant discourse on divorce often takes these and other gender differences into account.

Origins

What brings divorce about? In our dominant discourse, divorce is an "option" available to each of the partners. In fact, according to the General Social Survey, nearly 50 percent of Americans consider it "usually the best option when a couple can't seem to work out their marriage problems."[24] Thus books like Susan Gadoua's *Contemplating Divorce: A Step-by-Step Guide to Deciding Whether to Stay or Go* impress upon their audience that alternatives exist and choices must be made – much as we have the opportunity to decide what we want in many other dimensions of our lives. Gadoua has shared her expertise on divorce in traditional media outlets such as the *Wall Street Journal* and *USA Today*, and in newer virtual spaces such as TheModernWomansDivorceGuide.com and divorce360.com. As she puts it:

In this book, I will help you honestly assess the level of happiness and fulfillment in your marriage, and assist you in determining what more, if anything, you can do to improve your current situation. I'll call on you to choose to stay or go from a place of faith and following your truth, as opposed to staying or leaving out of fear

. . . By the end of the last chapter, I hope that, with the road map provided here, you will have a clearer sense of what direction to take regarding your marriage.

. . . While no option is ideal at this point in your marriage, all of your choices are fairly straightforward; you can stay married, you can separate, or you can divorce.[25]

Divorce stems from personal deliberations and initiatives. Outside factors – the quality of the marriage above all – of course matter a great deal, but ultimately the individual decides to divorce. Our legal context reinforces this perspective: all 50 states of the country along with the District of Columbia have no-fault divorce laws in place. California was first to adopt such laws in 1969; by 1983, all states but New York and South Dakota had followed suit (South Dakota joined the other states in 1985, and New York in 2010). Because of these laws, one partner can request the dissolution of a marriage without having to provide evidence that the other partner has committed a breach of the marital contract. Prior to no-fault laws, the requesting partner had to produce proof of adultery, abandonment, felony, or other similarly culpable acts.

Divorce reflects personal will and action. With this in mind, the primary narrative is that one – and not both – of the partners formally files for divorce. As Susan Gadoua puts it, divorce is seldom a "split" that is "mutual and amicable" out of a realization by both partners that they have "simply grown apart."[26] Perhaps the most typical image is of the man "messing up" – with extra-marital affairs or abusive behavior most often, but also addiction or other forms of behavior deemed deviant – and either the woman or the man moving to formally put an end to it. Stories of celebrity couples such as Tiger Woods and Elin Nordegren, Tom Cruise and Katie Holmes, Charlie Sheen and Denise Richards, and Senator John Edwards and his cancer-stricken wife Elizabeth (separated by the time of her death, because the state of North Carolina requires separation before granting divorces) reinforce this image. They receive intense media coverage and usually feature embarrassing public admissions of guilt and apologies on the part of the men.[27] Tiger Woods spent, for instance, a full 14 minutes on national television in 2010 apologizing for his "irresponsible and selfish" behavior; "I know," he stated, that "I have bitterly disappointed all of you." Thus, "for all that I have done, I am so sorry . . . I had affairs, I cheated. What I did was not acceptable, and I am the only person to blame."[28]

The same image of misbehaving men appears in books such as Erica Manfred's *He's History, You're Not: Surviving Divorce After 40*, which opens with the following account:

> Like September 11 or the Kennedy assassination, you never forget where you were in the moment it happened. It was Christmas Eve 2000, and I was in a flannel nightie getting ready for bed in the house we had bought in the woods of New York ten years earlier, when we'd left New York City for the adventure of country life . . . I asked him casually why he had been so distant lately. I expected to hear some mumbled answer about pressure at work, or lack of sleep due to the constantly active baby . . .
>
> "I want to leave you," he said.
>
> If you have ever heard these five words – and if you are reading this, I bet you either have heard them or said them – you know the sheer terror that accompanies this particular announcement.[29]

There appear to be empirical grounds for the idea that divorce is initiated by one of the partners and that men tend to be the ones to bear most of the responsibility for breaking the marriage. An AARP report in 2004, based on a survey of 1,147 individuals who divorced between the ages of 40 and 69, shows that the vast majority of divorces are initiated by one of the partners only,[30] and that two times out of three it is the woman who asks for the divorce[31] with abuse of some kind being the most frequent reason, as we already noted earlier.[32] The report also notes that women are also more apt than men to put their spouse at fault, while men are more likely to admit being at fault than women.[33]

The discourse, thus, sees individuals who are faced with unpleasant circumstances as initiators of divorce. "The choice you make today will determine the rest of your life! You are at a crossroad in your life," states California-based Cindy Holbrook, one of the many "coaches" for divorced women. "It is completely up to you what path you choose to take."[34] Divorce reflects personal will, resolution, and hope.

Past

A recent article in the *New York Times* (at one point in September 2012 the most emailed article on the newspaper's website) by culture critic Judith Newman discusses one of the latest divorce trends in the United States:

Planners of high-end parties are reporting a significant increase in the number of people celebrating the end of a marriage not with a whimper, but a bang . . . There are specialists in divorce-party planning, and there is also a Web site, divorcepartysupply.com, where you can "celebrate your new freedom" with light-up devil-horn tiaras, black long-stem roses and, for those trying to work off a little anger, penis piñatas.

"People don't usually bill them as divorce showers or divorce parties," said Marcy Blum, the events planner and an author of *Weddings for Dummies*. "It's more like, 'Come Celebrate My New Life (and Maybe Get Me a Present)'."

"In a way," continues Newman, "the rise of the divorce shower is not that surprising. With only about a 50-50 chance of a first marriage lasting – and the odds worse for second and third marriages, in case you were under the illusion that love is lovelier the second or third time around – there seems to be a societal desire to commemorate, and even celebrate, what has become an increasingly common milestone in people's lives."[35] Without question, divorce is often portrayed as a "milestone" in our everyday language: it is a sign of the road we have traveled and that is behind us for good.

On *Good Morning America*, *The Today Show*, and many other major media outlets, Americans thus recently had the chance to learn about Divorce Party Planner, a Los Angeles-based company. On the company's Internet homepage, the first answer to the question of why one should want to throw a divorce party is that "A Divorce Party [sic] is a way to mark the end of the pain and suffering that comes with divorce." Client testimonials on the same page attest to the usefulness of such parties. "Rhonda," the first featured customer, writes that "My divorce party brought much needed closure to a horrible time in my life. It helped me turn the corner and start living again."[36] Indicatively, the predominant color of the site is pink, and the only real-life image we see is of three attractive women laughing, celebrating, and having what appear to be tropical drinks at a club,[37] all of which reinforces the idea that women seem especially eager to leave behind their unhappy existences with inadequate husbands.

What about the past, exactly, is being left behind? In a sense, one's whole life as one knew it. "Being left when you're over 50 is like falling into a black hole in space," writes Manfred in *He's History, You're Not*. "My life – my past life – passed before my eyes."[38] Yet the discourse is often more specific than that. Once again we run into the language of "grief." Something has died, and this is usually the relationship of the two partners itself. Consider what we read in *Rebuilding: When*

Your Relationship Ends, written by Dr. Bruce Fisher in 1981 (with later additions by Dr. Robert Alberti). Since 1981, it has undergone seven rounds of printing and three editions, and became at one point the top online best-selling book on divorce. Millions of Americans have copies of the book, and the work has served as the basis of ten-week seminars all over the country. "Indeed, the divorce process," writes Alberti, "has been described by some as largely a grief process. Grief combines overwhelming sadness with a feeling of despair." This is because at the heart of divorce, we are told, is "loss:"[39]

> It's tough to let go of the strong emotional ties which remain from the dissolved love union. Nevertheless, it is important to stop investing emotionally in the dead relationship . . . To invest in a dead relationship, an emotional corpse, is to make an investment with no chance of return. The need instead is to begin investing in productive personal growth, which will help in working your way through the divorce process.[40]

The words "dead" and "corpse" describe the broken marriage. Judith Wallerstein and Sandra Blakeslee talk about divorce in their national bestseller *Second Chances* (based on a landmark study of 60 families and their experience of the first decade after the breakup) as the "coup de grâce of a stressful marriage,"[41] and again talk about "grief."[42] For their own health, the divorced partners must come to accept this very fact. They should leave it behind; at most, we learn in Fisher and Alberti's *Rebuilding*, one should conduct an "autopsy" of "your dead relationship," so as to learn what went wrong and not repeat the same mistakes.[43] Importantly, if the couple had children, then the "family" as everyone knew it is also gone, and this too must be dealt with.

At the same time, the discourse recognizes that some things from the past may in fact linger on, at least for a while. Wallerstein and Blakeslee point out that not everything can be left behind: "divorce," they note, "does not wipe the slate clean . . . small children, a low-paying job, and the ghosts of the failed marriage" may continue to be with us even if the two partners have parted ways.[44] The "ghosts" of the failed marriage can manifest in various ways. Negative criticisms received from the former spouse remain in one's head, for instance, and one must fight at first to quiet them. Considerable internal work is often required to let go of the anger and resentments. Thus, Manfred titles chapter 11 of *He's History, You're Not* "Forgiving the Bastard and Moving On: Forgive Yourself First."[45] A significant goal of "divorce recovery coaches" is accordingly to help new divorcees deal with whatever stays on with partners after the divorce is complete. With this in mind, Shelley Stile – a certified Divorce Recovery Life Coach, author, and speaker – certainly recognizes that divorce means the end of marriage but not the immediate closing of negative emotions, resentments, anger, and potentially harmful dynamics with the children. She urges those going through and beyond divorce to quiet the "mind chatter,"[46] control their anger,[47] and let go of negative emotions.[48] Certified Divorce Coach Cathy Meyer notes that "emotional" divorce may very well happen after the legal divorce has occurred.[49]

Such efforts of letting go are usually depicted as successful and ultimately needed only for a short while. In the American discourse, divorce is designed precisely to let one quickly move into a new phase in life. Its function is like that of a door shutting and the person walking away. Standard, formulaic language designed to signify the definitive dismissal of the past and the start of a new life is accordingly all around us. We have heard hundreds of times from hundreds of couples, for instance, the words that Tiger Woods and Elin Nordegren put in their joint press release about their split: "We are sad that our marriage is over and we wish each other the very best for the future."[50]

Self

Divorce, we are told, shakes one's sense of identity. As Gadoua puts it, "In all my work as a therapist, I have never seen a population as lost, thrown off center, and frightened as this lot who were divorcing and contemplating divorce . . . every other important life decisions or events my clients experienced – such as job transitions, major moves, loss of loved ones, and natural disasters – seemed less debilitating than divorce. It affected their sense of safety, well-being, community status, and comfort. Divorce *is* a big deal."[51] Wallerstein and Blakeslee make a similar point in *Second Chances*: "because a man's or woman's identity is often tied to a spouse, especially if the marriage has lasted many years, divorce may shake adult identity to the core." Thus, "people again must ask themselves, Who am I? What do I want? Whom do I want? . . . What are my priorities?"[52]

But the initial shock is expected to quickly turn into a much relished opportunity to explore one's self and seek new ways of being. The 2004 AARP survey found that the "buzzwords" of 76 percent of divorcees, when talking about the dissolution of their marriage, are "freedom, self-identity, and fulfillment."[53] Repeatedly, we encounter the concept of "rebirth." Divorce recovery coach Shelley Stile emphasizes to her clients that "within every loss is an opportunity to reinvent oneself."[54] She then observes:

> Life Transitions can be opportunities to re-invent ourselves. We can now be the Creator of a new way of being. It isn't easy to see that when you are in the midst of turbulence but it is true. Everything in life happens for a reason, and we can use this life transition as a catalyst for powerful and necessary change that can result in a life that we deserve, a life that is both fulfilling and perhaps, meant to be.[55]

Pointedly, she also stresses that "in order to be the person you want to be, you have to let go of the person you were! In order to live the life you want to live, you have to let go of the life you led."[56]

Thus, Sharon Wegscheider-Cruse, a nationally-known expert on divorce who has appeared on *The Phil Donahue Show*, *The Oprah Winfrey Show*, and *Good Morning America*, devotes a full chapter to a "New You for a New Life" in her book *Life after Divorce: Create a New Beginning*.[57] In Judith Newman's article in the *New York Times* on divorce trends in the United States, we read about "celebrants like Martha Torres of Thousand Oaks, Calif., who, after 30 years of marriage, lost 50 pounds and held a 'rebirth' party immediately upon filing for divorce. She followed it up a year later with an 'I'm still standing' party, to celebrate becoming independent financially."[58] An entire chapter of Manfred's *He's History, You're Not: Surviving Divorce After 40* is devoted to "Reinventing Yourself: How to Become Who You Really Are."[59] And Wallerstein and Blakeslee write that "divorce is much more than the coup de grâce of a stressful marriage. It is a new beginning that offers people second chances. It is no more and no less than an opportunity to rebuild their lives."[60]

What, then, does this rebuilding of one's self entail? What does "rebirth" mean? Our old marriage channeled and constrained us: we expressed certain parts of ourselves and not others. Most likely, because we were not happy and even the worst marriages last more than a few months, we became accustomed to living a suboptimal existence. We encounter stories of personally repressive marriages on divorce coaching and support groups' websites, and in counseling materials and books. "I lost my identity as a wife and unhappiness was like a chokehold around my neck," states Jeanette, a graphic designer from Portland, Oregon, in her testimonial for Divorce Recovery Coaching, a San Francisco company founded by Judy Cameron and offering "Rapid Divorce Relief" services.[61] "But I felt powerless," Jeanette continues, "to step out of my unhealthy marriage, afraid I would lose everything."[62] Such accounts are exceedingly common.

There appear at least two major aspects of the rebirth process. The first concerns our most intimate and personal side: it concerns the very core of our identity. We are wiser and more experienced now: What do we wish to become? What direction do we want to go in? Here adjectives such as "healthy," "beautiful," "caring," and "strong" are commonplace. A bad marriage compromised us in a negative manner. The transformation of our selves entails a move toward a much more positive self. Dr. Phil urges his many followers, for instance, to "take the catastrophic language out of your mind . . . and find your authentic self."[63] No longer "half of a couple," we must "find" our "passion"[64] and "all the things that are uniquely yours and need expression."[65] These include one's intimacy and sexuality. Every choice is acceptable, and the discourse emphasizes the process of exploration as key to a proper rebuilding of one's self. The exchange on Oprah Radio between host Dr. Laura Berman and a female caller in May 2011 is in this regard typical. In reply to the woman expressing her hesitation about having sex with other men after 25 years of marriage to her previous (unfaithful) husband ("I am not really sure . . . I just know that it's frightening for me to think about, you know, me having sex with, with another man after 25 years with the same person," the caller states), Dr. Berman characteristically replies: "I can understand that; I think that is completely normal and natural." Her co-host, Dr. Jeff Gardere, then adds: "I also think it's very natural . . . I have had patients who have been divorced for 5 or 6 years . . . they've waited a couple of years until they could sort things out."[66] Rebuilding one's self also involves careful exploration of our innermost self.

The second aspect of our rebirth has to do with our professional side. We have the opportunity, and in some cases the necessity, to rethink our careers. This is especially the case for women, who are more likely to have put on hold their professional development because of marriage and possibly children. Marriage may have constrained our time and geographical location. With divorce almost always come new financial pressures. Even so, it is incumbent upon us to think about who we wish to be as we move forward. Open-mindedness and exploration are in order. As divorce coach Cathy Meyer puts it:

> Think about what kind of work you've always wanted to do, and not only what you've done in the past. Many people limit themselves to the jobs

they have had experience in, or jobs that pertain to their degree. However, a job in a different field may be better for you, your children, and your new life. Don't limit your options.[67]

Coaches are not the only professionals talking about career reinvention: family law attorneys also point to it. On this point, for instance, New York state attorney Carol Most has developed a video series to help divorcees transition into their new lives. With women especially in mind (the "Center for Work Life Policy," she observes, "says that 60% of working women will step back in their careers or leave the workforce completely. The majority will want to reenter, often doing so in lesser positions or at lower earnings"), she talks about the risks of lower self-esteem and bruised senses of identity. But, as one might expect, she then urges the following:

> She might begin by creating an ideal job spec (e.g. restricted hours, light commute, interesting work, minimum compensation, strong career path, professional on-the-job training, or jobs in a growth industry). Remember this is a starting point – there is no perfect job (as there are no spouses!). She or he must know what can be flexible, what is non-negotiable and why. She will need to think out-of-the-box – picturing a different life with new freedom and new responsibilities. She will need to think ahead – how can these requirements change in the future? This may require advice from a therapist or career coach.[68]

Divorcees need to stop, clarify their values, and learn what's important to them in their life moving forward. The emotional turmoil and erosion of self-esteem incurred during divorce contribute to feeling helpless and overwhelmed. We must take stock of where we are and then, positively, craft a new sense of self.

Future

The future, our discourse tells us, often brings a good deal of uncertainty. In most cases, it immediately generates worries about financial health and independence. We hear this especially when the discourse focuses on women, as, for instance, in Erica Manfred's retelling of her reaction to hearing her husband's decision to leave her:

> The sensation was strange, like some weird crack in reality had occurred; things as I knew them were not as they seemed. I entered a world like Dali's, where watches and worlds, my world, could melt and slither away. It was like being told very matter-of-factly that someone dead had come back to life, or that Copernicus was wrong – the world was really flat.

"But I am fifty years old, we just adopted a kid, we spent my inherit-ance," I whined piteously. "How am I going to survive alone? I am too old to find someone else. I don't have a job. It's not fair."[69]

The passage is rich with information. The men find (younger) part-ners, for age matters less in their case. Women, on the other hand, have a much harder time. Women have sacrificed their careers for the family (something, incidentally, that can only occur in cases where the man earns enough to support the entire family – as happens in middle- and upper-middle-class families); thus, women are bound to face financial difficulties on top of romantic ones. "We [women over 40 who experience divorce] have lost both our happy memories of times past *and* the expectation of a secure, comfortable future," notes Manfred in *He's History, You're Not*.[70] The 2004 AARP report confirms that women are more likely than men to be "troubled about becoming financially destitute."[71] Thus, chapter 1 of Manfred's book is titled "Grieving Is a Full Time Job: How to Survive the First – Worst – Year."

The first phase of our new lives is therefore not without its risks. This goes beyond finance and includes emotional, psychological, rela-tional, and other challenges. A number of paths seem to be possible. Wallerstein and Blakeslee outline the multitudes of outcomes in the following way: "divorce can be a profound catalyst for psychological, social, and economic change. It can also be a stumbling block against such change or the beginning of psychological, social, and economic deterioration. Divorce opens up or closes off a multitude of opportu-nities. As ever, the journey begins with the first step."[72] They add that "divorce at the outset comprises a special category of life crisis in that it simultaneously engenders new solutions and new problems."[73]

We are accordingly advised that as divorcees we are bound to go through a number of steps. In *Rebuilding*, Fisher and Alberti envision the divorce process as consisting of 19 "rebuilding" blocks, arranged in a pyramid. The bottom ones include emotions and mental stances such as "denial" and "fear." Above those, in the second row, we find blocks such as "grief," "anger," and "letting go." In the third row are more positive blocks which include "openness," "love," and "trust." The fourth row consists of three blocks: "sexuality," "singleness," and "purpose." At the very top of the pyramid is one block: "freedom."

Thus, the discourse asserts that, after an initial phase of reorienta-tion, we come before a very open future. As with other transitions that in this book we categorize as *New Beginnings*, initial confusion brings one, if all goes well, to a point where everything is possible and one's responsibility is to decide what is next. The canvas is empty, awaiting the first stroke of paint. The building blocks "purpose" and "freedom" are therefore quite representative of this outlook. Purpose has to do with identifying one's new goals now that the marriage has died. "What are your goals?" we read in the book: "What do you plan to do with yourself after you have adjusted to the ending of your love relationship?" One should be in a position to say: "I have goals for the future now."[74] "Freedom" is in turn equated with reaching the top of the mountain, with the transformation "from chrysalis to butterfly." We learn that, as the final step of the transition, "you're becoming free to choose your path to a self-actualized life as a single person or in another love relationship."[75]

All this, of course, calls for celebration and even efforts to publicly assert our new position vis-à-vis life itself. The divorce party, to return to Newman's piece in the *New York Times*, serves precisely such a function: "But whether serious or silly, a gift is not always just a gift. A party's not always just a party. They really can be cathartic, truly a bridge to something new."[76] As Los Angeles' The Divorce Party Planner company puts it:

> The party is an opportunity to announce your new status in life. You are now single and available for new experiences and even new relationships. A whole new phase of life is just beginning. And that is something to celebrate![77]

We are moving forward, the future is undefined, and our task is to give it shape.

Actors

This is clearly a transition involving two, at this point separate, individuals. There are important differences in the depiction of men and women during the transition. Divorced men, for instance, are seen as helpless in taking care of themselves on certain basic fronts (eating healthily, keeping their homes tidy, etc.) but also as freed persons who are more likely to start dating again and have romantic affairs. Women, by contrast, are seen as more capable of taking care of themselves, even if they do face more financial strains. This is what we read, for instance, in "How to Protect Yourself from Bad Break-Ups," an article in the Money section of *US News*, as it quotes prominent researchers on the matter: "When you think about the things that are really challenges to health, women are really better at managing the healthcare system," University of Chicago sociologist Linda Waite states. Waite adds that "they are better at taking care of themselves." Rutgers University's Deb Carr is quoted as concurring: "for divorced people or widowed people who haven't remarried, the men are still worse off."[78]

"Others" besides the spouses also figure prominently in many divorces. One frequent actor on the stage is a lover. As Erica Manfred recalls in her personal account:

> "There's someone else," he said, naming a co-worker twenty five years younger than me who'd been his best friend at work for years. "I am in love with her."
>
> It's strange how clichés that you have heard countless times on soap operas and TV movies stop being clichés when they're spoken to you personally.[79]

Children also figure prominently. They are often portrayed as "caught in the middle of the animosity between the parents," as a popular book from the 1990s on the topic puts it,[80] with possible long-lasting effects harming them throughout their lives, as Wallerstein and Blakeslee argue in *The Unexpected Legacy of Divorce* – a book that spent three weeks on the *New York Times, San Francisco Chronicle*, and *Denver Post* bestseller lists.[81] Accordingly, a great number of resources are available for parents to look after the wellbeing of their sons and daughters. The divorcees must handle children with care. As Gadoua writes:

> Talk openly with your child about his or her needs, fears, thoughts, and so forth; and check in regularly. Then balance that with the needs of both of you as parents. Keep in mind that there are many professionals, books, and other resources out there to guide you in setting up a new life for you and your children.[82]

To aid parents, Gadoua lays out an exercise so that they may prepare a "script" to communicate effectively with their children.[83] Hence, inevitably, public admissions by celebrities come with statements about the importance of the wellbeing of whatever children might be present. The joint statement by Woods and Nordegren announcing their divorce is in this sense typical:

> We are sad that our marriage is over and we wish each other the very best for the future. While we are no longer married, we are the parents of two wonderful children and their happiness has been, and will always be, of paramount importance to both of us. Once we came to the decision that

our marriage was at an end, the primary focus of our amicable discussions has been to ensure their future well-being. The weeks and months ahead will not be easy for them as we adjust to a new family situation, which is why our privacy must be a principal concern.[84]

Importantly, the discourse on children itself comes with variations. Sociologist Terry Arendell argues that there exists a "masculine" interpretation of how children picture in the transition: irrevocably tied to the mother, so that the father–children relationship is always influenced by the presence of the mother. Mothers, on the other hand, appear to have their own, truly "unique and independent" relationship to their children.[85]

A list of secondary actors also exists. Gadoua's script for announcing the transitions to others comes with a list: "parents, stepparents, in-laws, brothers, sisters, stepsiblings, grandparents, aunts, uncles, and cousins . . ."[86] Friends, too, are sometimes mentioned, often as a source of support. On that front, journalist and NBG blogger Pamela Cytrynbaum humorously wonders what fate the couples' friends will endure: Whose friends will they continue to be? "Who will take 'custody' of those friends?"[87] On psychologytoday.com, in turn, sociologist Laurie Essig notes their role as judges and potential critics.[88]

Escape to Freedom

We have seen that the dominant discourse on divorce in the United States emphasizes individuality and freedom. By and large, divorce is seen as a liberating experience – as a logical answer to the challenges of a broken marriage and an undesirable situation. It amounts to a rejection and a move toward better things – toward all that the individual can, in fact, be. Thus, divorce is very much about a new beginning. Evidence from other countries suggests that other interpretations of divorce are certainly possible. As with the discourse for any given transition, the dominant discourse belongs – and is indeed a component of – a broader cultural context. Let us consider here the question of women and the emancipatory effects that, according to the American discourse, divorce can have for them, despite the financial difficulties that they, more than men, typically encounter (and have encountered for decades)[89]. Indeed, it is worth noting that we encountered little in our analysis of the American discourse that might depict divorce as a transition that stigmatizes either of the partners involved.

Dominant discourses elsewhere point to important differences. For instance, in a recent analysis of Great Britain, psychologist Anna Sandfield reports a "high level of pro-marital conventionality and anti-divorce rhetoric," and the "prevalence of traditional expectations about marriage and women's roles and identities, reflected in the disapproval and isolation experienced by the divorced."[90] Recent work on the "dominant discourses" in South African society about women and their worth after undergoing a divorce points to the existence of a narrative of failure, shame, and becoming social outcasts.[91] Divorce may be largely frowned upon, often with important negative consequences for women in particular. The discourse may have been similar in the United States decades ago, but it no longer is.[92]

Perhaps more intriguing is a recent exploration of the discourse on divorce in China. Hui Faye Xiao, a China specialist at the University of Kansas, begins by noting that Chinese divorce rates have experienced unprecedented growth in the last decade or so. Until 2004 married couples needed the permission of their work units to obtain a divorce. The relaxation of that rule led to a tremendous spike in divorce rates: in that year alone, over 1.61 million Chinese couples went through the divorce procedure. This constituted a 21.2 percent increase from the prior year. 2004 became the "year of divorce" in the popular media.[93] Overall, following the country's turn toward a market economy, rates have been increasing dramatically since the 1980s, but especially in the last 10 years or so.

In tandem with years of market liberalization and an increased emphasis on individualism, Xiao points out that women are seen as having acquired more control over their marital affairs. However, when it comes to divorce, she stresses that this does not translate into women being depicted as initiators of divorce or, following the divorce, as being in a position of great potential for renewal, as is the case in the United States. On the contrary, Xiao states that:

> There is an unprecedented huge increase in the production of popular narratives of divorce. Most of these popular representations tend to reduce the complexity of the social issue of divorce as a result of political, economic and legislative changes to a personalized victim narrative of the "abandoned woman."[94]

Media reports accordingly labeled 2005 "the year of abandoned women."[95] This may appear to be a rather conservative, male-oriented discourse: the woman is seen as hopeless victim. In fact, the situation is more subtle: women can manage themselves. The dominant discourse depicts them as being capable, if willing to invest time and energy and eager in doing so, to prevent divorce from happening in the first place. Thus, Xiao writes, "domestic fiction, women's magazines, media reports, advertising, TV shows" have become "the educational tools to help women master the art of accruing and managing the symbolic capital of consum(er)ability, making 'free choices' about their lifestyle and emotional capacity to accomplish a certain quality of domestic life and sense of self-fulfillment." And, in this context, the general expectation is that they will use their new capabilities to change their dispositions and habits so as to prevent, in the first place, divorce from happening. This explains, therefore, the "sweeping popularity of various 'How-To' marriage guidebooks such as *Wife's Art of War* (Qizi bingfa), *How to Make a Man Love You for a Lifetime* (Ruhe rang nanren ai ni yisheng), and the Chinese translation of *Divorce is Not the Answer: A Change of Heart Will Save Your Marriage* (Lihun wuji yushi: ruhe tiaozheng yu wanjiu hunyin)."[96]

None of this suggests a particularly progressive understanding of women and power when it comes to divorce. The vision articulated in the American dominant discourse, while consistent with broader values of freedom and individuality in the country, is divergent from dominant discourses in other parts of the world. It involves, for men and women alike, empowering language, visions of freedom and recreation, and an embrace of change and new starts. It is indeed a very American story.

8　Parents' Death

Until approximately 20 years ago, little public attention or academic research concerned itself with the death of one's parents. As recently as 2004, award-winning journalist Le Anne Schreiber lamented in *O, The Oprah Magazine* that the 2001 *Handbook of Bereavement Research*,[1] "the bible of the field" of death and survivors published by the American Psychological Association, devoted only four out of 814 pages to the passing away of parents.[2] To this day, some major organizations dedicated to helping those who have lost a beloved one hardly mention parents. Mental Health America, one of the nation's leading promoters of psychological wellbeing, for instance, says nothing about parents when discussing "bereavement and the death of a loved one."[3] Only children, spouses, and the loss that may come from someone committing suicide are listed. Similarly, the Wendt Center for Loss and Healing, a prominent counseling and support organization in Washington, DC, when talking about "grief," has special sections for the loss of a child and of a spouse, but not for the loss of a parent.[4] "Ageism," a general tendency to care little for the elderly in American society, proposes Miriam Moss, a former researcher at the School of Public Health at Drexel University, may explain this broad disinterest in talking about this transition. "The attitude is," Moss observes, "Oh well, she was old. How old was she? Seventy-eight? Oh, I'm sorry. What else is new?"[5]

Yet, starting in the late 1990s, things did begin to change: more and more Americans started talking openly and publicly about death in general[6] and, in particular, the almost inevitable experience of having one's parents die. This shift may have been due to the millions of baby boomers (those born between 1946 and 1964) who started having elderly parents approaching the end of life – a demographic reality that remains relevant today.[7] It may also have resulted from the fact that, unlike decades ago when life expectancy was shorter and one's parents died much earlier in a person's life, the parent–child relationship can now easily last 50 or more years. As part of that change, the financial and emotional dependence of the son or daughter on the parents has lengthened in time significantly.[8] Anyone – from young children to, far more commonly nowadays,[9] mature adults – can now experience this transition.

Today, a multitude of voices – from Elmo on Sesame Street[10] to national public radio[11] – talk about death and parents. It is recognized as a major and noteworthy life transition: as researchers John Barner and Paul Rosenblatt (from the University of Georgia and the University of Minnesota respectively) recently put it, "an individual's experience of parental death is ... a significant developmental milestone" and it constitutes an "event of vital importance to the understanding of the self in a variety of contexts."[12] It is also seen as unexpectedly painful and disorienting. In the eyes of the American Hospice Foundation, for instance,

> When a parent becomes ill and is dying, the adult child can be a forgotten mourner. Friends, colleagues, and even other family members may assume the adult child has broken close ties with his/her parents, married, moved away, and therefore is not so affected by the illness or death of a parent. Not true. The illness and perhaps the death of a parent is extremely painful at any age.[13]

Experts such as Debra Umberson, who draws from national survey data and in-depth interviews, describe it as an "unexpected crisis for most healthy, well-functioning individuals."[14]

What, then, is the dominant discourse on this important transition? The discourse primarily speaks to adults who lose their parents. With that in mind, the death of one's parents is typically pictured as *an inevitable, cyclical event that is part of the natural unfolding of life and occasions the maturation of the surviving son or daughter into a freestanding and autonomous human being.* Here, the themes of life's cyclicality, phases, order, and boundaries are prominent. The transition is something that countless others have experienced before us: it is part of the human condition and amounts to one's final step into full adulthood. Thus, the origins are certainly external to us: as the surviving offspring, it happens to us. With this in mind, we should not (and in fact cannot) turn away from the past. On the contrary, we must accept and absorb it into the present and future. For the self, the task becomes not one of reinvention at all, but of refinement: the son or daughter must now claim his or her space in the world as a fully independent, complete person. The person must feel whole without the presence of the parents; for this, a revised version of the existing self needs to be crafted. How this is achieved is an open question, so the future is considerably open: little about the death of one's parents puts limits on what comes next. At the same time, the transition itself is not only about the surviving child: the actors include the parents (in their role of the departed) and whichever other siblings there might be, and, in a broader sense, humanity at large. On the whole, this transition is about continuity, life's cyclical nature, and order.

A Rite of Passage

Psychologist Alexander Levy's *The Orphaned Adult: Understanding and Coping with Grief and Change after the Death of Our Parents* became in the late 1990s one of the first popular books on parental death. As such, it helped frame the public discussion of this transition. Already on the back cover of the book we encounter language remarkably representative of the American perspective: "Losing our parents when we ourselves are adults is in the natural order of things, a rite of passage into true adulthood." Levy himself proposed the crucial idea that "perhaps only after parents have died can people find out what they are going to be when they grow up."[15] The language of "rite of passage" and true, complete "adulthood" has remained at the very center of our dominant discourse. Umberson would use very similar language a few years later in her groundbreaking book *Death of a Parent: Transition to a New Adulthood* – a work that summarizes data from the National Institute on Aging and in-depth interviews on this transition: "The loss of a parent," she asserts, "represents a rite of passage into a new adult identity."[16] This is very particular and consequential language that deserves careful unpacking and analysis. Let us consider the origin of the transition first.

Origins

In our dominant discourse, the death of one's parents is always considered an external event: it is experienced, but not brought about, by the son or daughter. In fact, the son or daughter becomes essentially the victim of this event and, if young, special steps should be taken to ensure that the child in no way starts feeling responsible for what has happened.[17] The death can be brought about by two rather different sorts of external causes: an accident or illness before real old age, or the natural process of aging and decline. In either case, responsibility for the death lies clearly beyond the son or daughter. Indeed, responsibility often lies beyond the parents themselves: it happens to them and, as a result, happens to the son or daughter.

Hence, in the case of premature deaths by way of accident or illness, Phyllis Silverman, a contributing expert writing for *Psychology Today*, suggests that, when explaining to children why a parent might have died, there be clarity about how this came about:

> What do these children need? They need to hear the word dead, they need to hear in a gentle quiet way that their parent is not coming back, although we can understand why they would like that to happen. It was not Daddy or Mommy's choice. A simple explanation of what happened is appropriate, for example, Daddy was sick and sometimes the doctors can't fix the problem.[18]

No one chooses to die. The discourse on parental suicide is, in other words, very secondary, even among academics.[19] Thus, a significant element of randomness is brought into the picture: unfortunate timing, a moment of poor judgment, or faulty genes, for instance, bring a parent's life to an end. We search for meaning but cannot find it easily: the cause is very much removed from us. Edward Myers, author of perhaps the first "guide" for adults who lose a parent, talks about "shock, bewilderment, and disbelief." He points to the "inability" on our part to acknowledge what has occurred.[20] Far less often do we find in the dominant discourse language that pins responsibility genuinely on the parent himself. These are the cases of alcoholic, drug-addicted, or otherwise self-destructive parents. In these cases too, however, the cause is obviously "external" when it comes to the son or daughter: the death of a parent *happens* to the surviving son or daughter.

The second, and perhaps most common, account of the origins of this transition is to define it as natural. On the website of Colorado-based HospiceCare (a nonprofit healthcare organization serving the city of Boulder and beyond), we read, for example, about the ideas of clinical psychologist Therese Rando.[21] Rando is the founder and clinical director of the Institute for the Study and Treatment of Loss in Rhode Island and an authority on mourning and loss:

> In today's society, in the cycle of human development, it is normal and natural to lose your parents when you yourself are an adult. The death of parents is the single most common form of bereavement for adults. Depending on their ages and on yours, death is usually more or less

expected. In contrast to the death of a child, it is consistent with the laws of nature. In contrast to the death of a spouse, it usually does not deprive us of our primary sources of companionship and identity. And in contrast to the loss of a brother or sister, it is usually less threatening to us personally.[22]

The reference to the "laws of nature" externalizes the cause of death in a different way than in the case of premature death: here, the transition is in line with the broadest and most fundamental aspects of life and the universe. There is a logic at work: this is the way that life as we know it on this planet unfolds. Because of this, the loss is made a bit more bearable, since we understand that such deaths are fundamental to the human experience.

This interpretation emphasizes inevitability and the cycle of life and death as something that we must come to terms with. Examples abound. Journalist and CNN producer Allison Gilbert, for instance, opens her book *Parentless Parents: How the Loss of Our Mothers and Fathers Impacts the Way We Raise Our Children* with a moving passage about walking with her beloved father in the streets of Manhattan and, before parting ways to head to their respective offices, hearing from her dad: "You better be okay when I die. Because it *will* happen."[23] And on the website of Columbia University's counseling services, in response to a student's distressed message about the death of her mother (the student signs her name as "Lonely and Depressed" and shares her sense that she was "abandoned"), Alice, Columbia health consultant, writes: "Death is a normal part of the life cycle, and something we all face sooner or later."[24]

Past

The past is incorporated into the present and future. The discourse tells us that we do not, and indeed cannot, dismiss our parents as irrelevant once they pass away. The incorporation can happen in a variety of ways. Memory and remembering are especially important: we are told it is natural as well as important to keep our parents in our minds. During a March 2012 radio episode of The Diane Rehm Show fully dedicated to young children experiencing the death of a parent, we therefore hear Gardiner Harris, a public health reporter for the *New York Times*, offer the following advice:

I think one of the great gifts that the surviving parent and family members can do is to continue to share stories and memories about the person who died, especially with such a young child. They may not have as many memories of their own so that really is a gift to keep talking about the person who died, using their name, letting the child know it's not a forbidden subject. They can ask their questions as they're ready. As they get older, they'll ask different questions and it's important to keep that conversation going.[25]

But even relatively young children *do* remember their parents, and these memories – positive or negative – are undeletable in the son or daughter's mind.[26] Neil Chethik, in his landmark book on sons who have lost a father, *Fatherloss: How Sons of All Ages Come to Terms with the Deaths of Their Dads*, boils down the learnings from his interviews with over 370 ordinary American men to a matter of memory and, in particular, memory about *"affection:"*[27] men, he concludes, remember all their lives the affection of their fathers. Hence memories and continuity are at the heart of Hallmark cards. The company offers six sympathy cards related to the loss of a father, for instance. The first is called *Nostalgic Photo*, and comes with the following text: "Of all the heroes we look up to in a lifetime, none stick with us quite like the first."[28] Another, called *Memories Keep Him Close*, states that "there are places in your mind that will forever remember his stories and traditions, his humor and generosity."[29] A third states that a "father's love is like a rock . . . solid, immovable, everlasting."[30] In a similar spirit, on the popular website *ehow*, we are told that "even though he is gone physically, your father lives on in your memory and in the acts you do in his honor."[31]

At the same time, we also encounter repeatedly the idea that one should almost "sift" through the available memories to decide what is worth keeping and what we should let go. This is what one can read, for instance, in the *Los Angeles Times*, as reporter Melissa Healy discusses the transition with Jeannie Safer, psychotherapist and author of *Death Benefits: How Losing a Parent Can Change an Adult's Life – for the Better*.[32] As Safer puts it:

> The adult intent on making the most of a parent's loss should be willing to examine her parents' emotional legacies carefully and consciously. Doing so, she argues, will better distinguish those parental legacies worth keeping – the ones that contribute to health and well-being – from those that no longer serve that end.[33]

On another level, parents become more explicitly part of the identity of the surviving child. The child may adopt new roles and behaviors that, according to Umberson, "emulate" the parents.[34]

Accordingly, on *WebMD* we read the personal story of Tom Valeo, a journalist keen on describing how his father's death affected him:

> But as I read the eulogy in front of the assembled mourners, I realized I was not just paying tribute to my father; I was reciting a credo of sorts, a list of beliefs and goals drawn from his life that I admired and wanted to keep alive in my own way. I commended his deep compassion for other people, his tireless raging against social injustice, his devotion to family and friends – and to my mother as she languished for years in a nursing home after a devastating stroke.
>
> Like so many sons, I had modeled myself after my father in many ways. And as I delivered his eulogy, I realized that, like it or not, he would live on through me.[35]

Our parents live through us, and we become all the more aware of this once they are gone.

On yet another level, we often encounter the idea that our parents' departure has long-lasting effects on our mental and emotional well-being. Hope Edelman, in her *New York Times* bestseller *Motherless Daughters: The Legacy of Loss* (which sold over 500,000 copies), emphasizes time and time again how it took her many years to truly come to terms with the loss of her mother. She also affirms that the loss of a mother creates a "void" in our lives "that is never completely filled again."[36] In his analogous book for sons who have lost a father, *Fatherloss,* Chethik talks about men mourning subtly for a long time: for the over 370 ordinary American men he interviewed, "the aftershocks went on for years."[37]

The discourse emphasizes that this is especially the case for young children: in their case, experts as well as survey-based reports underscore the fact that the death of parents can "reverberate" for decades, as a recent article in the *Wall Street Journal* put it.[38] This is the message found in Donna Schuurman's powerful *Never the Same: Coming to Terms with the Death of a Parent*[39] and is the core intuition at the heart of *Comfort Zone Camp,* the nation's largest (tuition-free) bereavement camp for children, which seeks explicitly to help young girls and boys deal with the "loss of a parent" (as well as sibling or primary caregiver).[40] Such loss, the organization's leaders emphasize, "is undeniably one of the most traumatic events a child can experience," with potentially very harmful consequences for the ability of those children to reach "their potential" in life and as members of their community.[41] The impact on adults is often not as extreme, but here too we encounter time and time again language about the long-term effects of this transition on grown men and women.

Self

The death of parents affords the self one of the most important occasions it ever encounters: the chance to finally *be*. This is the "shocking – almost sacrilegious" truth,[42] says Jeannie Safer when reflecting on this transition with Melissa Healy of the *Los Angeles Times*. As Safer puts it in the opening page of the book:

> The death of a parent – any parent – can set us free. It offers us our last, best chance to become our truest, deepest selves. Nothing else in adult life has so much unrecognized potential to help us become more fulfilled human beings – wiser, more mature, more open, less afraid. It creates opportunities for growth – possibilities unimaginable before and not available by any other means.[43]

This is not a matter of reinvention, of course, but rather of completion as well as refinement. Recent academic research based on in-depth interviews with surviving adults talks about a "reorganization of the self."[44] "With their parents gone," Safer observes in her interview with Healy, "many adults keenly sense that they are 'next in line' for decline, disability and demise. That often concentrates the mind on what's right, and wrong, in their lives – what traits and behaviors have served them well and which would better be abandoned."[45] Hope Edelman, in *Motherless Daughters*, observes that the "adult daughter, however, does confront the loss with a relatively intact personality . . . she understands at some level that adjusting to the death of a parent is a developmental task of middle age."[46] And in *Fatherloss*, Chethik talks about a "significant reordering" of one's "inner landscape."[47]

Orphaned adults themselves give voice to this perspective. In her *O, The Oprah Magazine* article, Schreiber reports on her interviews with a small sample of women, ages 46 to 66, about losing a parent. "Although the stories they told, and the parent–child relationships they described, were highly individual," she notes, "a remarkable consistency began to emerge. Without exception these women described profound changes, both internal and external, which they directly attributed to their parents' deaths. Most surprisingly, they characterized the changes as positive. That, in fact, is why they seldom, if ever, had talked in detail about their reactions to becoming motherless or fatherless."[48] The changes varied a good deal, but most in the end dealt with the theme of reaching full adulthood. The reflections of Maggie, one of the interviewees, are representative. Maggie talks about "a new seriousness:"

Certainly a new sense of my own mortality, but that's not the whole picture. It's sort of like when your mother used to choose your clothes, and then the time came when you chose your own clothes but there was still that little voice in the back of your head going, Would my mother like this? And even if the answer was Hell no, that's exactly why I'm getting it, the thought was there. After the death, you don't ask yourself the question. You're on your own. In some way, the pressure's off, and in some ways the pressure is on. Because you have no one to answer to but yourself.[49]

The American Hospice Foundation points to the same idea with perhaps more sober words: "You may be ready to pick up on the other aspects of dealing with the death of your parent, such as loneliness, feelings of being an orphan, and the fact that you are now the 'older generation.'"[50]

These are themes that are central to many books on the subject as well. Umberson, for instance, writes in *Death of a Parent* that

We may implicitly believe that once we reach adulthood, particularly if we have children of our own, that our development is more or less complete. We do not expect that there will be major changes in the way we experience the world or react to it . . . the death of a parent is a turning point in the emotional, personal, and social lives of most adults – an event that initiates a period of substantial change and redirection in the way we view ourselves, our relationship to others, and our place in the world.[51]

The transition, she continues, qualifies as a major life event, and as such provides one with "opportunities to recast self-conceptions, values, and beliefs."[52] Tellingly, she then adds that a "parent's death propels the social and psychological transition from childhood to adulthood. We suddenly recognize that there is no longer a parent to turn to; that there is no longer a choice about whether or not to be self-reliant. Even adults who did not rely greatly on their parent may experience the feeling of being on their own for the first time."[53]

And, in *Always Too Soon: Voices of Support for Those Who Have Lost Both Parents,* journalist and CNN producer Allison Gilbert writes that "the death of a parent often creates a developmental push."[54] Myers, in his "guide" for adults who lose a parent, quotes several of his interviewees on this very point. One states that "my parents' death made me grow up . . . suddenly I was in charge." Another admits that "I believe that my father's death began a period of maturity that I would not have achieved otherwise . . . there was no more 'passing the buck.'" Yet another affirms that she "grew and emerged a much stronger, self-reliant, and capable person."[55]

Remarkably often, then, this transition is depicted as a positive opportunity for self-development. What is described as a terribly painful event is also presented as potentially profoundly beneficial for the self. Not coincidentally, the impact of parental death on the bereaved son or daughter has, according to Barner and Rosenblatt, been the focal point of "much of the existing scholarship on the subject of parental death."[56]

Future

The future is open, but as is the case with many other transitions, the death of one's parents occasions a number of predictable steps immediately following the event. Three such steps are often mentioned. The first concerns grief – and the language here is not too different from the one we encounter about job loss or divorce, both transitions that are ultimately about an open future. The National Funeral Directors Association employs rather typical language:

> When your mom or dad dies, it may be one of the most emotional losses you'll experience in life. It is only natural to feel consumed by a combination of pain, fear and deep sadness at the loss of such a significant influence in your life.
>
> The specifics of how you grieve will depend on a number of personal factors, including your relationship with your parent, age, gender, religious beliefs, previous experience with death, and whether or not you believe it was time for your parent to die. But there are some common reactions that people often experience after the loss of a parent. They include:
>
> - Shock
> - Denial
> - Numbness
> - Guilt
> - Preoccupation with the memory of your parent
>
> . . . After the initial shock fades, you will experience what is called secondary loss. This is when you may begin to think of all the upcoming experiences that your parent will not be there to share in. Things like career accomplishments, watching your own children grow, and other milestones.[57]

Variations of this account can be found in virtually every resource or book on parental loss.

A second commonly discussed step is a rethinking of one's relationship with one's parents. The common image is of love but also often regret: the child recognizes how much more loving, present, or responsive he should have been toward the parents when they were alive. Guilt, in other words, plays a role. We read, for instance, in *Elle* this personal account of Holly Millea, who covers beauty and fashion for the magazine:

> Packing up her room, I found a tower of ELLE magazines, every one of my stories dog-eared. I'd spent 20 years interviewing celebrities and never interviewed the most beautiful, fascinating woman the world will never know. Which has left me overwhelmed with unanswerable questions and regret and guilt that I never gave her the kind of attention I'd given to total strangers. Shame on me that the only story I've ever written about my mother was her obituary.[58]

Guilt figures prominently as well in the memories that *New York Times* reporter Harris shares on *The Diane Rehm Show*. He described in painful detail, "to my great undying shame," how he and his brother would play rock, paper, scissor to see which of the two would respond to their mother's requests for help during the last few months of her life, which were spent mostly in her bedroom in slow decline.[59] In the same spirit, on *WebMD*, Valeo reports the view of Robert Glover, author and marriage and family therapist in Bellevue, Washington, that "a son's failure to make a connection with his father can be a source of lingering grief that easily breeds depression after his father dies."[60] Remorse is a major problem for at least the short-term future.

A third predictable step, we are often told, has to do with our recognizing the finiteness of our lives: our parents' death serves as a warning sign of our own mortality "in a way that no other death can," as Umberson puts it.[61] In *Always Too Soon*, Gilbert agrees, adding that "there is a gap between understanding that people die and internalizing the statement 'Someday I will die.' As long as both parents are alive, we are buffered from the reality of death."[62] We become, as the American Hospice Foundation puts it, the "older generation."[63] In a similar vein, the National Funeral Directors Association notes that "if you are older, the death of a parent may even bring up issues of your own mortality."[64]

Yet, all these are steps that define in only a very limited fashion our future. Even in the case of young children losing a parent, the grieving process is expected to be relatively short, and in the first longitudinal study of its kind (and one that received considerable media attention),[65] researchers at the University of Pittsburgh School of Medicine describe the majority of those children as able to cope with their grief within one year of the loss.[66] By and large, the broader consequences of becoming a truly full, autonomous adult for the first time in our lives – the central interpretation of this transition in the dominant discourse – have much to do with *openness*. There are few obvious limitations, in fact, that the transition imposes on us, at least when it comes to adult orphans. Indeed, the notion of full "autonomy" implies that the individual is free, for the first time, to move about without constraints. In a very real sense, the transition is ultimately about freedom – a fact which explains in part why so often the transition, as tragic as it is, is often cast as being profoundly positive in some respects.

This is precisely the message, for example, on the website *ehow*. In a piece titled *What to Do after a Parent's Death*, contributor Genevieve Van Wyden stresses that "you may have felt emotionally tied to your parents and were unable to follow your dreams or live your life as you had wished. You have to resolve your feelings so you can move ahead." She then continues:

> Take stock of who you are and follow your dream. If you have always wanted to be an architect, decide whether you wish to pursue your dream. First, look at how your parents influenced your decisions before their deaths and why they did so. Some parents who may have been children of the Depression truly felt they were protecting their children in steering them away from their dreams – they wanted to protect them from a potential financial or economic disaster ... Don't be angry with them because, even as they were keeping you from achieving your dream, they did so out of love for you.[67]

Myers, in his "guide" for adults who have lost a parent, while actually acknowledging that some may not find the transition positive at all, proceeds to state something quite similar: "you are now free to proceed," he writes. "Whatever duties may have burdened you, whatever roles may have confined you, whatever expectations may have restrained you, you can now move on in whatever direction you want your life to take."[68] The road is open, and all we have to do is decide where to head as we move forward.

Representative in this regard are also the final words of Edelman's book *Motherless Daughters*. "There is no shame in turning loss into life," she asserts. "Like the phoenix, the mythological bird that ascends from the ashes of its own destruction," she continues, "every motherless daughter has the potential within herself to arise from tragedy and take flight." The daughter, she reasons further, "has every right to that future,"[69] and should in the last analysis capitalize on this opportunity. With the same idea in mind, in *Fatherloss*, Neil Chethik writes that "the experience of losing a father" in the "best" of circumstances "can inspire in the son a new appreciation for his life and move him with urgency to make the most of his remaining years."[70]

Actors

This is a collective transition on many levels. Parents die and in this regard they are the inevitable protagonists in this transition. At the same time, the change is to a very real extent about the son or daughter who lives through this difficult time, as he or she stands alone as well as in relation to the parents, siblings, and others. In a broader sense, the experience of parental death is described as involving a connection to humanity as a whole: the bereaved son or daughter joins, as it were, countless other human beings who have gone through this transition before and, ultimately, participates fully in the human condition. The discourse emphasizes relationships and others over exclusive individuality.

Central to this transition, then, are the parents and the surviving child. The parents die, and the child for some time must find ways to adapt to this enormous change. The adaptation is in many regards about one's relationship to one's parents: what it was but, also, what it will be going forward. As Edelman puts it in the case of women and mothers, for instance, "a motherless woman continues to renegotiate her relationship with her mother throughout her life."[71] Psychologist Alan Pope talks about "'holding on to' the deceased parents," and about "an ongoing relationship to the deceased parent [which] serves several vital psychological and developmental functions."[72] The parents may have passed away in a physical sense, but they endure in the minds of their sons and daughters.

Yet others are also present. Umberson notes, for instance, that "bereaved adults experience a change in relationships with others."[73] Levy, in his classic book, devotes an entire chapter to "Changes in Relationships to Others after Parents Die."[74] This is a core dimension of the transition. Who, then, are these others? Above all, they include one's siblings and, if one of the parents is still alive, that parent. We can see this in the work and words of Alan Wolfelt, Founder and Director of the Center for Loss and Life Transitions in Colorado, who runs workshops throughout the United States and is the author of a series of very popular brochures (distributed via numerous channels, such as funeral homes and counseling centers) on various kinds of losses. *Helping Yourself Heal When a Parent Dies* is one of those brochures, and there Wolfelt deals with the question of "others" in very typical fashion:

> If you have brothers or sisters, the death of this parent will probably affect them differently than it is affecting you. After all, each of them had a unique relationship with the parent who died, so each has the right to mourn the loss in his or her own way.
>
> The death may also stir up sibling conflicts. You and your brothers and sisters may disagree about the funeral, for example, or argue about family finances. Recognize that such conflicts are natural, if unpleasant. Do your part to encourage open communication during this stressful family time. You may find, on the other hand, that the death of your parent brings you and your siblings closer together. If so, welcome this gift.
>
> Finally, when there is a surviving parent, try to understand the death's impact on him or her. The death of a spouse – often a husband or wife of many decades – means many different things to the surviving spouse than it does to you, the child of that union. This does not mean that you are necessarily responsible for the living parent; in fact, to heal you must first and foremost meet your own grief needs. But it does mean that you, a younger and often more resilient family member, should be patient and compassionate as you continue your relationship with the surviving parent.[75]

Importantly, the discourse underscores the fact that those relationships may change in a variety of ways and, in the simplest way, for either the better or the worse. Hence, Myers, in his "guide" to adults who have lost a parent, writes that "you may end up growing closer to your other parent, or you may drift away. You and your brothers and sisters may rediscover each other after years of mutual indifference, or you may become estranged."[76]

Other characters figure in this transition as well, but in their case their role is truly secondary: they do not experience the transition as much as feel its effects through the protagonists. Those "others" are, for instance, the partners of the bereaved sons or daughters,[77] as well as the children of the surviving offspring. The relationship to those children, we are told, undergoes important change. Thus, Gilbert tells us in *Parentless Parents* – one of the most comprehensive analyses to date on the topic, which leveraged focus groups, in-depth interviews, and other data sources, including the opinions of well-known experts – that the loss of parents affects the way we as parents conduct and feel about our own parenting. Parentless parents can feel more isolated, for instance, sensitive to the fact that their spouses' parents (the children's grandparents) may still be alive and have a lively relationship to the children in question.[78]

The Optimist's Perspective

Once again, we see in the dominant American discourse an effort to insert positivity into a painful and negative transition in life. Yet, in the case of parental death, this optimism is not accompanied by a celebration of individuality. Surely this is a story about personal becoming and how, as single human beings, we experience the world. At the same time, the transition is depicted at its very *core* as being about the human condition. Our connection to our parents is one of the strongest bonds that exist in life; death, in turn, is an inherent component of life. The bereaved son or daughter is asked to recognize these fundamental truths. As psychologist Pope puts it, the transition is understood to foster "a greater sense of interconnectedness to others," even a "transcendence of egoistic concerns."[79] We are part not only of our parents but of humanity in general, and the death of one's parents places us squarely into the midst of the human experience. We become full, complete human beings. Accordingly, the discourse emphasizes the concepts of life's cycle, the laws of nature, and the inevitability of certain things in life. It also emphasizes our place in the broader scheme of things.

Elements of this perspective – which, like all other perspectives considered in this book, is fundamentally cultural – can certainly be found in other countries, too. The event is considered important in probably every society on earth, and is also very often seen as a critical step in a person's development – psychological but also physiological. However, what is remarkable in this case is that at least in some of those contexts a well-developed public discourse on this transition as a major part of a person's life – including, and especially, as it concerns grown adults – seems to be largely missing. If in the United States a dominant discourse began developing in the 1990s in response to the situation of many baby boomers and their aging parents, the same cannot be said, for instance, of several other major industrialized countries in the world. There, it appears that the passing of one's parents has not been objectified, for the moment at least, as something that necessitates wide-open dialogue, reflection, and guidance – and has thus not given rise to a dominant discourse. This is the case even when it comes to the more confined world of academia. As recently as 2004, Helen Marshall, Research Fellow in the Centre for Research on Ageing and Gender (CRAG) at the University of Surrey in the United Kingdom, stated that "virtually all known research concerning the experience of midlife loss of parents is based in the United States and has not been addressed in the United Kingdom or wider Europe."[80] Why this difference exists between the United States and these other countries is unclear, and is certainly deserving of investigation by comparative sociologists, anthropologists, and others capable of investigating cultural divergences when it comes to perspectives on life, death, and generational changes across countries.

With this said, in the last few years there seems to be emerging, in very limited form, in Europe and beyond a discourse with regard to young children and their experience of parental loss. The discussions seem focused for now on the best ways to *explain* to those children in simple language what has happened and on identifying ways of *supporting* effectively those children. We can see an example of this in the Spanish and Italian sites of amazon.com – which otherwise offer no significant resources on this transition. On each site we find a book for children, though both are admittedly translations of American books. The Italian one is *Il Lutto Infantile*,[81] a 2007 translation of *Losing a Parent to Death in the Early Years*,[82] written by a team of researchers at the University of California at San Francisco. Far from being aimed at a broader audience, it is a psychological resource for adults intent on helping children. The Spanish book is *Ante la Pérdida de Nuestros Padres*,[83] a 2011 Spanish translation of Daniel Fitzpatrick's *When Your Parent Dies*;[84] this is a short, Christian self-help book which actually speaks as much to young children as to adults.

Additional evidence of a growing interest in the experience of young children concerns academic research on their long-term physiological wellbeing (a theme that, of course, is also prevalent in the United States).[85] Researchers have examined, for example, the cardiovascular health of bereaved children in Guangzhou, China,[86] the educational achievements of orphaned children in South Africa,[87] and the mortality rates of children who have lost a parent in Sweden.[88] We can expect this body of research to grow further and, at some point perhaps, to inform a broader discourse on parental death and young children.

Still clearly missing in many countries, then, is a well-developed, dominant discourse on parental death and bereavement. We can conclude by offering a broader observation about cultural – if not discourse-related – differences. Evidence from sub-Saharan Africa points to a widespread practice to deal with parental loss that differs, in spirit, from the values we find articulated in the American discourse. Research shows that in the case of children orphaned by the HIV/AIDS epidemic, local practices urge those children to *forget* their parents and their past. This is seen as a critical step in the recovery of those children.[89] Unsurprisingly, it has been heavily criticized by Western donors and observers as ineffective. Regardless of effectiveness, the approach differs markedly from the American one and points, at least from a cultural (if not dominant discourse) perspective, to how differently this painful transition can be approached.

9 Retirement

In 1900, life expectancy in the United States was around 47. Back then, retirement hardly existed as a practical or conceptual reality. During the Great Depression and the establishment of Social Security in 1935, the government began recognizing a sort of "finish line" in a person's career and the existence of a brief, declining period of life that required financial support.[1] Indeed, until the 1950s or even the 1960s, "people just worked until they dropped dead,"[2] as Marc Freedman puts it in *The Big Shift: Navigating the New Stage Beyond Midlife*.[3] In recent decades, with life expectancy greatly increasing and now reaching almost 80 in the United States according to the World Bank and government sources,[4] and with many men and women stopping to work in their sixties, retirement has become a whole new phase in life.

In fact, according to a report by the US Social Security Administration Office of Retirement and Disability Policy, the average life expectancy for the average man and woman after retiring in 2011 at the age of 62 was 21.4 and 23.8 years, respectively. Americans, the report notes, are bound to spend more time in retirement than they did through grade school.[5] A handout available online from New York-Presbyterian, the hospitals of Columbia and Cornell universities, makes a similar point:

> Retirement is a major event in most people's lives. It usually signifies the end of one phase of life and the beginning of a new one. Today a person can be retired for as long as 20–30 years or more due to longer life expectancies. For many of us, the years spent in retirement will be longer than those of childhood and adolescence combined.[6]

This new life phase, most obviously embodied at the present time by the baby-boomer generation,[7] has caught the attention of a variety of individuals, service providers, government agencies, financial counselors, and others. The reasons vary: some are concerned about ensuring the health of retirees, others about their financial independence, happiness, and fulfillment. Yet the vast majority articulate and subscribe to (and in fact are motivated by, at least in part) a rather specific view of what this new transition is about.

In our dominant discourse, though old age and other factors certainly play a role, individuals are seen as contemplating their options and then choosing to retire. Upon retiring, the past – typically decades of active employment or some form of occupation that is viewed in hindsight as constraining though also rewarding – comes to an end, and with it a major part of our selves is set aside. Rather than signaling decline, however, the transition ushers in a supposedly long and surely the freest period of our lives. The self is now at liberty to be what it wants for the last and certainly most unencumbered time. The future is awaiting definition and can include anything, from traveling across the world to returning to school to actually continuing to work in some form or another. Though a spouse is often part of the picture, the protagonist is the retiree. *Retirement is depicted as the decisive end to the bounded structure and limitations of everyday working life and as the arrival of a period of intense freedom.* Thus conceived, retirement is at its essence about *New Beginnings*.

The Arrival of Unlimited, Free "Me" Time

John Nelson and Richard Bolles, authors of one of the most popular books on retirement – *What Color is Your Parachute? For Retirement: Planning Now for the Life You Want* – write that "society is irrevocably remaking the *old* retirement into a *new* retirement as a life stage."[8] In their view, a primary characteristic of this new stage is the largest amount of free time that a person experiences in a lifetime.[9] Such free time means, among other things, the liberty of not having to be anywhere at any given time and not having to relate to anyone in any particular way. The retiree tosses away the constraining mantle of an active, working life. In a *US News Money* article, we read that Americans view retirement as leaving behind "the days of the alarm clock and gridlocked traffic, giving way to lazy days on the golf course or in the motorhome."[10] Data from the Bureau of Labor Statistics shows that individuals from 25 to 54 years of age spend 8.8 hours a day on tasks that pertain to their full-time job:[11] those hours diminish greatly as one enters retirement age, to the point where most of the time besides sleeping is spent on leisure activities, as Figure 9.1 illustrates.[12]

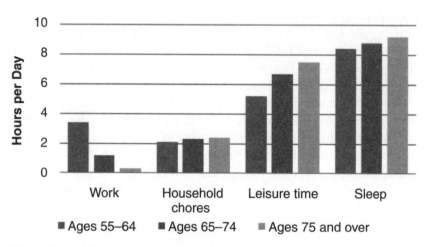

Figure 9.1: Retirement and Leisure

Source: Adapted from the Bureau of Labor Statistics

What is characteristic of such freedom is the focus on "me:" the language stresses retirement as a sort of release, of being able to concentrate on one's self, of doing away with many of those extraneous and ultimately foreign things that for too long have interfered with one's wellbeing. It is telling, in this regard, that the Merriam-Webster Dictionary defines retirement as the "withdrawal from one's position or occupation or from active working life:"[13] one *withdraws* from the public sphere, performing, and having to conform to expectations and roles. There is then an uptake in activities that fulfill more authentically one's ambitions and inclinations. The New York-Presbyterian Hospitals pamphlet asserts that "retirement is different today. In the past, it meant a slowing down of activity and the completion of work life. Retirement was generally used in reference to men. Now for both men and women it can mean having the opportunity to take up hobbies, travel, start a new career, go back to school, spend time with family, take care of grandchildren, or work only part-time."[14] Barbara Waxman, in her book *How to Love Your Retirement: The Guide to the Best of Your Life*, talks about "retirement" as being "about purpose, passion and the place where the two intersect. It's about strengthening bonds with friends, family members and those causes that we relate to."[15]

Importantly, such language does not necessarily imply that one will stop working altogether or correspond to how all Americans envision their late years in life. A 2012 Wells Fargo study involving

1,000 individuals with a yearly income below $100,000 showed that roughly 300 of the respondents planned to work past their eighties.[16] Overall, 70 percent of the respondents expected to work during retirement. Such plans may be unrealistic in practice, due to health and other considerations, but they may point to an important trend. As of May 2012, there were 7.2 million Americans over the age of 65 still in the workforce. This number has doubled from just 15 years ago; roughly 18.5 percent of Americans over the age of 65 are still in the labor force.[17] A strand in the dominant discourse recognizes this possibility, as part of what is called "phased-retirement" or simply a recognition that the freedom retirement brings can include, depending on the circumstances, some type of partial employment. With this in mind, let us consider the various elements of the discourse more closely.

Origins

What prompts an individual to retire? In our dominant discourse, the individual *decides* to retire. Old age certainly plays a role; so do the stock market, the minimum age for Medicare (65),[18] and the specifics of one's retirement accounts, as Prudential Financial, a Fortune 500 company, for instance observes.[19] Ultimately, however, all these are just some factors among many that one must weigh to arrive at a decision, and none, we are told, should force us to retire at any given point. Thus we read in the #1 best-selling book in early 2013 on retirement planning on amazon.com – Ernie J. Zelinski's *How to Retire Happy, Wild, and Free* – that "You are never too young to retire,"[20] and "If deep down you know you are ready, just do it!"[21] In the same vein, the US Social Security Administration's website contains a header for retirement aid that reads, "Your decision is a personal one;" it then adds that "there is no one 'best age' for everyone and, ultimately, it is your choice."[22] It informs readers that once an individual reaches the full retirement age, their social security benefits will not be reduced if they plan to continue working: retirement does not need to happen at any particular age, in other words, for those benefits to be available. Karen Chan, an Extension Educator of Consumer Economics at the University of Illinois, who coordinates programs on retirement planning and investing, points out that the decision to retire is a "very individual one," and something that "will require an informed decision."[23]

Because of this, Americans are confronted with a plethora of tools to help them reach a decision. Experts talk about "self-checks." The AARP provides a 12-question *Ready for Retirement Self-Assessment Tool*. The results of the test allow potential retirees to know if they are in one of three categories: a modest retirement lifestyle, a standard retirement with enough money to get by, and a retirement that is very expensive.[24] This is a pressing question for many, understandable in part in light of the fact that – as Jonathan Gruber, a Professor of Economics at the Massachusetts Institute of Technology, points out – in the United States social security retirement benefits typically amount to a mere half of the income earned when working (as opposed to two-thirds in Europe on average, for instance).[25] The Employee Benefit Research Institute, a major non-partisan research organization based in Washington, DC, suggests paying attention to the expected costs of medical and long-term care.[26] The Retirement Living Information Center in Redding, CT, along with other popular retirement information sources, presents potential retirees with "access to an array of resource materials, including reports on great places to retire, tax information on each state, monthly reports on new retirement communities" to help them decide on retirement.[27] The US Social Security Administration urges potential retirees to take into consideration family circumstances as a key factor for when to start receiving social security benefits.[28] And New York-Presbyterian Hospitals emphasize that "a smooth transition to retirement depends on financial circumstances, health, and attitude, as well as the reaction and behavior of loved ones and friends."[29]

Spouses in particular deserve special consideration. Given that retirement is an individual choice, a big question is whether preferences can be coordinated between partners. Thoughtful consideration of what a spouse might want is encouraged. At the same time, many experts claim that Americans do not appear to be doing a particularly good job on this front. Kathleen Murphy, President of Personal Investing at Fidelity, recently described the tendency of potential retirees not to involve their spouses in the decision-making process: "millions of American couples have worked very hard to save for retirement. However, far too many don't take the time, or have the comfort level, to jointly discuss their plans for the future."[30] In a 2011 study of 648 married couples, Fidelity found that nearly half of couples that are near retirement cannot agree on a specific time when they both will retire. Only 41 percent of couples had agreed to handle their investment decisions together.[31] Others paint a different picture. Alicia Munnell, Director of the Center for Retirement Research at

Boston College, for instance believes that "husbands and wives like to coordinate their retirement."[32] Coordination, of course, does not mean interference: the choice remains a personal one throughout.

The calculation is complex, then, but it remains a calculation nonetheless. Little in the American discourse suggests that retirement "happens" to someone.[33] It is a decision one makes following deliberation and consideration of various factors. "You may be asking yourself if you *should* retire," Jan Cullinane writes in an AARP-sponsored book (and #3 on amazon.com for Retirement Planning as of early 2013) on retirement and women. "If you are unsure, or just for fun, take the 'Are You Ready for Retirement Quiz' in Appendix 1."[34] The language is about personal choice and freedom, and, with that, prompting young workers especially to start saving early on precisely to be in a position to retire when they want later in life, as a recent article in the *Wall Street Journal* urged readers to do.

Past

Retirement signifies closure and therefore a dismissal of the past. The discourse juxtaposes one's working life as a time of constraints and regimented routines *with* the freedom that retirement ushers in. "Retirement can set you free,"[35] is the title of one section of Zelinski's popular book, *How to Retire Happy, Wild, and Free*. He advises retirees to "let go of the past, and find peace and happiness within"[36] and submits that work is "a barrier to the lives they wanted; now they're free to live to the fullest."[37] Hallmark cards on retirement come with similar messages: one reads "A New Journey Begins . . . The open road awaits,"[38] another defines it as "a time to relax, to play, to feel happy."[39] Similarly, in *Supercharged Retirement: Ditch the Rocking Chair, Trash the Remote, and Do What You Love*, a book recommended by the US Department of State for its staff,[40] Mary Lloyd portrays retirement as "[t]he end of mindless meeting, stuck-in-traffic commuting, irritating interference from the office nemesis, and other such negatives."[41] Zazzle.com, one of the fastest-growing technology companies in Silicon Valley,[42] in turn has over 5,000 t-shirts on retirement for purchase. The slogans on the shirts capture rather clearly how the past should be conceived: "Retired, Goodbye Tension! Hello Pension!"[43] And Mary Lloyd, author and CEO of Mining Silver, a company dedicated to capitalizing on the talent of retirees, compares retirement to the Grand Canyon, a sight that you cannot foresee until you are at the edge: "[o]n horseback and going fast, a cowboy or desperado might have found himself in freefall before he knew that it was happening."[44] The same can be said of retirement: "we come roaring up to it at top career speed and pitch headlong into a world much different than the one we were in three seconds ago without realizing the magnitude of the change."[45]

The past, then, will amount to something very different from what retirement brings. Especially illustrative, in this regard, is a 2012 special edition of CNN's *State of the Union with Candy Crowley: Yielding their Time*. Crowley spoke with retiring Senators Jon Kyl, Kay Bailey Hutchison, Joe Lieberman and Representative Barney Frank about their pending retirements. In one way or another, all put forth visions of retirement as a major break from their working lives. In her last question, Candy Crowley asked the lawmakers to "complete this sentence: after I retire I am most looking forward to . . ." Senator Kyl responded that he was looking forward to more time chopping wood at the cabin. Senator Frank (the most prominent gay politician in the United States) remarked that it will allow him to spend more time with his husband and work at marriage "full-time." The ability to control her own schedule is what appealed to Senator Hutchison. Finally, Senator Lieberman simply said that "I'm looking forward . . . to doing something different. I mean change is, is very healthy in life."[46] These are images of moving on.

We may say that with retirement one finally shifts away from the public view and retreats into a private world. The professional performance is over and a more intimate self can step in. Importantly, while such images have historically been applied to men more than women, given that the latter were less likely to have careers outside the home, today they readily address women as well. For women, too, retirement means leaving behind demanding, even if very rewarding, careers. Books like Gail Rentsch's *Smart Women Don't Retire – They Break Free: From Working Full-Time to Living Full-Time*[47] and Jan Cullinane's *The Single Woman's Guide to Retirement*[48] speak directly to women, as do numerous support organizations, life coaches, and others.

Now, while breaking from the past is the primary image associated with retirement, in the dominant discourse we also find plenty of warnings that the separation from our past may in fact prove very difficult if too abrupt. After all, a working life often holds profound psychological (and not only financial) significance for a person. We leave behind not only grueling schedules, unwanted meetings, and demanding tasks: we also separate ourselves from our professional identity. This can be unsettling. With women especially in mind, Gail Rentsch writes that "[a]s we faced the desire to retire from our jobs and leave the prestige and pride in accomplishment that each of us enjoyed from them, we struggled with the question What comes next?"[49] She adds:

> Work is our identity, our label. It is how we reveal ourselves when we meet others for the first time; it is our defining elevator speech. Telling someone that we teach high school or college math, or direct a project for the government, is shorthand for what we can do, who we know, and how we fit into the general scheme of adulthood.[50]

The question may have special salience for women, since their ability to affirm themselves in the workplace is more recent and thus, in a sense, more relished, as Claudia Goldin, economic historian at Harvard University, pointed out in her 2006 Richard T. Ely lecture at the American Economics Association's annual meeting.[51] They also tend to be healthier and live longer as well, and thus appreciate continuing being active well into their old age.[52]

But the language often addresses male and female retirees without distinction. Kathleen Gurney, an expert in money management, warns that the transition to retirement can bring about "a huge change" in anyone's life.[53] The Livestrong Foundation stresses that the transition can be "sudden and drastic."[54] And Stacy Julien, a writer for AARP, even advises anyone thinking about retiring not to "go cold turkey:" perhaps a part-time job before retiring fully can serve as a healthy way of ending one's career.[55] Her advice is the same as that offered by the Center for Retirement Research at Boston College: "Workers approaching retirement often say they want to retire gradually, rather than going straight from full-time employment to complete retirement." The reason is the drastic change that occurs in an individual's social, economic, and mental life. Most Americans, the Center notes, are often not ready to experience such a major change in short order.[56] As Bart Rutherford notes in his book, *Phased Retirement: Transitioning from Employment to Retirement,* "work can provide social and psychological benefits that can't be met in retirement years. Today's older Americans aren't heading to the shuffle board courts with glee. You value your careers and want to challenge yourself."[57]

Thus, retirement does imply a major break from the past but the departure is seen as potentially taking some time. This logically has implications for the other dimensions of the transition, such as the self and the future.

Self

On bankrate.com, one of the leading aggregators of financial rate information on the Internet, a full section is devoted to retirement. There, we learn about the thinking of Joan Carter, "a certified retirement coach and co-founder of Life Options Institute, an online lifestyle resource for people over 50."[58] Carter believes that "so much of our identity is caught up in our job title, the company that we work for, and our business card . . . When people ask you what you do, they ask 'who are you?' After you retire, you have to create a new identity."[59] This idea of a new identity often comes with an important qualification: that new identity should be more *authentic* or *genuine* than our previous one. With the constraints of having to conform to the requirements of the workplace gone and, consequently, of our professional role in the public sphere also gone, we have the unprecedented opportunity and almost the obligation (toward ourselves) to give expression to our truer selves. By implication, this depicts our previous identity as somehow contrived or in some ways not truly genuine. A variation of this is to urge us to think much harder about the person we have always wanted to be – and thus have never been, even in a repressed form. The reader will remember that we encountered these themes in the discourse on surviving a life-threatening disease. There, too, calls (almost of a moral nature) to be truer to our inner or desired selves abounded. If survival represents a second chance at life and genuine being, retirement is depicted as our final chance to do the same. A recent *New York Times* article thus reports that Americans view retirement as a "second act," as the "encore phase" and "golden years" of life.[60]

Consider the words of Dorian Mintzer, a Boston-based retirement coach and public speaker, and founder of Revolutionize! Retirement™:

> Drop the masks and get to know the real you. How much of the identity you've been carrying around all these years is the real you, and how much of it has been masking who you are in your soul? How much of your personality did you leave at home every day? How much were you able to express the "real" you in your career? This is the grand opportunity in the transition into retirement: to finally get to know your true self, the identity at your core, your essence, and then find ways to express it fully in the world.[61]

Thus, former psychology professor and now life transitions coach Nancy Schlossberg titles her best-selling book (published by the

American Psychological Association) *Retire Smart, Retire Happy: Finding Your True Path in Life*[62] (a 2007 PBS special, "Retire Smart, Retire Happy," was based on this book). In the same spirit, Seattle-based retirement coach Janice Williams points out in her blog that "the empty space between ending your full time employment and beginning your new retirement lifestyle is a good time to contemplate and reflect on your true identity. Make time to engage in activities that stimulate self-discovery."[63] And Zelinski, in his #1 bestseller (also on the US Department of State's list of recommended resources on retirement[64]), writes that "retirement is the perfect time to become the person you would like to be and do the things you have always wanted to do."[65] He then entitles a section of *How to Retire Happy, Wild, and Free* "Create your new Identity because your old one won't do."[66] This is especially so given that, as a *US News & World Report* article states, "tales of old victories won while working quickly lose their impact over time . . . in retirement you need a new story to spin."[67] And that spin should be about our attempts to pursue what is closest to our selves, our "lifetime dreams," as bankrate.com puts it.[68]

How, then, is this identity makeover to take place? The advice varies. One strand is aggressive: retirees are urged, or are simply seen as eager, to take control of the situation. Sydney Lagier, author of the blog *Retirement: A Full-Time Job*, tells retirees to become entrepreneurs in all sorts of areas of their lives. It is important to take the time during retirement to discover or rediscover an athletic ability, and try to engage in new disciplines of study that interested us in school but we never had the chance to explore. She urges retirees to be open to anything; they should submerse themselves in a new place to live and reinvent their social persona.[69] Indeed, one should become a "social butterfly" because "retirement is the beginning of discovering who it is you really want to be."[70] Bonnie Louise Kuchler tells her readers that "You're the Boss!," and that retirement is in fact a full-time job that requires our active management and attention.[71] Such reflections are often made with baby boomers in mind, which are often conceived as especially active and restless. As an article on foxbusiness.com puts it, "Watch out world, the Woodstock generation is about to move into retirement communities . . . Baby boomers want more from their communities than just bingo and shuffleboard, and will shun anything associated with growing older."[72]

A second strand is perhaps gentler. Zelinski, for instance, reasons that retirees should take their time to get closer to themselves spiritually, materially, and psychologically.[73] The image here is of slow and careful self-investigation. Janice Williams's advice is typical of this approach:

> Spend time enjoying the beauty of nature. Journal your thoughts as they flow freely without judging them. The practice of meditation can calm the chatter of your mind so that you can become aware of new understanding [sic] about who you really are. Allow yourself to become very still so you can connect with your inner truth.[74]

Regardless of specific path, the direction is the same: self-discovery and ultimately the expression of a new or otherwise repressed for far too long self.

Future

Our dominant discourse is unequivocal about retirement: it is, or at least should be, a time of endless options. "Believe. Anything is possible," is the header on retirement coach Dorian Mintzer's website.[75] Zelinski defines retirement as "an opportunity to live life like never before."[76] Nelson and Bolles describe it as a time "To design the life you want to live, [for which] you'll need to do some real research and make some important decisions."[77] And Dave Bernard of *US News & World Report* simply asserts that "[r]etirement offers the promise of living the life you have always wanted to."[78] The US Department of Labor reminds retirees that the average American spends around 20 years in retirement and that therefore this is a time of great potential.[79] Examples of such a mindset abound – something that scholars have recently been examining in good detail.[80]

What sorts of options are especially envisioned? Barbara Waxman is the founder of the Odyssey Group, an executive and life coaching company. She characteristically defines herself as a coach for "adults midlife and better."[81] In her *How to Love Your Retirement: The Guide to the Best of Your Life*, she rejects the word "retirement" and coins instead the term "pro-tirement" to describe a time of growth, meaning, and renewal.[82] Education, volunteering, and exercising are but a few of the possible activities during pro-tirement:

> Today's retirees are blazing new trails. Look at colleges bursting with older adults. Look at gyms filled with mid-lifers. Look at organizations (both volunteer and for pay) that are actively recruiting for part-time support.[83]

Learning new things is especially prized. Dave Bernard, for instance, is the founder of the Osher Foundation, an organization that donates to life-long learning, operating 116 life-long learning institutes across all 50 states.[84] He believes in the power of continuing education.[85] Life-long learning provides a time where the individual is no longer required to take certain courses to fill graduation or major requirements: pure interest and curiosity push us to explore.[86] In the same spirit, the Tufts Institute for Lifelong Learning considers retirees "third agers" capable of enriching their lives with an enormous variety of learning experiences,[87] and the University of Kentucky offers retirees 65 years old or older the opportunity to take for free regularly scheduled classes if these are not fully enrolled. The University of Texas at Austin, in turn, has a "Road Scholar" program featuring a senior educational group traveling to promote the idea of life-long learning.[88] Learning keeps retirees within the mix of society: extended learning, we read on *US News & World Report*, allows retirees to keep a sharp mind and in the process remain fully engaged in the world.[89]

Geographical mobility is also highly valued. Americans are quite mobile to begin with, but movement, and freedom it implies, are especially central to the idea of retirement. The motorhome heading into the sunset is one of the most iconic images: new vistas, landscapes, climates, and adventures await. Many retirees simply think of moving to warmer or more pleasant places, prompting the AARP to list "9 Questions to Ask before You Relocate."[90] And often retirement can entail a move to one of countless communities scattered throughout the country. The marketing materials of these communities reveal much about the dominant picture of retirement. Rather than representing a sort of decline, the move to such a place is very often depicted as promising stimulation, growth, and exploration. There are popular destinations indeed: according to the 2000 census, roughly 35 million Americans age 65 or older lived in senior living arrangements.[91] Consider in this regard the branding used by Leisure Care Retirement Communities, one of the nation's largest retirement and assisted living communities. The homepage of their website states the following:

Retire like you mean it.
You've got dreams. You're going to make 'em happen.
Freedom. The open road. Vroom. Head out to the highway. Not to the laundry room. You're in the driver's seat. Completely.
You're over 62? So what!? Nothing's stopping you now. Over the hill? Not even close.
Grab it by the horns and show it who is boss. Do it your way. Have fun.[92]

Other retirement communities send a similar message. Mather LifeWays, an organization known for its Ways to Age Well℠ approach, caters to the "young-at-heart" and describes in the following way one of its residences in Evanston, Illinois:

> The Mather is a residence for those 62 and better located in a lively-yet-serene North Shore neighborhood. People living here aren't looking for a conventional retirement living experience; at The Mather, we offer Repriorment™ – not retirement. Repriorment is about rediscovering all of those pushed aside (but not forgotten!) passions and dreams. It means doing the things you want to do – not those you have to do. Curious?[93]

In line with this, a survey of 107 senior-living organizations in 13 states conducted by the Mather LifeWays Institute on Aging in collaboration with Caring Communities Shared Services and Life Services Network (LSN) of Illinois, the state affiliate of the American Association of Homes and Services of the Aging and the Assisted Living Federation of America, indicates that those organizations "will continue to expand partnerships in order to meet and exceed expectations of the next generation of older adults. Potential partnerships include other Continuing Care Retirement Communities, colleges/ universities, for-profit ventures, Naturally Occurring Retirement Communities, active adult communities, and state and local government agencies."[94] According to Wesley Homes™ Retirement Resources, retirement communities have to change the programs that they offer to match the needs of newly retired individuals: no longer are retirees satisfied with the basic perks of retirement.[95]

Yet another, increasingly popular, choice is phased retirement. Consistent with the notion that many individuals are not fully ready to let go of their past immediately, counselors and experts alike talk about an initial mix of activities that includes work in some form. The United States Government itself supports it: in 2012, Public Law 122-141 was approved, entitling federal employees to "partially" retire while working part-time.[96] As Rutherford writes in *Phased Retirement*, "depending on your needs and preferences, your phased retirement could be anything from a new part-time career to a seasonal job to a relaxed work schedule with your current employer."[97] And a recent AARP study found that 40 percent of workers who are 50 or older are interested in the phased retirement option.[98] According to Rutherford, "phased retirement is the perfect 'in between' step that allows them to take part of their career, but make more time for non-work activities."[99]

Now, because the choices abound, a strand of the discourse recommends prospective retirees to take time to ponder their options.
Typical language comes from The Transition Network (TTN), an
organization with chapters in over ten cities (from San Francisco to
New York) catering to women over 50. The purpose of the organization is the following:

> *As I look ahead to the changes in my life, what can I do with all this experience*
> *that will be challenging and fulfilling?*
>
> Does this sound familiar? It does to the thousands of TTN women who
> are looking ahead to "what's next," just like founders Charlotte Frank and
> Christine Millen did over ten years ago.
>
> After long and successful careers, Charlotte and Christine were ready
> to refocus themselves on something new, something more flexible and
> something gratifying. But what? And how would they go about discover-
> ing and following that new passion?[100]
>
> We believe this is our time to pursue the interests that may have been
> put on hold for family or career purposes. We are enriching our lives by
> seeking out new skills, engaging in a healthy lifestyle and following our
> intellectual passions . . . Here you will find resources to help you discover
> and embrace your path.[101]

The future should include some time for reflection, research, and
exchanging of ideas as well.

Actors

There is little doubt that the dominant discourse on retirement focuses
almost exclusively on the person directly undergoing the transition.
Once again, as we have seen with many of the transitions examined
in this book, we encounter a highly individualistic paradigm. Even
if retirees are thought of as belonging to an entire generation, like
baby boomers, the only protagonist is really the single retiree: it is
an individual transition above all, experienced by millions of single
individuals. What is at stake – the emotional, psychological, financial,
and other implications, consequences, possibilities, etc. – concerns
each retiree. Others witness and may celebrate the transition, but they
are not participating in it. All calculations and attention turn to the
person undergoing the transition. "Retire the way you want," the ING
Group, the world's seventeenth largest corporation, tells retirees.[102]
New-Presbyterian Hospitals simply state that "[r]etirement is a personal experience."[103] Consider the language in Nelson and Bolles'
What Color is Your Parachute?:

> It's about you, and all the parts of your life. For example, most retirement books focus on finances, and come from the narrow perspective of money . . . other books focus on health, and come from the narrow perspective of medicine and managing your physical body. Still others focus on happiness, and come from the narrow perspective of your relationship with yourself and others. *This book is unusual because it integrates all those aspects of your life.* So, instead of coming from one of those narrow perspectives, this book takes your perspective. It's you-centered . . .[104]

The authors recognize that the existing resources are about the retiree, but often focus on only one aspect of his or her life. Their approach is different only in quantitative terms: it considers all aspects of the retiree's life. "It's About You," is the caption on Dorian Mintzer's website, right above the picture of a retirement-age lady pointing the finger at the reader viewing the site.[105]

Virtually all obtainable resources for potential retirees offer the same prospective. This means not only that the transition itself is individual, but that the outcome of the transition is also understood to be an individual matter: whatever choices one ends up making, they are going to translate into the retiree finding herself in a given situation as a single individual: one becomes *a* life-long learner, not a permanent and integral member of a stable group of individuals who are bound to each other, much like one is unlikely to go and live with her sons or daughters and their families (a move that could easily turn those relatives very much into central actors of the transition). Others are peripheral to retirement, at best second-order actors.

Given this, how do these others figure in the picture? One way is that they can serve a particular function *for* the retiree. According to the AARP and its 10 *Steps to Get You Ready for Retirement: Start planning now for your ideal retirement,* an individual should "build and maintain . . . [a] network before retirement." This could entail "spending an hour a day on Twitter or LinkedIn 'conversing' with people who share your skills and interests, or starting a morning meet up group at a local coffee shop." The purpose of this, of course, is "to discuss ideas with other soon-to-be retirees."[106] Others, other retirees included, can inspire us and many, of course, will take on a second role as well: they will become our new neighbors and friends, for instance.

A third way is for others to figure as someone whom retirees will visit more often. Children and grandchildren fall into this category, as do friends and more distant relatives. "Visit" is an important word here: as we will see shortly, retirement does not mean joining anyone's family. Free from professional schedules and constraints, the retiree is in fact in the enviable position to move around the country to connect in some contained fashion with others. Finally, surrounding the retirees are those supporting figures that provide the retiree with very practical help: health professionals, caretakers of various sorts, government agencies, and the like. One has worked hard and is therefore hopefully in a position to benefit from the support of others as needed. Others figure, then, in the broader picture of retirement, but truly as secondary actors.

A New You

The dominant American discourse affirms retirement as a time of personal discovery, authenticity, and reinvention. It reflects personal volition and choice, and should usher in a long period of exciting exploration and adventure. The past is left behind, and a new sense of purpose and direction drives us forward. This is an individual transition: others support it and witness it, but it does not truly concern them.

At the start of the chapter, we learned that this depiction of retirement as a *New Beginning* is relatively novel. Indeed, according to a Harris Interactive survey commissioned by SunAmerica Financial Group, as recently as 2001 "62 percent of people approaching retirement age viewed retirement as a winding down or continuation of life . . ." but by 2011 "a majority (54 percent) [of survey respondents] viewed retirement as a whole new chapter in life filled with opportunities and new challenges."[107] While according to some, such as Michelle Barnhart, a Professor of Marketing at Oregon State University, negative stereotypes – such as being forgetful or unwilling to change – are still associated with retirees,[108] the dominant discourse paints a more positive and optimistic picture of this phase of life. Briefly put, the message is that Americans seem headed toward "Supercharged Retirement," as we read on Silver Mining's homepage.[109] All this has, it is worth noting, implications not only for how Americans are encouraged to live upon retiring but also for gerontologists and other scholars of late life: they must reckon with the (biological and cultural) fact that an essentially new phase in life is being crafted and shaped.

Throughout this book, we had the opportunity to see significant differences between the American discourse on transitions and the perspectives found in other cultures. Retirement is no exception:

the explicitly individualistic, supposedly exciting, novelty-rich image characteristic of the American discourse is often missing (or is greatly reduced) in many other cultural contexts. Let us consider briefly the case of Japan and the question of where retirees choose to live. The rapid increase in the number of retirees in the United States is similar to the current situation in Japan, which happens to have the oldest population among industrialized nations.[110] Life expectancy for the Japanese is extremely high as well: men are expected to live for 75.9 and women for 82.1 years.[111] The Japanese have similar concerns on what to do with their retirement years and the discourse is focused, like the American one, on filling the end of life with meaning.[112] Yet, part of the answer points toward maintaining the family structure. Indeed, the Japanese tend to retire with their children:[113] more specifically, 46 *percent of the elderly actually live with their children.* While this number has certainly dropped over the years,[114] it remains far greater than can be said of the United States. Retirement is accordingly about intimate reconnection with family, and thus continuity and the cyclical nature of life, rather than novelty, new homes, new selves, and new adventures.

Something similar can be said of many other countries, even if they are moving to some extent toward a more American worldview. Hence observers of India, for instance, point out that retirement there is often seen as something that strengthens family bonds,[115] and certainly the idea of moving to a vibrant and stimulating retirement community for a golden period of personal renaissance is far-fetched. "In the South [of India], there is still a strong sense of family," according to K.S. Girish, local director at Jones Lang Laselle, a global real estate service firm: "elders are still an important part of most social and religious functions, as a result of which they think twice before settling down in a senior citizens community."[116] In much of the country, it is expected that the retirees stay with their nuclear family for retirement. The resulting picture differs from the American concept of dramatic, sudden change, and reinvention.

In fact, according to an HSBC Group study of global attitudes toward retirement and the aging process involving more than 11,000 people across the world, the overall outlook in the United States toward retirement finds some parallels perhaps in Canada but differs remarkably from the perspectives that seem dominant in many other countries, including Japan and India. The study offers brief synopses of those perspectives. "Brazilians," it reports, "view later life as a time for slowing down, relaxing, and spending time with their families, relatives, and friends, and they expect significant support from their children." In the case of Hong Kong, "respondents . . . view it as a time for rest, relaxation, and the enjoyment of accumulated wealth." As to India, respondents "view later life as a time to live with and be cared for by their families." By contrast, and not surprisingly given all that we have learned in this chapter, Americans view retirement as "a time for opportunity, new careers, and spiritual fulfillment, but are less focused on family or health than are other countries." Canadians seem to share some of the spirit of adventure found in the American perspective: "Canadians," the study found, "view their later years as a time of reinvention, ambition, and close relationships with friends and family."[117] Clearly, rather different images of retirement are very much in place across the world and cultures.

Part III
Conclusion

10   Transitions in America

Transitions usher change into our lives. They accordingly function as markers of the passing of time: as we think back to our past, we recall leaving home to attend college, for instance, or getting our first job, ending a romantic relationship, moving home, or losing a close relative. Transitions open and close phases in our lives and, in so doing, give texture to our existence. We may say that a life without transitions would unfold seamlessly without significant alterations in our experiences. Monotony would rule: we would discern little difference between the present and 10 or 20 years ago, other than perhaps our age. But this is not the case. Time inevitably brings changes, and each change colors how we experience life.

How we interpret transitions is therefore of great consequence for us. Interpretation entails the definition of, and attribution of meaning to, transitions: What are they? What do they represent? What implications do they have for those directly involved and society more broadly? In a sense, each life transition is unique: getting married, for instance, has little to do with surviving a life-threatening disease. The positive and negative emotions, problems, and opportunities associated with each transition are unique. In a given cultural context, each transition is interpreted in a unique manner. Each transition "means," to use Max Weber's language,[1] something particular, something that is different from other transitions. At the same time, all transitions are alike in one important respect: in each case we face a moment of significant change in our lives. Something is no more, and something new presents itself. We sense some sort of closure but also the beginning of something different. The passing of time itself stares at us directly.

Given this, it stands to reason that in any given cultural context there exist certain shared fundamental tendencies or inclinations for making sense of not only any given transition but all transitions

– for making sense, that is, of all those moments that bring about major change in our lives and present us with the passing of time itself. Since societies are complex and include a multiplicity of economic, ethnic, racial, gender, and other groups, we can expect a corresponding multiplicity of tendencies and inclinations. The larger and more diverse the society, the greater the multiplicity is likely to be. Yet, multiplicity does not mean infinite variety, and it therefore follows that much could be gained by learning more about what those tendencies and inclinations might be. How are transitions – all transitions – approached and understood in a given cultural context? Do we observe certain basic perspectives and viewpoints, certain attitudes and answers?

This is obviously no small investigative task. Psychologists, as we discussed in chapter 1, have largely preoccupied themselves with individual transitions and the mind as it operates for the most part independently of cultural contexts. For this reason, they have not generated insights that can be particularly useful for an investigation of the basic interpretative guidelines available in any given society to make sense of transitions. Sociologists have primarily been interested in how social structures shape transitions, and how they make it more or less likely for certain segments of the population (the wealthy, for instance, or minority women) to experience any one transition. The question of culture – of the basic cognitive tools that inform and shape how members of a society make sense of transitions – has been of interest to them, but almost invariably in relation to selected, particular transitions. This means that, if we wish to identify the deeper conceptual tendencies and inclinations that exist toward all transitions in a cultural context, much work remains to be done. The resulting findings will likely be of value to psychologists and sociologists alike: they will speak to the basic cultural material that is available to individual minds to make sense of their life experiences. There are good reasons to undertake this investigation.

In the preceding chapters, I offered an initial step toward that investigation. The focus was on the *dominant American discourse* on life transitions: those ideas and concepts which are constantly articulated in the popular media, the statements of leading public figures, the stances found in the policies and programs of powerful organizations, the opinions and perspectives found in major websites and blogs, the language of counselors and coaches, the views expressed by business and major associations, the majority opinions in survey polls, and so on, and which interpret those transitions and thus help

Table 10.1: The Dominant American Discourse on Eight Transitions

	Dominant Discourse
Group I: New Beginnings	
Starting College	*The first, most explicit and public, opportunity for self-definition in one's life*
Losing a Job	*A personal tragedy that becomes a catalyst for potentially exciting and liberating individual change*
Surviving a Life-Threatening Disease	*An event that creates for survivors the freedom, and in a sense the moral duty, to craft the life they really want to live*
Divorce	*Unshackled from a bad situation, the individual gains a new freedom to willfully pursue his or her dreams*
Retirement	*The decisive end to the bounded structure and limitations of everyday working life ushering in a period of intense freedom*
Group II: Continuity with Others	
Getting Married	*The reduction of uncertainty in our lives via the permanent embrace of continuity through bondage to another soul*
The First Child	*Becoming "settled" with one's partner, with a special appreciation for completion, life's cycle, and inevitability*
Parents' Death	*The final rite of passage into true adulthood, in line with the natural order of things*

us make sense of and organize those transitions. Throughout, I recognized that the dominant discourse is certainly not readily embraced by everyone in American society. Alternative perspectives exist: at several points in the book, when especially noteworthy or relevant, I discussed those alternative perspectives. Throughout, I also noted that at times the dominant discourse comes with important variations – ones that reflect variables such as religious orientation, class, and gender. When relevant and possible, I examined those variations.

The investigation – structured around five questions related to the origins, past, self, future, and actors in each transition – generated useful findings. Table 10.1 offers a high-level summary of the content of the dominant discourse for the eight selected transitions.

As we saw, the dominant discourse on transitions can be seen as putting forth two basic perspectives: *New Beginnings* and *Continuity with Others*. The first perspective represents perhaps the primary, most typical approach to transitions. With *New Beginnings*, in a number of nuanced and rich ways, transitions are presented as opportunities for individual reinvention. Whether brought about by internal or external causes, these transitions are seen as powerful occasions for the recreation of the self. The past is left behind – that is, it is essentially relegated to irrelevance – as the individual in question is catapulted into an open-ended future awaiting definition. These are exciting, riveting moments in an individual's life (others play a role, but typically as supporting or secondary characters). In the most fundamental sense, this interpretation amounts to a conscious, creative leveraging of time: the passage of time is something positive, promising, and generative, even if the transition itself may have started off as something negative (losing a job, for instance, or the death of one's parents).

We observed throughout how such an approach is consistent with other broadly celebrated values in American culture and history. These include the myth of individuality, self-directed realization, new starts, and optimism. In the words of blogger and statistician Nate Silver, "if there is one thing that defines Americans – one thing that makes us exceptional – it is our belief in Cassius's idea that we are in control of our own fates."[2] America, we often hear, is the land of opportunity and freedom. It seems worthwhile to observe here that the Self-Help section of amazon.com for books is divided into 18 sub-sections. The topics vary a great deal, from "Motivational" to "Abuse." The smallest section is "Inner Child," with 257 books. The second largest is "Stress Management," with 6,100 books. The biggest section, however, includes more books than all the other sections combined: this is "Personal Transformation," with over 35,000 books.[3] American readers are deeply interested in, and probably very thirsty for, major change in their lives.

With *Continuity with Others*, something rather different – though in fact complementary to the above – is being promoted and celebrated. Certain transitions are depicted as having much to do with inevitability and certainty; life appears cyclical, so that we find ourselves doing the same things that our parents and ancestors did before us. Regularity, order, predictability come to the fore, and the transition in question is embraced as a celebration of precisely the opposite of reinvention and newness. Indeed, these transitions offer respite from an otherwise unsettling and perhaps exhausting view of life as demanding constant change of us. Here we have the opportunity to actually follow a pre-established path. The past is folded intimately into the future, as the self finds itself connected to others in a time of refinement and adjustment rather than rebirth. We should note here that the transitions that fall into this category seem more family-oriented or as having to do with the private spheres of our lives.

We saw that this approach, too, resonates with other elements of American culture, including a widespread interest in celebrating traditions, an appreciation for predictability, and faith in God and an orderly universe. It seems appropriate here to add that far more Americans than not favor maintaining order in the nation over ensuring freedom of speech or giving people more say,[4] and that nearly 50 percent of Americans identify religion as very important in their lives (the figure is 21 percent in Great Britain, 13 percent in France, and only 11 percent in Germany).[5] By and large, despite their love of novelty and change, Americans on the whole also appear to subscribe to many conservative values, even when compared to Europeans, as Fareed Zakaria, CNN journalist and Editor-at-large of *Time* magazine, recently noted.[6] In such a context – one where "family values," for instance, remain dear to a great percentage of the population[7] – a view of transitions as explicit demonstrations of the orderly unfolding of life probably has a certain appeal.

The combination of *New Beginnings* and *Continuity with Others* may at first seem contradictory. There is certainly a tension between the two approaches. In practice, however, the two outlooks are rather complementary. The dynamism and uncertainty associated with *New Beginnings* are balanced by the calm that characterizes transitions understood to offer *Continuity with Others*. Those looking for direction and interpretation as life unfolds and inevitably brings about change have at their disposal two perspectives that essentially play off each other: for certain transitions, they are called to act and create something new; for others, they are encouraged to embrace and adjust to the rhythms and natural progression of life. One approach requires, in a sense, more energy, activism, even aggression toward life; it is, as a result, more exhausting in spirit. The other approach, by contrast, emphasizes understanding, appreciation, and adaptation. We may say that the second approach offers a certain *relief*, especially since the first approach is probably more dominant in society. Let us also not overlook the fact that ultimately the worldview found in *New Beginnings* promotes ideas about individuality, freedom, and self-realization that are ultimately, and ironically, collectively shared, at least in part. They are ideas that define in part the essence of being American, and thus in subtle ways also have much to do with belonging, connecting to others, and continuity.[8]

Throughout, we observed that many alternative interpretations for these eight transitions exist in the dominant discourses present in other countries. Above all, perhaps, we noted a lesser tendency toward making transitions into opportunities for individual *New Beginnings*. But something else emerged as well: in other cultures there appears to be less of an interest in objectifying transitions as something to be highly conscious of in the first place. We learned in chapter 1 that Americans tend to be especially preoccupied with transitions. Very simply put – and at the risk of making too sweeping a statement – life seems to unfold without need for explicit discussion or public reflection much more in, for instance, Europe than in America. Americans seem instead to be very, almost hyper, conscious of transitions: with talking about, pointing out, actively ritualizing, interpreting, and advertising those transitions as major markers and milestones. Hence, to go back to our eight transitions, the American laid-off worker who recreates herself, the college freshman who leaves home to step into adulthood, the optimistic orphaned adult who capitalizes on his parents' death to finally affirm himself, or the divorcee who throws himself a party to signal to the world the start of a new life, simply do not appear in the dominant discourse found in other cultural contexts. Some transitions, such as getting married, of course, do appear in the dominant discourses pertaining to those contexts. But here, too, we note important differences: the presence of long-established rituals, and not explicit and wide-open public discussions aimed at making sense of or demarcating those transitions. Thus, William Bridges observes correctly in the introduction to the preface of the revised 25th anniversary edition of his classic *Transitions: Making Sense of Life's Changes* that, when comparing the United States with older, traditional societies,

> We can wish we had such rituals and celebrations, but we do not. We are going to have to learn *individually* and *consciously* for ourselves what once was done for people automatically and collectively by their society [emphasis added].[9]

All this suggests that transitions likely play an especially particular and important function in the definition of a person's identity in the American context – at least when it comes to the picture we find in the dominant discourse. Transitions are actively depicted as having specific and major consequences for individual growth and development: *for this reason, they enjoy a privileged position in American public culture.* Now, as we have noted on several occasions throughout this book, the existence of a dominant discourse does not mean a blind acceptance of its content on the part of everyone in society. At the same time, and especially in light of the fact that it *is* reaching millions of Americans (as measured, for instance, in copies sold of best-selling books or visits to websites such as those of retirement or career coaches), the dominant discourse in America can be said to inform at least in part how many Americans approach transitions. Americans likely see transitions as influential for their personal development, and at least in part as involving elements of individualism and forward-looking renewal on the one hand, and appreciation for connections and life's cycle on the other.

Importantly, this means that, to return to our disciplinary discussion in chapter 1, life transitions, especially in the American case, have at once deep social *and* psychological dimensions: a socially constructed paradigm of what transitions (not just single transitions, but all transitions) mean advances very specific views of personal identity, the significance of time, our relationship to the world, and our connections to others. The dominant discourse provides Americans with instructions for how they, as individuals, should manage and leverage transitions for their own personal evolution – for the making of their own sense of self and personal trajectories. The traditional focus on the mind as an isolated entity by psychologists, and on structural variables of the life course by sociologists (along with their concern with culture, but only in relation to specific life transitions), has so far yielded limited fruitful cross-disciplinary insights into an interpretation of transitions. Given what we have learned here, however, it seems that much could be gained by *joint psychological and sociological* examinations of life transitions, at least in the American context.

With all this in mind, two questions seem especially deserving of discussion in the remaining pages of this book. First, how readily does the dominant discourse in the United States as described throughout this book apply to other transitions not considered in the previous chapters? Let us briefly consider here the following four transitions: graduating from college, the empty-nest phase, menopause, and the death of a close relative other than a parent. Together with the eight transitions examined earlier in this book, these four transitions qualify, in the dominant discourse, as among the most important changes Americans are likely to face in their lives.

To start, we see that with all four transitions there clearly exists a great deal of discussion in the public sphere by mainstream media, professional counselors and coaches, associations, and others. The American dominant discourse has certainly not overlooked these moments in the life of countless Americans, though we should note that menopause has become the subject of attention only in the last two decades or so. A precursory analysis of those voices, in turn, reveals how well the discourse on each transition conforms to the two

Table 10.2: The Dominant American Discourse on Four Additional Transitions

	Group I: New Beginnings			Group II: Continuity with Others
	Graduating from College	Empty Nest	Menopause	Death of Close Relative (Other than Parent)
Origins	External	External	External	External
Past	Incorporated	Dismissed	Dismissed	Incorporated
Self	Reinvention	Reinvention	Reinvention	Refinement
Future	Open	Open	Open	Defined
Actors	Individual	Individual	Individual	Collective

approaches of *New Beginnings* and *Continuity with Others* – with the first approach again being the more prevalent one. Table 10.2 offers an overview of the four transitions.

Despite the fact that college graduates face great uncertainty in the labor market, for instance, the dominant discourse depicts the end of college as a moment of great potentiality for young adults to define, before society and themselves, who they are. If college itself allowed for exploration, leaving college is seen as the first moment of professionalization and, in financial and other logistical terms, full independence from parents. It is, as many sources (from counselors to college fraternities) describe it, the moment we become an adult and therefore face ourselves and the "real" world for the first time.[10] Patrice Bending, a recent graduate, in an article in the *Huffington Post*, calls it a "Crash Course into Adulthood."[11] The self, despite the obvious challenges that come with this transition, accordingly faces a fantastic opportunity for long-term definition. "Life after college" writes life coach Jenny Blake in her widely praised book (now the basis for a popular blog)[12] *Life after College: The complete guide to getting what you want*, "is about realizing that you are in the driver's seat, and that you have full responsibility for your life from here on out. My hope is that this book will help you feel empowered and inspired to create the life you really want."[13] The difficulties associated with a bad labor market, if anything, should strengthen the resolve that graduates have to capitalize on this opportunity.

The origins of the transition are of course external: the four-year course of study is now over. Curiously, for a transition that is really about *New Beginnings*, the past is partly incorporated into the future:

one's future is very much shaped by being a college graduate (indeed, that is the purpose of going to college), though the actual subject matter of one's studies (one's major) is often of limited importance. This means, in turn, that in principle at least one should now give careful thought to next steps: alternatives abound (career choices are multiple, and one can always go to graduate school), and one's choices will indeed be definitional. But there is little that is constraining about the end of college. The canvas, graduates are told, is still empty: "I say," we read on the College Aftermath blog (a thoughtful virtual space where Reanne Wright, 2006 graduate from the Rochester Institute of Technology, shares her thinking about the transition) "now is the time to 'Seize the Day' . . . find your own path."[14] The site averaged over 10,000 unique visitors per month in late 2012.[15]

With millions of young Americans leaving home to attend college, millions of parents are left, for the first time in many years, alone at home. If married, this transition could be construed as a return to the life of a couple without children. If the parent is single, it could be presented as a return to the relatively solitary life that most of us experienced as young adults at one point or another. The dominant discourse, however, turns what it admits might be seen as a melancholic or otherwise problematic moment into a valuable occasion for a new lease on life. Resources abound, from support services from specialized counselors, such as Natalie Caine's *Empty Nest Support Services* in Los Angeles (the services include newsletters and an open-access chat room),[16] to popular books such as *Chicken Soup for the Soul: Empty Nesters – 101 Stories about Surviving and Thriving When the Kids Leave Home*[17] and *Barbara & Susan's Guide to the Empty Nest: Discovering New Purpose, Passion & Your Next Great Adventure.*[18]

We have seen this positive interpretation of unpleasant transitions at work in other transitions, such as losing a job. The origins are external: the child has reached the age for college. The past – the life of a family, with all that that means – is now forever gone and, despite one's temptation to hold on, one should let go. Now the parents' time has been freed and, more importantly perhaps, their role as educators and nurturers is essentially over. The discourse insists that their reinvention is therefore not only desirable but inevitable. For this very reason, parents should seize the opportunity and give thought to what their future will look like. "I am enjoying a new freedom and joy I never imagined," writes Caine in one of her newsletters.[19] Importantly, this is typically depicted as a future of late middle age: that is, a time when the parents are still young enough to entertain a huge variety of possibilities. And this is above all an individual transition: though both parents experience it, the newly acquired freedom concerns each parent separately: the point is precisely that the time they gave to their child can now be taken back. "Now that the perfect child has left home," writes Christie Mellor in her new guide for empty-nesters, "it's time to create your perfect life."[20] This is a standard transition of *New Beginnings*.

Menopause, too, is portrayed as offering *New Beginnings*, though it could clearly be construed as something altogether different. The emphasis is on complete (and invigorating) physical and mental change – one that has traditionally been seen as a sign of decline but should no longer be viewed as such. *New York Times'* best-selling author Christiane Northrup notes in the opening page of her book dedicated to menopause that "nor did I know that by the time I began to actually skip periods and experience hot flashes, my life as I had known it for the previous quarter century would be on the threshold of total transformation." She talks about her body "being, quite literally, rewired," of an "entirely new and exciting relationship with my creativity and vocation," and of her brain as "changing."[21] Coaches, advisors, and health professionals make ample use of terms such as "power" and "wisdom." The rise of a new self – this time biological as much as psychological – is, of course, caused by circumstances not stemming from personal choice and is accompanied by a necessary dismissal of the past (the transformation requires it) and, in turn, a wide open future full of possibilities and novelty. This is without question an individual transition. The language we encounter on epigee.org, a leading education resource on women's health issues, captures well the essence of the discourse:

> Menopause actually signals a new beginning in a woman's life. Yes, the time of menstruation is over, but with each end there is a new cycle that starts. This is a time to focus on you. In the past, you were expected to cater to everyone [. . .] your partner, your children, your coworkers, and your friends. Now is the time to answer your own needs and wants. The energy that you once had to dedicate to others is now yours to use. Take this opportunity to do things that you have always wanted to do. This is the beginning of new spiritual maturity.[22]

By contrast, the last transition – the death of a close relative other than one's parent – conforms instead readily to *Continuity with Others*. We should note here that there exists only a dominant discourse for close relatives: not much is said about relatives toward whom we do not feel close. Who, then, are these close relatives? Typically they are one's own children, siblings, and grandparents. The picture is quite similar in all cases and *differs* in one important respect from the picture concerning the death of parents: in none of these cases is there an emphasis on the openness of the future. When one's child dies, for instance, the discourse does not stress the opportunities that this tragic event generates for the parents. On the contrary, counselors and others make clear that the future will now be defined by certain powerful characteristics: the parents will be incomplete for the rest of their lives, and a terrible void will be forever present.

Thus, bereaved mother Ann Finkbeiner, author of *After the Death of a Child: Living with Loss through the Years*, puts forth two conclusions about the long-term effects of losing a child after interviewing a wide range of parents who have experienced this terrifying loss. "One," she says, "is that a child's loss is disorienting . . . children's deaths make no sense, have no precedents, are part of no pattern . . . the other thing I learned is that letting go of a child is impossible."[23] For siblings and grandparents, attention similarly goes to recognizing the void created by the death of the relative, but virtually nothing is said about openness or possibilities. On the website of health insurance company Cigna, we accordingly read the following:

> The death of a brother or sister in later adulthood is frequently thought of as having virtually no effect on the siblings left behind. This is based on the assumption that the loss to the sibling's children or spouse outweighs the loss that a sibling feels . . . Although you might not have had constant contact with the sibling, you feel a deep loss for a person who was a constant presence in your life, for one who shared your family history, culture, and connections since childhood.[24]

In all cases, the past is never dismissed but incorporated – to one degree or another – into the future. And, in all instances, these are shared transitions: the protagonist is not only the survivor but also the person that passed away along with the others who might be closely affected by the turn of events.

The second question we should consider here concerns causation. Why, it seems logical to ask in closing, is there in the United States such a well-developed dominant discourse on transitions, with its dual focus on individual reinvention and an appreciation for connections with others and continuity? Why such preoccupation with transitions? A proper investigation of these matters certainly requires a great deal of research and probing. Still, we can at least point to three related reasons as possible explanations. The first two have to do with what we may call the "demand" side of the equation; the third concerns the "supply" side.

First, we should recall the young age of the United States itself: it is a relatively new culture and, as such, perhaps still lacks deeply-rooted, taken-for-granted, widely-shared interpretations of the passing of time and change in our lives. Americans may not know with a fair degree of almost instinctive cognitive certainty how to make sense of any given transition. Competing interpretations could in principle apply and perhaps a certain amount of confusion may be in place. The fact that the United States has a large and ethnically diverse population, and is thus home to a heterogeneous cultural environment, may further intensify this feeling that there is perhaps an unsettling absence of a cohesive set of cultural tools to make sense of transitions in life. With competing outlooks around, and with none having its roots in several centuries of local history, Americans may be especially interested in gaining cognitive guidance – firm, clear instructions for how to approach some of life's most challenging and possibly rewarding moments.

There is surely something liberating about this possibility: much still awaits definition, and this means that there is still considerable freedom for the individual. One can choose, in a sense, how to live one's life, and this relates to a second, still "demand"-related factor. We know that the United States is a country of significant geographical, occupational, and (until recently) class mobility. Americans also change homes, divorce, and have religious conversions more frequently than individuals in most other countries in the world. Many adolescents, moreover, leave their families and homes to attend college far more often (and for farther destinations) than their counterparts elsewhere. The social safety net, in turn, is weaker than in other countries: those who lose a job, have no health insurance, or fall on hard times for any number of reasons are left to their own devices much more than in most of the developed world. Given all this mobility and risk surrounding Americans, it seems reasonable that there be a real need for a large-scale, highly developed discourse on how to approach transitions in life and that that discourse should emphasize, on the one hand, individuality and openness and, on the other hand, the possibility of continuity and connection.

Yet, a third reason points in a rather different direction. Much of life in the United States is subject to extraordinary commodification. This applies to virtually every sphere of life – from the need to meet basic needs such as eating to more abstract things such as entertainment. Commodification is not unique to the United States, of course, but it may very well be most developed there. The size of the market and the potential for profits are enormous; given the possible need for cultural signs and guidance that may be present in the United States, it seems quite possible that a variety of actors have sought to capitalize on such need. Books, life coaches, companies, associations, and entire industries can reap enormous benefits from helping Americans make sense of the transitions they face. These forces are quite likely responsible for fueling in part, if not creating, the need for their services and products in the first place. As Harrington and Bielby recently put it when thinking about the role of the media in shaping our understanding of adulthood and aging, "media texts and technologies help unite cohorts, define generations and cross-generational differences, and give structure and meaning to our lives as they unfold."[25] The media, businesses, industry associations, not-for-profit organizations, authors, and many others have an interest in objectifying and talking about transitions.

None of these answers are intended to be conclusive. They are instead initial reflections on some of the many questions that the analysis presented in the previous chapters is hopefully bound to generate. The objective of this book was, in fact, to explore fundamental cultural elements in the American discourse on transitions: as such, it also sought to lay the groundwork for new and exciting research on American values, practices, and beliefs on some of the most fundamental challenges related to life and the passing of time.

Appendix:
Data Sources Overview

This appendix lists the most important data sources used for each chapter to identify and analyze the dominant discourse on life transitions in the United States. Each chapter also relies on additional sources not explicitly mentioned here.

Chapter	Major Data Sources
2. Starting College	• Higher Education Institute at UCLA: report (2007) on Americans' opinions about college as a financial investment.

- Higher Education Research Institute: survey (2007) on college freshmen's views of college as a chance to improve their financial wellbeing.
- National Center for Education Statistics: data (1975–2009) on the percentage of Americans that attend college after high school.
- Organization for Economic Co-operation and Development: survey (2009) of individuals aged 25–64 estimating the percentage that have completed tertiary education in the United States.
- Pew Research Center: study (2011) of the relationship between college and variables such as success, personal growth, intellectual growth, maturity, and parents' ability to afford tuition.
- United States Department of Education: survey (2008) of college undergraduates to identify how many choose to live at home while attending college.
- University and college websites: specific statements from a selected number of colleges

on the transition facing entering freshmen; college as transition to adulthood.

- Popular blog: a post on a *New York Times* blog on the merits of going to college.
- *UnCollege.com* and other higher education-focused websites: resources and opinions advocating self-directed learning instead of college.
- Speeches by leading public figures (university officials, Barack Obama): illustrative statements placing the student at the very center of the college experience, and affirming the purpose of college is personal transformation and discovery.
- Personal Counseling Program at Brooklyn College: advice on time management skills required for success in college; college as an individual experience to be managed and used.
- Best-selling books: visions of college as a time for personal reinvention and discovery; college representing a clear break from life in high school and before.
- Academic research: college as the transition to adulthood in the United States but not other countries.

3. Getting Married
- Center for Applied Research in the Apostolate at Georgetown University: data (2007) on young Catholics' views on reasons for marrying.
- Pew Research Center: data on the increase in inter-racial marriage (2012), the number of individuals married (2007), and the primary reasons for marriage (2012); marriage as choice.
- National Longitudinal Survey of Youth: survey (1979–current) on marriage as a status symbol and personal accomplishment.
- Music by *Heartland*: a popular song (2006) about a father's feelings for his daughter getting married; emphasis on continuity and generational change.

- 1996 Personal Responsibility and Work Opportunity Reconciliation Act: law changing the distribution of federal cash assistance to the poor designed to promote marriage.
- Federal Marriage Amendment of 2006: an attempt in the United States to label marriage as a union between a man and a woman.
- US Census Bureau: data (2010–11) on couples' tendency not to move after marriage.
- Covenant Life Church in Gaithersburg, Maryland: a senior pastor from a large conservative church expressing views of marriage as a binding union between a man and a woman.
- National Survey of Family Growth: survey (1954–2002) showing the high propensity of Americans to have sex before marriage; marriage as posing limits to sexual freedom.
- CBS's sitcom *How I Met Your Mother*: popular TV show on CBS depicting marriage as settling down, and setting boundaries and order.
- California Family Code: code defining marriage as a civil contract between a man and a woman where consent is necessary.
- General Social Survey: data (1972–94) on marriage as a gateway to having children.
- World Value Survey: data (2005–8) on Americans' belief in the worthiness of marriage.
- Best-selling books: depictions of marriage as a personal choice leading to a more defined, bounded, and stable future; marriage as desirable and the norm, though singlehood is increasingly accepted; marriage as requiring self-adjustments in identity and daily life.
- Academic research: scholarly analyses of societal views on marriage, trends, and class and other variables shaping propensity to marry.

4. The First Child
- National Center for Health Statistics: data (2012) on fertility rates in the United States.
- General Social Survey: data (1972–94) on the

ideal number of children couples prefer in the United States and cross-tabulation data (1975–2010) on trends over time.

- US Census Bureau: data (2000–10) on the number of same-sex, unmarried, and interracial households in the United States.
- National Association of Evangelicals: view of children as gifts from God.
- Pastor Joel Osteen of Lakewood Church: pastor of the largest congregation in the United States preaching that children are a gift from God.
- Pew Research Center: study (2010) on Americans' views on family and data (1965–2000) on the significant increase in the amount of time fathers spend with their children; parenting as requiring identity adjustments.
- Gallup: data (2007) on the ideal number of children a family should have.
- *WebMD*: reassurance for individuals and couples who do not want to have kids that, though surely parenthood brings joy, they are not alone in their preferences; normality is having children.
- 123greetings.com greeting cards: humorous depictions of new child as posing limits to parents' future.
- Pop star Jay-Z: plans and ideas about generational continuity.
- Center for Disease Control and Prevention: federal guideline asking all females capable of conceiving a baby to consider themselves "pre-pregnant."
- Montefiore Medical Center in the Bronx: medical checkup forms requesting females to indicate whether they "plan on becoming pregnant in the next year."
- MOMS Club®: viewpoints supporting women who choose to stay at home and raise their children; reproduction as personal choice.

- United States Department of Agriculture (Center for Nutrition Policy and Promotion): data (1960–2011) on the average cost of raising a child.
- Best-selling books: depictions of getting married as being ultimately about willful continuity and connection with another person, and introducing a new element of security and predictability in our lives.
- Academic research: scholarly research showing that life with a partner does not increase a person's happiness.
- Popular blogs: discussions on the theme of "mutuality" in marriage.

5. Losing a Job
- US Bureau of Labor Statistics: data (2006–12) on unemployment trends.
- University of Southern California Center for Work and Family Life: a help-book to aid families experiencing job loss.
- RiseSmart, Corporate Warriors, and other outplacement firms: advice that job loss is not the end of one's career or a sign of decline; optimistic language of reinvention.
- New York State Department of Labor: public materials on job loss as a positive event.
- National Employment Counseling Association: how to grieve when a job is lost.
- North Carolina Office of State Personnel: handout to help state workers and their families cope with job loss and let go of the past.
- One Stop Career Centers (Colorado), United States Department of Labor: language acknowledging and accepting the emotions of laid-off workers; the past should be left behind.
- Christian Networking Group: logic for accepting shock, denial, anger, anxiety, and embarrassment following job loss.
- Career counselors: leading voices urging reinvention and open possibilities following job loss.

- National Veterans' Training Institute: arguments for positive interpretation of job loss as fostering new opportunities for the self.
- Colorado Bar Association: job loss as a wakeup call for reinvention and self-discovery.
- Financial Planning Association: advice on how to get through job loss successfully.
- Larimer County Workforce Center (Colorado): arguments urging individuals to pull themselves up and find a new career.
- 2012 Democratic National Convention: Michelle Obama stating job loss is not impossible to overcome; America has tradition of overcoming.
- International Labor Organization: a study (2012) of forced labor in the United States, Canada, and Europe compared to Latin America, Africa, the Middle East, and Asia-Pacific.
- University employee career websites: help is available to avoid falling into a "blame" cycle.
- Popular blogs: posts on jobs that are disappearing quickly from the economy, and what one can do about it.
- Best-selling books: illustrative arguments on how to accept emotions and feelings regarding job loss, and move beyond the grieving process to build new identities and careers; job loss as "gift" and a "blessing."
- Newspaper and magazine articles: data and information on the loss of jobs in the economy and ways to face this challenge.
- Academic research: scholarly research on sudden job loss, unemployment trends, and creation of new jobs in the American economy.

6. Surviving a Life-Threatening Disease

- National Cancer Institute: illustrative booklet available to cancer survivors to help with the transition, financial concerns, and their new life after cancer.
- American Cancer Association: advice to the patient to avoid excuses and pursue activities that produce good and positive feelings;

cancer as a personal battle that must be faced and can be won.

- National Eating Disorders Association: estimate on the number of Americans suffering from eating disorders at some time in their lives.
- South Carolina Department of Mental Health: data (2013) on the number of Americans suffering from eating disorders.
- *American Journal of Psychiatry*: study (2009) on the number of fatalities due to eating disorders.
- National Association of Anorexia Nervosa and Associated Disorders: data (1999 and 2004) on deaths within 20 years from the onset of anorexia.
- General Social Survey: data (1972–94) on the number of people returning to normal after suffering from an eating disorder.
- Institute of Medicine: discussion of the impact of a life-threatening disease on the patient's family, friends, and caregivers.
- Idaho Department of Health and Welfare: video interviewing survivors of a life-threatening disease; leaving the past behind and moving toward a new future.
- MD Anderson Cancer Center: language and clinics on surviving cancer.
- Dana-Farber Cancer Institute: information on cancer survivorship as possible and increasingly common.
- Lance Armstrong Foundation: language about optimism and survival.
- National Comprehensive Cancer Network: programs and information on beating cancer.
- National Coalition for Cancer Survivorship: a proceeding (2006) dedicated to the delicate phase of post-treatment.
- Danish Cancer Society: evidence of discourse on survivorship in Denmark beginning as late as the mid-1990s.

- Academic research: data on survivorship and the role that others, with their support, play for patients.
- Magazine and newspaper articles: emphasis on personal hope and determination as key for survival.
- Popular blogs: encouraging survivors to take on and beat cancer; past as important but ultimately something that should not inform the future.

7. Divorce
- US Census Bureau: data (2011) on the percentage of Americans that have experienced divorce.
- National Marriage Project: report (2011) on divorce as an important transition in American life.
- US Department of Health and Human Services: data (2012) on marriages lasting more than 20 years.
- General Social Survey: data (1972–94) on divorce as an "option" available to each partner.
- Divorce laws across America: no-fault divorce laws in all 50 states.
- Tiger Woods and Elin Nordegren: celebrity divorce featuring embarrassing public admissions of guilt, apologies, and determination to leave the past behind and move on.
- AARP: survey (2004) showing divorcees using "freedom," "fulfillment," and other similar terms to describe their new status as singles.
- Divorce coaches: language on renewal, personal renaissance, and endless possibilities.
- Divorce Party Planner: service to help new divorcees celebrate their new freedom and positions in life.
- Divorce Recovery Coaching and other counseling organizations and companies: advice on how to end repressive marriages and launch into a new phase in life.
- Oprah Radio: advice on rebuilding one's self after divorce.

	• Academic research: data on divorce trends, associated costs, divorce as an "American tradition."
	• Magazine and newspaper articles: language and arguments on divorce as something liberating and worthy of celebration.
8. Parents' Death	• *O, The Oprah Magazine*: interviews with middle-aged women on losing a parent; language about positive consequences of this transition for the surviving offspring.
	• *Handbook of Bereavement Research*: evidence that little public discourse about parental loss has historically existed.
	• Mental Health America: example of how one of the nation's leading promoters of psychological wellbeing does not mention the loss of a parent.
	• Wendt Center for Loss and Healing: leading organization on loss pays little attention to parental loss.
	• Sesame Street: example of how a new discourse is emerging recognizing the death of a parent as a noteworthy life transition.
	• HospiceCare (Colorado): view of loss of parent as a normal event in one's life and natural evolution.
	• The Diane Rehm Show: show on loss of parents in childhood, power of memories, and continued attachment to parents.
	• *WebMD*: on how parental death can strengthen one's awareness and feelings for those parents.
	• American Hospice Foundation: on the life cycle, parental death, and generational change.
	• National Funeral Directors Association: language about parental death and the natural order of things.
	• Family therapists and counselors: advice on grieving but also moving on and becoming one's own full person for the first time; stepping up to fill the void.
	• Center for Loss and Life Transitions

(Colorado): description of the collective nature of this transition.

- Italian and Spanish books on parental death: examples of limited discourse in other countries.
- Academic research: scholarly research on the reorganization of self after the loss of a parent and the long-term wellbeing of children.
- Magazine and newspaper articles: views emphasizing the freedom and call for full personal expression following parental death.
- Popular blogs: language about memories and continuity, but also personal assertion and unprecedented freedom to be.

9. Retirement

- World Bank: data (2010) on life expectancy in the United States.
- US Social Security Administration Office of Retirement and Disability Policy: depiction of retirement as an individual choice.
- US Department of Labor: average number of years that Americans spend in retirement.
- US Department of State: list of recommended retirement books encouraging individuals to seize and enjoy this valuable phase in life.
- United States Census: data (2000) on the number of individuals 65 or older that live in retirement communities.
- Fidelity: a study (2011) of how prospective retirees tend to consult spouses on their retirement choices.
- HSBC Group: data (2012) on global attitudes toward retirement.
- New York-Presbyterian, the hospitals of Columbia and Cornell universities: visions of retirement as signifying the end of one phase of life and the beginning of a new one.
- United States Senate: a discussion (2012) with former United States senators on how they plan to spend their retirement.
- AARP: data (2007) on the number of Americans interested in "phased" retirement;

urging proper planning and thinking prior to retirement.

- Employee Benefit Research Institute: examples of how retirees are asked to plan for their retirement; retirement as a deliberate, calculated individual choice.
- Hallmark cards: popular illustrations of retirement as a new beginning in life.
- Leisure Care Retirement Communities: one of the nation's largest retirement and assisted living communities describing the freedom and empowering qualities of retirement.
- Retirement Living Information Center: data and materials to support thoughtful deliberations and planning for retirement.
- Mather LifeWays Institute on Aging: language on personal fulfillment, great expectations, and invigorating qualities of retirement.
- The Transition Network: resources for women over the age of 50 to plan and have a successful retirement.
- Academic research: scholarly analyses of the "reorganization of the self" during retirement.
- Popular blogs: posts emphasizing that retirees are in charge of their identity makeover; retirement as a time to reflect on and finally express one's true identity.

Notes

Chapter 1: Discourse and Transitions in Life

1 Hajer (1995). See also Harrington & Bielby (2010).

2 Giddens (1991).

3 For "Aging," see http://www.barnesandnoble.com/s?view=grid&sort=SA&FMT=physical&dref=1%2C5%2C310. For "Divorce," see: http://www.barnesandnoble.com/s?view=grid&sort=SA&FMT=physical&dref=1%2C5%2C318. For "Addiction & Recovery," see: http://www.barnesandnoble.com/s?view=grid&sort=SA&FMT=physical&dref=1%2C5%2C309. And for "Personal Transformation," see: http://www.amazon.com/s/ref=sr_nr_n_3?rh=n%3A283155%2Ck%3Apersonal+transformation%2Cn%3A%211000%2Cn%3A4736&bbn=1000&keywords=personal+transformation&ie=UTF8&qid=1327071265&rnid=1000

4 For *Divorcio*, see http://www.amazon.es/s/ref=nb_sb_noss_1?__mk_es_ES=%C3%85M%C3%85Z%C3%95%C3%91&url=search-alias%3Dstripbooks&field-keywords=divorcio&x=0&y=0. For *Jubilación*, see: http://www.amazon.es/s/ref=a9_sc_1?rh=i%3Astripbooks%2Ck%3Ajubilacion&keywords=jubilacion&ie=UTF8&qid=1327071542

5 See http://www.amazon.co.uk/Self-Help-Books/b/ref=amb_link_44135865_15?ie=UTF8&node=532458&pf_rd_m=A3P5ROKL5A1OLE&pf_rd_s=left-1&pf_rd_r=0Y2E1CSN0ST16562CEFV&pf_rd_t=101&pf_rd_p=266917767&pf_rd_i=74

6 For an entertaining discussion on books on self-help, including transitions, in America, see Hollandsworth (2003).

7 See Brennan (2008).

8 See, for instance, the offerings of Atlanta-based *Create Your Career Path* (http://www.halliecrawford.com/aboutus.html)

9 See, for instance, http://www.judysmithdivorcecoach.com/

10 See, for instance, http://www.familytransitionscoaching.com/empty nest.htm

11 Thus, for around $2,500, for instance, one can buy the Retirement

Coach Kit from the Purposeful Entrepreneur Institute in Oregon (http://www.purposefulentrepreneur.com/retirementcoachtraining.html)

12 LaRossa & Sinha (2006).

13 The General Social Survey collects data on demographic characteristics and attitudes of residents of the United States. The survey is conducted by the National Opinion Research Center at the University of Chicago. It involves face-to-face in-person interviews of a randomly-selected sample of adults (18+). All references to the survey in this book refer to cumulative data from 1972 (the first year of the survey) to 2010 (the most recent year available) unless otherwise noted. For all references, I report the relevant survey question by its variable code.

14 Fifty-seven percent of Americans believe that moving out of the parents' house is either "quite" or "very" important for becoming an adult, with another 25 percent thinking it "somewhat" important, and only 17 percent of respondents thinking of it as either "not too important" or "not at all important." Variable ownhh.

15 Variable ftwork.

16 Sixty-two percent of respondents to the survey believe that having children in one's life is either "one of the most important" or a "very important" thing to them, with another 19 percent thinking it "somewhat important." Variable impkids.

17 The World Values Survey is an ongoing project funded by the United States government and directed by a team of social scientists investigating the cultural, moral, religious, and political values of people from over 90 countries around the world. Most of the data is available on the project's Internet website (http://www.worldvaluessurvey.org/). All claims and comparisons I make in this book come from my own analysis of the data, unless otherwise stated.

18 Question V58 in the survey (2005–2008 Wave).

19 Variable worryjob in the General Social Survey.

20 One third of all Americans left their home states at least once since the age of 16. Nearly 60 percent of Americans have moved cities since the age of 16. Variable mobile16 in the General Social Survey.

21 See Giddens (1991), Cerulo (2008), and Swidler (2001).

22 See, for instance, Diewald & Mayer (2009), Dannefer & Settersten (2010), and Settersten & Trauten (2009).

23 See, for instance, Rumberger et al. (1990), Mitchell & Lovegreen (2009), Cruickshank (2009), Crosnoe & Elder (2002), and Elder (1994).

24 For representative works, see Aminzadeh et al. (2009) and Srivastava et al. (2009).

25 See, for instance, Sherman (1987).

26 There surely exist cultural analyses of particular, selected transitions. On parenthood, for instance, see LaRossa & Sinha (2006). On career

changes, see Chudzikowski et al. (2009). These analyses recognize that transitions happen in cultural contexts, but are not concerned with unveiling the broader cultural material that members of any given society have at their disposal to make sense of any given transition.

27 Geertz (1973).
28 See, for instance, Swidler (2001) and Greenfeld (2006).
29 See, for instance, Potter (2003).
30 See, for instance, Harrington & Bielby (2010) on the contribution of modern media to the discourse on adulthood and aging.
31 Question V80 in the survey (2005–8 Wave). The percentage of respondents who thought that being creative or thinking up new ideas was "somewhat like me," "like me," or "very much like me" was 74 percent in the United States, 73 percent in Great Britain, 70 percent in Germany, 67 percent in France, and 42 percent in Japan.
32 For French, see, for instance, Cassagne & Nisset-Raid (1995). For Spanish, see Pierson (1985).
33 See   http://www.npr.org/2012/08/30/160357612/transcript-mitt-romneys-acceptance-speech
34 When it comes to satisfaction (question A170 in the Four-Wave Aggregate, 1989–9/2000 survey), Americans came in thirteenth, behind countries such as Denmark and Puerto Rico. When it comes to happiness (question A008 of the same survey), Americans came in thirteenth again.
35 See, for instance, Ritzer (1996) and Beardsworth & Bryman (1999).
36 Question V88 in the survey (2005–8 Wave). The percentage of respondents who thought that being supportive of traditions was "somewhat like me," "like me," or "very much like me" was 70 percent in the United States, but only 63 percent in Great Britain, 55 percent in Germany, 51 percent in France, and 26 percent in Japan.

Chapter 2: Starting College

1 See http://nces.ed.gov/programs/coe/indicator_trc.asp
2 Turley (2006).
3 Hoover & Keller (2011).
4 See http://www.whitehouse.gov/photos-and-video/video/2012/05/04/president-obama-speaks-college-affordability#transcript
5 Taylor et al. (2011).
6 Taylor et al. (2011).
7 Turley (2006).
8 See Vedder (2010).
9 Epstein Ojalvo (2012).
10 See http://www.uncollege.org/
11 See http://uncollege.org/academicdeviance.pdf

12 For another example, see Lee (2001).
13 Higher Education Research Institute (2007).
14 Zhao (2010).
15 Taylor et al. (2011).
16 Nearly 60 percent of Americans, according to the General Social Survey, believe that formal schooling was either very important or important as a source of the skills they use in their job. Variable schooling.
17 Nearly 85 percent of Americans think that a good education is either essential or very important for getting ahead. Variable opeduc in the General Social Survey.
18 Harrison (2008).
19 See, for instance, the discussion in Villar and Albertin (2010).
20 Higher Education Research Institute (2007).
21 Taylor et al. (2011).
22 See http://www.nakedroommate.com/
23 Cohen (2011).
24 Lombardo (2005, emphasis added).
25 Gabriel (2010).
26 Lee-St. John (2008) and Messina (2007).
27 Tognoli (2003).
28 Tinto (1987, 1988).
29 Elkins et al. (2000).
30 http://news.stanford.edu/news/2004/september22/henconvo-922.html
31 http://www.grinnell.edu/offices/president/missionstatement
32 http://www.weinberg.northwestern.edu/advising/liberalarts.html
33 http://www.artsci.washington.edu/mission.asp
34 Taylor et al. (2011).
35 Brint (1998).
36 http://www.sparknotes.com/college/life/page23.html
37 http://campushealth.unc.edu/healthtopics/academic-success/developing-your-college-identity.html
38 Agliata & Renk (2008).
39 Karp & Holmstrom (1998).
40 Adams et al. (2006).
41 http://www.sparknotes.com/college/life/page23.html
42 Syed & Azmitia (2009).
43 Cox & McAdams (2012).
44 Babineau & Packard (2006).
45 http://news.stanford.edu/news/2004/september22/henconvo-922.html
46 Jackson (2005).
47 Eom et al. (2009). The sample included students from all four undergraduate years and some graduate students (around 23 percent of total respondents).

48 Newbold (2010).
49 Kowarski (2010).
50 See http://sofo.colorado.edu/SOFOsdg.php
51 See http://slc.engr.wisc.edu/organizations.html
52 See http://hae.slc.engr.wisc.edu//
53 Jacobs & Hyman (2010).
54 http://pc.brooklyn.cuny.edu/TIMEMAN.HTM
55 Hicks & Heastie (2008); LaBrie et al. (2009); Parade et al. (2010); Smith & Zhang (2008); and Zhao (2010).
56 Savage (2003).
57 Coburn & Treeger (2009).
58 Jones (2002).
59 Rosenthal & Marshall (1988).
60 Taylor et al. (2011).
61 Karp & Holmstrom (1998).
62 Karp & Holmstrom (1998).
63 Organization for Economic Co-operation and Development (2011).
64 Johnson (2011).
65 Galland & Oberti (2000).
66 Lanz & Tagliabue (2007).
67 Scherger (2009).
68 Karp et al. (2004).
69 Buhl & Lanz (2007).
70 McVeigh (2002).
71 Labi (2011); Van der Wende (2011).
72 Tocqueville (2010).

Chapter 3: Getting Married

1   Arnett (1998).
2   Arnett (1998); Coontz (1992).
3   Lee & Payne (2010).
4   Torr (2011).
5   Corliss et al. (2004).
6   Lupia et al. (2010); Torr (2011).
7   Wang (2012).
8   Kefalas (2011).
9   Cohn et al. (2011).
10 Chambers & Kravitz (2011).
11 Carr (2008); Davis (2009).
12 Lee & Payne (2010).
13 Pearcey (2005).
14 Waite & Gallagher (2001).
15 Variable marlegit.

16 Jones (2011).
17 Donaldson (2001).
18 Batshaw (2009).
19 Smith (2000).
20 Cherlin (2004).
21 Carr (2008).
22 Kefalas (2011).
23 Torr (2011).
24 Taylor et al. (2007).
25 Pew Research Center (2010).
26 Whelan (2008).
27 Ingraham (2008).
28 Miller et al. (2011).
29 Chapman (2010); Wright (2004).
30 Greenfeld (2006).
31 Wallace (2004).
32 Leahy (2004).
33 Cohn et al. (2011).
34 Schneider (2011).
35 Cherlin (2004).
36 New Oxford Review (2012).
37 The song appears, for instance, in the top ten list of father-daughter dancing songs on the popular fatherhood site http://fatherhood.about.com (see http://fatherhood.about.com/od/fathersandweddings/tp/Top-Ten-Father-Daughter-Wedding-Dance-Songs.htm)
38 Montemurro (2003).
39 Barnes (2008).
40 Barnes (2008).
41 Besel et al. (2009).
42 Oswald (2000).
43 Gregson & Ceynar (2009).
44 Waite & Gallagher (2001).
45 Scheuble & Johnson (2005).
46 Burke & Cast (1997).
47 McClain (2006).
48 Baker et al. (2009).
49 Harris (2011).
50 Springer (2012).
51 Baker et al. (2009).
52 Schwartz (1995).
53 Bartley et al. (2005); Cunningham (2008); Mason & Lu (1988).
54 Waite & Gallagher (2001).
55 Waehler (1996).
56 For instance, a recent study found that welfare-recipient women

believe quite strongly that the road to self-sufficiency requires them to be single. Being single for them is a source of pride, not shame (Scott et al., 2007).

57 Lee & Bulanda (2005).
58 Carr (2008).
59 Page (2002).
60 Cove (2010).
61 Amador & Kiersky (1999).
62 Gilliam (2005).
63 Waite & Gallagher (2001).
64 Madkour et al. (2010).
65 Ross, Godeau, & Dias et al. (2004).
66 Madkour et al. (2010).
67 Abbott et al. (2010).
68 Finer (2007).
69 Madkour et al. (2010).
70 Simring & Simring (2001).
71 Observations derived from data from the General Survey. Variables xmarsex, race, and class.
72 Galland & Oberti (2000); Lanz & Tagliabue (2007); Scherger (2009).
73 Kennedy & Bumpass (2008).
74 Olds & Schwartz (2009).
75 Klinenberg (2012).
76 See Table 7 at http://www.census.gov/hhes/migration/data/cps/cps2011.html
77 See Table 1 at http://www.census.gov/hhes/migration/data/cps/cps2011.html
78 Season 3, Episode 7.
79 Variable marlegit.
80 Question V59 in the survey (2005–8 Wave).
81 http://weddings.weddingchannel.com/wedding-planning-ideas/wedding-ceremony-ideas/articles/wedding-vows-jewish.aspx
82 http://weddings.weddingchannel.com/wedding-planning-ideas/wedding-ceremony-ideas/articles/wedding-vows-buddhist.aspx
83 Cherlin (2009).
84 See http://www.leginfo.ca.gov/cgi-bin/displaycode?section=fam&group=00001-01000&file=300-310
85 Allen & Harmon (1994).
86 Coontz (2005).
87 Candeub & Kuykendall (2011).
88 Waite & Gallagher (2001).
89 Coontz (2005).
90 Greenfeld (2005).
91 Question V58 in the World Values Survey (2005–8 Wave).

92 Mauceri & Valentini (2010).
93 Coontz (2005).
94 Diamond (2012); Kamo (1990).
95 Takagi & Silverstein (2008).
96 Ingraham (2008).

Chapter 4: The First Child

 1 Martinez et al. (2012).
 2 Spearman & Murphy (2007).
 3 Variable chldidel.
 4 O'Connell & Feliz (2011).
 5 Riley (2001).
 6 Ventura (2009).
 7 Goldberg et al. (2012).
 8 LaRossa & Sinha (2006).
 9 LaRossa & Sinha (2006).
10 Matthews & Hamilton (2009).
11 Matthews & Hamilton (2009).
12 Variable febear.
13 Moon (2010).
14 Osteen (2011).
15 Calculations based on data from the General Social Survey. Variables relpersn and hhtype1.
16 Calculations based on data from the General Social Survey. Variables relpersn and hhtype1.
17 Calculations based on data from the General Social Survey. Variables hhtype1 and year.
18 Calculations based on data from the General Social Survey. Variables hhtype1 and year.
19 Goldberg et al. (2012).
20 Singer (2011).
21 Newton et al. (1992).
22 Goldberg et al. (2012).
23 Meade & Singh (1973).
24 Goldberg et al. (2012).
25 Goldberg et al. (2012).
26 Goldberg et al. (2012).
27 Mayle (2000).
28 Coontz (1992).
29 Waite (2000).
30 Pew Research Center (2010).
31 Pew Research Center (2010).
32 Pew Research Center (2010).

33 Shukert (2008).
34 Park (2002).
35 Park (2002).
36 Park (2002).
37 Variable nokids in the General Social Survey.
38 Variable childidel in the General Social Survey.
39 See Carroll (2007).
40 Wright (2008).
41 http://www.hallmarkcards.com.au/how-to/celebrate-new-babies/baby-traditions
42 Goldberg et al. (2012).
43 Shira (2012).
44 LaRossa & Sinha (2006).
45 Leavitt (1986).
46 Orenstein (2000).
47 Orenstein (2000).
48 Orenstein (2000).
49 Park (2002).
50 Payne (2006).
51 Zappert (2001).
52 Jay & Kovaric (2007).
53 Zappert (2001).
54 See http://www.workingmother.com/
55 Mason (2007).
56 LaRowe (2009).
57 Slaughter (2012).
58 See http://www.momsclub.org/goals.html
59 Schlessinger (2009).
60 Livingston & Parker (2011).
61 Settersten & Cancel-Tirado (2010).
62 Settersten & Cancel-Tirado (2010).
63 Olmstead et al. (2009).
64 Sears & Sears (2006).
65 Settersten & Cancel-Tirado (2010).
66 Medina (2010).
67 LaRossa & Sinha (2006).
68 http://www.babycenter.com/0_top-ten-surprises-of-new-parenthood_3656981.bc
69 Stamp & Banski (1992).
70 variable wrkbaby.
71 See   http://www.123greetings.com/congratulations/new_baby/new baby6.html
72 See http://www.webmd.com/parenting/what-happened-to-my-life
73 Lino (2012).

74 See, for instance, Lino (2007).
75 Dickler (2011).
76 Paul (2008).
77 Bjerga (2012).
78 See http://www.babycenter.com/cost-of-raising-child-calculator
79 http://www.babycenter.com/baby-cost-calculator
80 Mowder (2005).
81 Settersten & Cancel-Tirado (2010).
82 Paul (2011).
83 Johnson (2006).
84 See http://www.betterdads.net/
85 Myles (2007).
86 Mowder (2005).
87 Mowder (2005).
88 Mowder (2005).
89 Mowder (2005).
90 Dye (2010).
91 Meyerhoff (2006).
92 The site was recognized by *Time Magazine* as one of "25 Web Sites
    We Can't Live Without" in 2006 and 2007, and has been one of *PC
    Magazine*'s "Top 100 Web Sites" four times.
93 http://www.earlymoments.com/Promoting-Literacy-and-a-Love-of-Read
    ing/Benefits-of-Reading-to-Babies/
94 Berman (2010).
95 Stamm (2008).
96 Medina (2010).
97 See, for instance, the language used by the Department of Health and
    Human Services (Centers for Disease Control and Prevention) on the
    need to vaccinate newborns and young children: http://www.cdc.gov/
    vaccines/vac-gen/howvpd.htm#why
98 Banham (2010).
99 Simons et al. (1993).
100 Simons et al. (1993).
101 Morrill et al. (2010).
102 McEntire (2006).
103 Murphy (n.d.).
104 Mauceri & Valentini (2010).
105 For evidence on the United Kingdom, see Langdridge et al.
    (2005).
106 Warburg (2008).
107 Sidner (2012).
108 Kennedy (2012).
109 Iacovou & Tavares (2011).
110 Testa (2006).

111   United Nations (2010).
112   Davies (2012).
113   Davies (2012).

Chapter 5: Losing a Job

1   Abraham (1993); Mead (2012); Saint-Paul (1997).
2   Addison (1986); Norris (2010).
3   http://www.staffingindustry.com/Research-Publications/Daily-News/Lists-Search-Direct-Hire-Outplacement-Firms-Ranked
4   Quadagno et al. (2001).
5   http://data.bls.gov/timeseries/LNS14000000
6   Goldman (2009).
7   Zuckerman (2011).
8   Leonhardt (2009).
9   Zuckerman (2011).
10 See, for instance, Uchitelle & Leonhardt (2006) for a report on men who have left the labor market.
11 Newman (1999).
12 Gunn (2011).
13 Froehls (2011).
14 Newman (2009).
15 http://www.usc.edu/programs/cwfl/assets/pdf/Coping_with_Losing_Your_Job.pdf
16 See, for instance, http://www.dartmouth.edu/~eap/coworkers.pdf and http://hr.unlv.edu/tar/pdf/first_days.pdf
17 https://edis.ifas.ufl.edu/fy222
18 http://cap.illinois.edu/images/job_loss_coping.pdf
19 O'Donnell (2012).
20 Stelter (2009).
21 Shaiken (2009).
22 http://www.job-hunt.org/layoffs/surviving-a-layoff.shtml
23 Sellers (2010).
24 Finney (2009).
25 Finney (2009).
26 http://www.risesmart.com/Solutions/TC/Overview
27 Wolfelt & Duvall (2010).
28 Dance (2011); Russell (2011).
29 Variable impwork in the General Social Survey.
30 http://www.labor.state.ny.us/careerservices/findajob/handle.shtm
31 Browning (2010).
32 Pinsky (2012).
33 Wolfelt & Duvall (2010).
34 Dance (2011).

35 See, for instance, Jim Davis' *The Job Loss Guide* (http://familycorner. net/jobloss/index.htm). Davis is a career coach based in Tennessee and founder of familycorner.net. His work on career and family life has brought him national prominence.
36 Russell (2011).
37 http://www.osp.state.nc.us/RIF/EERif/coping.pdf
38 Blau (2008).
39 Dance (2011).
40 http://cap.illinois.edu/images/job_loss_coping.pdf
41 Ballard (2009).
42 Straits (2009).
43 http://www.washington.edu/admin/hr/roles/ee/layoff/resources/coping.html
44 http://www.labor.state.ny.us/careerservices/findajob/handle.shtm
45 Rich et al. (1999).
46 Cimino (2011).
47 Matuson (2009).
48 Matuson (2009).
49 http://www.labor.state.ny.us/careerservices/findajob/handle.shtm
50 http://www.nvti.ucdenver.edu/resources/resourceLibrary/pdfs/Coping JobLoss.pdf
51 Froehls (2011).
52 http://www.buildyourleaders.com/pdf/TenTipsJobLoss.pdf
53 Dance (2011).
54 Rhodes (2011).
55 Freeman (2011).
56 Mrosko (2010).
57 http://careerplanning.about.com/od/jobloss/a/job_loss.htm
58 http://www.fpanet.org/docs/assets/B246F92F-1D09-67A1-7A19DFC16 CF17FAC/3-1-10JobLoss.pdf
59 Parent (2011).
60 Straits (2009).
61 http://www.nanrussell.com/seminar_next.php
62 http://fcs.uga.edu/ext/pubs/hace/HACE-E-23-10.pdf
63 Hannon (2012).
64 http://www.youtube.com/watch?v=UF8uR6Z6KLc
65 Hannon (2012).
66 Chase (2010).
67 http://familycorner.net/jobloss/index.htm
68 McCarren (2009).
69 http://www.joblossrecovery.com/index.html
70 Joseph (2003).
71 http://www.myskillsmyfuture.org/
72 Browning (2010).

73 Joseph (2009).
74 http://www.labor.state.ny.us/careerservices/findajob/handle.shtm
75 Winerip (2011).
76 http://www.labor.state.ny.us/careerservices/findajob/handle.shtm
77 http://www.washington.edu/admin/hr/roles/ee/layoff/resources/cop
    ing.html
78 Salpeter (2011).
79 McCarren (2009).
80 See   http://www.npr.org/2012/09/04/160578836/transcript-michelle-
    obamas-convention-speech
81 Pinsky (2012).
82 Chudzikowski et al. (2009).
83 See, for instance, Russell (2011).
84 Abraham (1993); Smith (2009).
85 Addison (1986).
86 Economist (1997).
87 Norris (2010).
88 See   http://www.ilo.org/global/about-the-ilo/press-and-media-centre/
    news/WCMS_181961/lang--en/index.htm

Chapter 6: Surviving a Life-Threatening Disease

1   The National Cancer Institute (2010).
2   http://www.cancer.org/Research/ResearchProgramsFunding/Epidem
    iology-CancerPreventionStudies/CancerPreventionStudy-3/index
3   Pecorino (2011).
4   http://www.nationaleatingdisorders.org/get-facts-eating-disorders
5   http://www.state.sc.us/dmh/anorexia/statistics.htm
6   Crow et al. (2009).
7   Herzog & Dorer (1999); Stewart (2004).
8   Variable terminal.
9   http://www.cancer.gov/cancertopics/coping/life-after-treatment/
    page1
10 Hewitt et al. (2006); Kaiser (2008).
11 See, for instance, Kaiser (2008).
12 Coreil et al. (2012).
13 Pecorino (2011).
14 LeMouse (n.d.).
15 Idaho Department of Health and Welfare (2008).
16 http://www.mdanderson.org/patient-and-cancer-information/guide-to-
    md-anderson/patient-and-family-support/patient-and-caregiver-stories/
    katherine-hale.html
17 Cutts (2009).
18 Golden (2011).

19   O'Brien (2011).
20   http://www.nlm.nih.gov/medlineplus/magazine/issues/summer06/
     articles/summer06pg6-9.html
21   http://www.youtube.com/watch?v=zmtPPnEcMeE
22   Arinde (2008).
23   http://www.aa.org/lang/en/subpage.cfm?page=12
24   http://www.nationaleatingdisorders.org/information-resources/wom
     en-and-girls.php
25   See, for instance, Eib (2002), founder of the Cancer Prayer Support Group.
26   Gallia & Pines (2009).
27   http://www.dana-farber.org/Adult-Care/Treatment-and-Support/Treat
     ment-Centers-and-Clinical-Services/Lance-Armstrong-Foundation-
     Adult-Survivorship-Program.aspx
28   http://www.dana-farber.org/For-Adult-Cancer-Survivors/Cancer-Sur
     vivor-Stories/The-Importance-of-Vigilance.aspx
29   McMillan (2012).
30   Rechis & Boerner (2010).
31   Feuerstein & Findley (2006).
32   Cutts (2009).
33   http://www.nccn.com/index.php?option=com_content&view=article&
     id=130:dfci-nccn-survivorship-overview&catid=69
34   http://www.nccn.com/component/content/article/65/135-dfci-nccn-sur
     vivorship-family-and-friends.html
35   http://www.cancer.org/Treatment/SurvivorshipDuringandAfterTreat
     ment/BeHealthyafterTreatment/moving-on-after-treatment
36   Feuerstein & Findley (2006).
37   http://www.nccn.com/component/content/article/65/135-dfci-nccn-sur
     vivorship-family-and-friends.html
38   Frank (1993).
39   Schaefer (2009).
40   http://www.anad.org/get-information/recovery/
41   Schaefer (2009).
42   Golden (2011).
43   Moorjani (2012).
44   Coreil et al. (2012).
45   http://www.beingcancerfree.com/surviving-cancer/
46   Cutts (2009).
47   Cutts (2009).
48   Hewitt et al. (2006).
49   The National Cancer Institute (2010).
50   Silver (2006).
51   http://www.dana-farber.org/Adult-Care/Treatment-and-Support/Treat
     ment-Centers-and-Clinical-Services/Lance-Armstrong-Foundation-
     Adult-Survivorship-Program.aspx

52 http://www.dana-farber.org/Adult-Care/Treatment-and-Support/Treat
ment-Centers-and-Clinical-Services/Lance-Armstrong-Foundation-
Adult-Survivorship-Program.aspx

53 See, for instance, http://www.cancer.org/Treatment/Survivorship
DuringandAfterTreatment/UnderstandingRecurrence/LivingWith
Uncertainty/index

54 http://www.cancer.org/acs/groups/cid/documents/webcontent/0020
14-pdf.pdf

55 http://www.cancer.org/Treatment/SurvivorshipDuringandAfterTreat
ment/UnderstandingRecurrence/LivingWithUncertainty/fear-of-can
cer-recurrence-add-res

56 Feuerstein & Findley (2006).

57 Galbraith (2012).

58 Bonner (2007).

59 The National Cancer Institute (2010).

60 Moorjani (2012).

61 http://www.nlm.nih.gov/medlineplus/magazine/issues/summer06/
articles/summer06pg6-9.html

62 Halvorson-Boyd & Hunter (1995).

63 O'Brien (2011).

64 The National Cancer Institute (2010).

65 Hewitt et al. (2006).

66 The National Cancer Institute (2010).

67 Cutts (2009).

68 Snyder & Pearse (2010).

69 http://www.anad.org/get-information/recovery/

70 Golden (2011).

71 http://www.nccn.com/component/content/article/65/135-dfci-nccn-sur
vivorship-family-and-friends.html

72 http://www.mdanderson.org/patient-and-cancer-information/cancer-
information/cancer-topics/survivorship/survivorship-clinics/index.
html

73 http://www.cancer.org/Treatment/SurvivorshipDuringandAfterTreat
ment/SurvivorshipCarePlans/index

74 McCabe et al. (2003).

75 Teeley (2005).

76 The National Cancer Institute (2010).

77 http://www.nccn.com/component/content/article/65/135-dfci-nccn-sur
vivorship-family-and-friends.html

78 Coreil et al. (2012).

79 Sekse et al. (2009).

80 Drew (2007).

81 Hansen (2008).

82 Hansen (2008).

83 Duina (2011).
84 http://www.canceradvocacy.org/toolbox/
85 Clark (1999).
86 Kaiser (2008).
87 http://www.dana-farber.org/Adult-Care/Treatment-and-Support/Treat
ment-Centers-and-Clinical-Services/Lance-Armstrong-Foundation-Adult-
Survivorship-Program.aspx
88 Hansen (2008).
89 Kaiser (2008).
90 Hansen (2008).
91 Shahid & Thompson (2009).

Chapter 7: Divorce

1 Milstead (2012).
2 Kreider & Ellis (2011).
3 Jayson (2005); Time (2007).
4 Miller et al. (2011).
5 See data from the US Census Bureau as well as Kreider & Ellis (2011).
6 Jayson (2005).
7 Wilcox & Marquardt (2011).
8 Wilcox & Marquardt (2011).
9 Copen et al. (2012).
10 See, for instance, data from the US Census Bureau: http://www.
census.gov/compendia/statab/2012/tables/12s1336.pdf and from the
United Nations (Goldwert, 2010).
11 Riley (1991).
12 Whitehead (1996).
13 Whitehead (1996).
14 Riley (1991).
15 Riley (1991).
16 Riley (1991).
17 Miller et al. (2011); Trail & Karney (2012).
18 Trail & Karney (2012).
19 Wilcox & Marquardt (2011).
20 Miller et al. (2011).
21 Newman (1999).
22 Montenegro (2004).
23 Montenegro (2004).
24 Variable divbest.
25 Gadoua (2008).
26 Gadoua (2008).
27 Regarding Edwards, for instance, see Myers & Austin (2010). Regarding
Sheen, see: http://www.huffingtonpost.com/2012/07/20/charlie-sheen-

denise-rich_n_1690237.html
28 http://articles.cnn.com/2010-02-19/us/tiger.woods.transcript_1_elin-behavior-core-values?_s=PM:US
29 Manfred (2009).
30 Montenegro (2004).
31 Montenegro (2004).
32 Montenegro (2004).
33 Montenegro (2004).
34 http://www.coachingfordivorcedwomen.com/
35 Newman (2012).
36 http://divorcepartyplanner.com/
37 http://divorcepartyplanner.com/package_info.html
38 Manfred (2009).
39 Fisher & Alberti (2008).
40 Fisher & Alberti (2008).
41 Wallerstein & Blakeslee (1994).
42 Wallerstein & Blakeslee (1994).
43 Fisher & Alberti (2008).
44 Wallerstein & Blakeslee (1994).
45 Manfred (2009).
46 http://www.lifeafteryourdivorce.com/benefits-of-divorce-recovery-coaching/taming-mind-chatter
47 http://www.lifeafteryourdivorce.com/benefits-of-divorce-recovery-coaching/emotional-awareness-anger-tips
48 http://www.lifeafteryourdivorce.com/benefits-of-divorce-recovery-coaching/letting-go
49 Meyer (n.d.).
50 Zinser (2010).
51 Gadoua (2008).
52 Wallerstein & Blakeslee (1994).
53 Montenegro (2004).
54 http://www.lifeafteryourdivorce.com/divorce-recovery-coaching/loss-felt-in-divorce
55 http://www.lifeafteryourdivorce.com/benefits-of-divorce-recovery-coaching/life-after-divorce
56 http://www.lifeafteryourdivorce.com/benefits-of-divorce-recovery-coaching/letting-go
57 Wegscheider-Cruse (1993).
58 Newman (2012).
59 Manfred (2009).
60 Wallerstein & Blakeslee (1994).
61 http://www.divorcerecoverycoaching.com/
62 http://www.divorcerecoverycoaching.com/
63 http://www.drphil.com/articles/article/213

64 http://www.drphil.com/articles/article/213
65 http://www.drphil.com/articles/article/73
66 http://www.oprah.com/oprahradio/The-Fear-of-Dating-After-Divorce-Audio
67 Meyer (n.d.).
68 Most & Wexler (2008).
69 Manfred (2009).
70 Manfred (2009).
71 Montenegro (2004).
72 Wallerstein & Blakeslee (1994).
73 Wallerstein & Blakeslee (1994). ˘
74 Fisher & Alberti (2008).
75 Fisher & Alberti (2008).
76 Newman (2012).
77 http://divorcepartyplanner.com/
78 Moeller (2011).
79 Manfred (2009).
80 Garrity & Barris (1994).
81 Wallerstein et al. (2000).
82 Gadoua (2008).
83 Gadoua (2008).
84 Zinser (2010).
85 Arendell (1992).
86 Gadoua (2008).
87 Cytrynbaum (2012).
88 Essig (2011).
89 Weitzman (1985).
90 Sandfield (2006).
91 Van Schalkwyk (2005).
92 Wegscheider-Cruse (1993). According to Essig, stigma may now be starting to return among the ranks of educated, middle- and upper-middle-class Americans who divorce (Essig, 2011).
93 Xiao (2010).
94 Xiao (2010).
95 Xiao (2010).
96 Xiao (2010).

Chapter 8: Parents' Death

1 Stroebe et al. (2001).
2 Schreiber (2004).
3 http://www.nmha.org/index.cfm?objectid=C7DF9618-1372-4D20-C807F41CB3E97654
4 http://wendtcenter.org/grief/what-does-it-feel-like-to-grieve.html

5   Schreiber (2004).
6   Kearl (1989).
7   See, for instance, Brent (2011), Rosenblatt (2010), and Grinberg (2012).
8   Healy (2008); Umberson (2003).
9   Marks et al. (2007).
10 See http://www.pbs.org/parents/whenfamiliesgrieve/
11 http://thedianerehmshow.org/shows/2012-03-05/death-parent
12 Barner & Rosenblatt (2008).
13 Fitzgerland (2003).
14 Umberson (2003).
15 Levy (1999).
16 Umberson (2003).
17 See, for instance, Schlozman's (2003) article in *Educational Leadership*.
18 Silverman (2010).
19 See, for instance, Ratnarajah and Schofield (2007).
20 Myers (1997).
21 http://hospicecareonline.org/images/pdfs/education/adult_loss_of_a_parent.pdf
22 Rando (1991).
23 Gilbert (2011).
24 http://goaskalice.columbia.edu/grieving-parents-death
25 http://thedianerehmshow.org/shows/2012-03-05/death-parent/transcript
26 See, for instance, Biank & Werner-Lin (2011).
27 Chethik (2001).
28 http://www.hallmark.com/products/veterans-day/greeting-cards/nostalgic-photo-1PGC4034_DK/
29 http://www.hallmark.com/products/sympathy/greeting-cards/memories-keep-him-close-1PGC2616_DK/
30 http://www.hallmark.com/products/sympathy/greeting-cards/fathers-love-like-a-rock-1PGC2614_DK/
31 Garrett (n.d.).
32 Safer (2008).
33 Healy (2008).
34 Umberson (2003).
35 Valeo (2012).
36 Edelman (2006).
37 Chethik (2001).
38 Zaslow (2010).
39 Schuurman (2003).
40 http://www.comfortzonecamp.org/about-us
41 http://www.comfortzonecamp.org/about/lynnes-story
42 Healy (2008).
43 Safer (2008).

44 Pope (2005).
45 Healy (2008).
46 Edelman (2006).
47 Chethik (2001).
48 Schreiber (2004).
49 Schreiber (2004).
50 Fitzgerland (2003).
51 Umberson (2003).
52 Umberson (2003).
53 Umberson (2003).
54 Gilbert (2006).
55 Myers (1997).
56 Barner & Rosenblatt (2008).
57 http://nfda.org/consumer-resources-cremation/194.html
58 Millea (2010).
59 http://thedianerehmshow.org/shows/2012-03-05/death-parent/tran
    script
60 Valeo (2012).
61 Umberson (2003).
62 Gilbert (2006).
63 Fitzgerland (2003).
64 http://www.nfda.org/index.php/consumer-resources-aftercare/194
65 See, for instance, http://www.cbsnews.com/2100-500368_162-2010
    2154.html
66 Melhem et al. (2011).
67 Van Wyden (n.d.).
68 Myers (1997).
69 Edelman (2006).
70 Chethik (2001).
71 Edelman (2006).
72 Pope (2005).
73 Umberson (2003).
74 Levy (1999).
75 http://www.newingtonmemorial.com/support/grief-words/helping-
    yourself-heal-when-a-parent-dies
76 Myers (1997).
77 See, for instance, Rosenblatt and Barner (2006).
78 Gilbert (2011).
79 Pope (2005).
80 Marshall (2004).
81 Lieberman et al. (2007).
82 Lieberman et al. (2003).
83 Fitzpatrick (2011).
84 Fitzpatrick (2009).

85 See, for instance, Luecken & Roubinov (2012) and Schafer (2009).
86 Schooling et al. (2011).
87 Case & Ardington (2006).
88 Rostila & Saarela (2011).
89 Hutchinson (2011).

Chapter 9: Retirement

1 http://www.ssa.gov/policy/docs/ssb/v69n2/v69n2p55.html; Hamilton (2011).
2 Tugend (2011).
3 Freedman (2011).
4 Waxman (2010); http://data.worldbank.org/indicator/SP.DYN.LE00.IN; Shrestha (2006).
5 http://www.socialsecurity.gov/policy/docs/ssb/v71n4/v71n4p15.html
6 http://www.cornellcares.org/pdf/handouts/rct_retirement.pdf
7 Waxman (2010); Shrestha (2006).
8 Nelson & Bolles (2007).
9 Nelson & Bolles (2007).
10 Taylor (2011).
11 http://www.bls.gov/tus/charts/
12 http://www.bls.gov/tus/charts/chart4.pdf
13 http://www.merriam-webster.com/dictionary/retirement
14 http://www.cornellcares.org/pdf/handouts/rct_retirement.pdf
15 Waxman (2010).
16 Ellis (2012).
17 Greenhouse (2012).
18 http://www.socialsecurity.gov/pubs/10043.pdf
19 http://www3.prudential.com/email/retirement/IMFPWeb/0212570-00 001-00.pdf
20 Zelinski (2009).
21 Zelinski (2009).
22 http://www.socialsecurity.gov/pubs/10147.html#a0=0
23 Chan (2012).
24 http://www.aarp.org/content/dam/aarp/money/budgeting_savings/ 2011-12/Consider-your-savings-your-pension-and-your-earnings-before-you-retire-AARP.pdf
25 Wisenberg (2012).
26 Helman & Greenwald (2012).
27 http://www.retirementliving.com/about-us
28 http://www.socialsecurity.gov/pubs/10147.html#a0=0
29 http://www.cornellcares.org/pdf/handouts/rct_retirement.pdf
30 http://www.fidelity.com/inside-fidelity/individual-investing/couples-2011

31 http://www.fidelity.com/inside-fidelity/individual-investing/couples-2011
32 Brandon (2011).
33 Jasen (2012).
34 Cullinane (2012).
35 Zelinski (2009).
36 Zelinski (2009).
37 Zelinski (2009).
38 http://www.hallmark.com/products/retirement/party-plates/retire ment-travel-5PBD2141_DK/
39 http://www.hallmark.com/products/retirement/greeting-cards/retire ment-time-to-relax-1PGC3163_DK/?searchTerm=retirement
40 http://www.state.gov/m/fsi/tc/79698.htm
41 Lloyd (2009).
42 http://www.lead411.com/silicon-valley-companies.html
43 http://www.zazzle.com/retirement+tshirts
44 Lloyd (2009).
45 Lloyd (2009).
46 http://cnnpressroom.blogs.cnn.com/2012/11/25/retiring-lawmakers-reflect-on-their-careers-on-state-of-the-union/
47 The Transition Network et al. (2008).
48 Cullinane (2012).
49 The Transition Network et al. (2008).
50 The Transition Network et al. (2008).
51 Farrel (2011).
52 See, for instance, http://www.huffingtonpost.com/elizabeth-fideler/ retirement-age-women-working-over-50_b_1862156.html
53 https://www.wellsfargo.com/beyondtoday/ages-stages/60s/prepare mentally
54 Colbert (2009).
55 Julien (2012a).
56 Calvo et al. (2007).
57 Rutherford (2007).
58 See www.whatsnextinyourlife.com
59 Waldrop (2007).
60 Tugend (2011).
61 http://www.revolutionizeretirement.com/articles/identitycrisis.htm
62 Schlossberg (2003).
63 Williams (2012).
64 http://www.state.gov/m/fsi/tc/79698.htm
65 Zelinski (2009).
66 Zelinski (2009).
67 Bernard (2012b).
68 Waldrop (2007).

69   Lagier (2010).
70   Lagier (2010).
71   Kuchler (2009).
72   Dowd (2011).
73   Zelinski (2009).
74   Williams (2012).
75   http://www.revolutionizeretirement.com/
76   Zelinski (2009).
77   Nelson & Bolles (2007).
78   Bernard (2012b).
79   http://www.dol.gov/ebsa/publications/10_ways_to_prepare.html#.UK RGZ8U738Q
80   Gergen & Gergen (2005).
81   http://www.barbarawaxman.com/Main/BarbaraWaxman.html
82   Waxman (2010).
83   Waxman (2010).
84   http://www.osherfoundation.org/index.php?olli
85   Bernard (2011).
86   Bernard (2011).
87   http://ase.tufts.edu/lli/about/index.htm
88   McMackin (2010).
89   Bernard (2011).
90   Julien (2012b).
91   Day (2012).
92   http://www.leisurecare.com/#aboutUs
93   http://matherlifeways.com/residences
94   http://www.seniorliving.com/news/senior-living-communities/140-the-future-of-senior-living-communities
95   http://wesleyretirementresources.com/http:/wesleyblog.org/2011/04/07/what-do-new-retirees-want-in-a-retirement-community/
96   Zawodny (2012).
97   Rutherford (2007).
98   Rutherford (2007).
99   Rutherford (2007).
100 http://www.thetransitionnetwork.org/about-ttn/
101 http://www.thetransitionnetwork.org/discover/
102 Ingyournumber.com
103 http://www.cornellcares.org/pdf/handouts/rct_retirement.pdf
104 Nelson & Bolles (2007).
105 http://www.revolutionizeretirement.com/
106 Fuscaldo (2012).
107 Bernard (2012a).
108 Bernard (2012a).
109 www.silver-mining.com/about/index.pnp

110 Campbell & Campbell (1991).
111 Campbell & Campbell (1991).
112 Campbell & Campbell (1991).
113 http://www.fpanet.org/journal/BetweentheIssues/LastMonth/Articles/
     TheFutureofRetirementAroundtheWorld/
114 Chira (1982).
115 http://www.fpanet.org/journal/BetweentheIssues/LastMonth/Articles/
     TheFutureofRetirementAroundtheWorld/
116 Bhattacharya & Ghorpade (2012).
117 http://www.fpanet.org/journal/BetweentheIssues/LastMonth/Articles/
     TheFutureofRetirementAroundtheWorld/

Chapter 10: Transitions in America

1 Weber (1978).
2 Silver (2012).
3 See   http://www.amazon.com/s/ref=sr_nr_n_20?rh=n%3A283155%2
   Ck%3Abooks%2Cn%3A%211000%2Cn%3A4736&bbn=1000&key
   words=books&ie=UTF8&qid=1341599441&rnid=1000
4 Question V71 in the World Values Survey (2005–8 Wave).
5 Question V9 in the World Values Survey (2005–8 Wave).
6 Zakaria (2009).
7 Park (2002).
8 Hall & Lindholm (1999).
9 Bridges (2004).
10 See, for instance, *How to Survive the Real World: Life after College*, which
   offers advice from over 700 college graduates on everything from spirituality to cooking and credit cards (Syrtash, 2006). See also the language
   used on the website of the Sigma Phi Epsilon fraternity, in its space
   dedicated to the transition: http://www.sigep.org/leadershipevents/
   life-after-college/
11 Bendig (2012).
12 See http://www.lifeaftercollege.org/blog/
13 Blake (2011).
14 http://www.collegeaftermath.com/
15 Estimate provided by Reanne Wright to the author in November 2012.
16 See http://www.emptynestsupport.com/
17 Canfield et al. (2008).
18 Rainey & Yates (2008).
19 http://www.emptynestsupport.com/newsletter/may2009.pdf
20 Mellor (2012).
21 Northrup (2012).
22 http://www.epigee.org/pregnancy/aboutus.html
23 Finkbeiner (1996).

24 http://apps.cignabehavioral.com/web/basicsite/bulletinBoard/brothers
    AndSistersUnderstandingSiblingLoss.jsp
25 Harrington & Bielby (2010).

References

Abbott, D. A., White, J. M. & Felix, D. S. (2010). Not ready for sex: An endorsement for adolescent sexual abstinence. *International Journal of Sociology of the Family,* 36(2), 159–79.

Abraham, K. G. (1993). *Job Security in America: Lessons from Germany.* Washington, DC: Brookings Institution.

Adams, G. R., Berzonsky, M. D. & Keating, L. (2006). Psychosocial resources in first-year university students: The role of identity processes and social relationships. *Journal of Youth and Adolescence,* 35(1), 81–91.

Addison, J. T. (1986). Job security in the United States: Law, collective bargaining, policy, and practice. *British Journal of Industrial Relations,* 24(3), 381–418.

Agliata, A. K. & Renk, K. (2008). College students' adjustment: The role of parent–college student expectation discrepancies and communication reciprocity. *Journal of Youth & Adolescence,* 37(8), 967–82.

Allen, P. & Harmon, S. (1994). *Getting to "I Do": The Secret to Doing Relationships Right!* New York: Avon.

Amador, X. & Kiersky, J. (1999). *Being Single in a Couple's World: How to be happily single while looking for love.* New York: Free Press.

Aminzadeh, F., Dalziel, W. B., Molnar, F. J. & Garcia, L. J. (2009). Symbolic meaning of relocation to a residential care facility for persons with dementia. *Aging & Mental Health,* 13(3), 487–96.

Arendell, T. (1992). The social self as gendered: A masculinist discourse of divorce. *Symbolic Interaction,* 15(2), 151–81.

Arinde, N. (2008). Survive and thrive, part 1. *New York Amsterdam News,* August 21, 16, 39.

Arnett, J. J. (1998). Learning to stand alone: The contemporary American transition to adulthood in cultural and historical context. *Human Development,* 41(5/6), 295–315.

Babineau, M. E. & Packard, B. W. (2006). The pursuit of college in adulthood: Reclaiming past selves or constructing new? *Journal of Adult Development,* 13(3), 109–17.

Baker, E. H., Sanchez, L. A., Nock, S. L. & Wright, J. D. (2009). Covenant marriage and the sanctification of gendered marital roles. *Journal of Family Issues*, 30(2), 147–78.

Ballard, L. (2009). Overcoming job loss hurdles. Retrieved July 11, 2012, from   http://www.christiannetworkinggroup.com/Articles/article_grief.html

Banham, R. (2010). Why life? Retrieved June 13, 2012, from http://www.massmutual.com/planningtools/research-insights/insights/article display?mmcom_articleid=48163af0b44e0310VgnVCM100000c06a06aaRCRD

Barner, J. R. & Rosenblatt, P. C. (2008). Giving at a loss: Couple exchange after the death of a parent. *Mortality*, 13(4), 318–34.

Barnes, M. W. (2008). White weddings and modern marriage in a postmodern family context. Conference Paper, American Sociological Association, Boston, MA.

Bartley, S. J., Blanton, P. W. & Gilliard, J. L. (2005). Husbands and wives in dual-earner marriages: Decision-making, gender role attitudes, division of household labor, and equity. *Marriage & Family Review*, 37(4), 69–74.

Batshaw, M. (2009). *51 Things You Should Know Before Getting Engaged*. Nashville, TN: Turner Publishing Company.

Beardsworth, A. & Bryman, A. (1999). Late modernity and the dynamics of quasification: The case of the themed restaurant. *Sociological Review*, 47(2), 228–57.

Bendig, P. (2012). Life after college – my crash course into adulthood at 22. Retrieved November 16, 2012, from http://www.huffingtonpost.com/patrice-bendig/quarter-life-crisis_b_1444426.html

Berman, J. (2010). *Superbaby: 12 ways to give your child a head start in the first 3 years*. New York: Sterling.

Bernard, D. (2011). Seniors benefit from lifelong learning. Retrieved December 15, 2012, from http://money.usnews.com/money/blogs/On-Retirement/2011/12/30/seniors-benefit-from-lifelong-learning

Bernard, D. (2012a). How society misunderstands the elderly. Retrieved December 29, 2012, from http://money.usnews.com/money/blogs/On-Retirement/2012/11/26/how-society-misunderstands-the-elderly

Bernard, D. (2012b). How to reinvent yourself in retirement. Retrieved November 30, 2012, from http://finance.yahoo.com/news/reinvent-your-self-retirement-172349582.html

Besel, A., Zimmerman, T. S., Fruhauf, C. A., Pepin, J. & Banning, J. H. (2009). Here comes the bride: An ethnographic content analysis of bridal books. *Journal of Feminist Family Therapy*, 21(2), 98–124.

Bhattacharya, S. & Ghorpade, S. (2012). Here's to spending sunset years in retirement homes. Retrieved December 12, 2012, from http://www.dnaindia.com/bangalore/report_heres-to-spending-sunset-years-in-retirement-homes_1739871

Biank, N. M. & Werner-Lin, A. (2011). Growing up with grief: Revisiting the death of a parent over the life course. *Omega: Journal of Death & Dying*, 63(3), 271–90.

Bjerga, A. (2012). Child born in 2011 may cost $234,900 to raise, USDA says. Retrieved June 12, 2012, from http://www.bloomberg.com/news/2012-06-14/u-s-child-born-in-2011-may-cost-234-900-to-raise-usda-says.html

Blake, J. (2011). *Life after College: The complete guide to getting what you want*. Philadelphia, PA: Running Press.

Blau, G. (2008). Exploring antecedents of individual grieving stages during an anticipated worksite closure. *Journal of Occupational & Organizational Psychology*, 81(3), 529–50.

Bonner, C. (2007). What I want next. *Woman's Day*, 70(4), 62–3.

Brandon, E. (2011). Average retirement age grows. Retrieved November 27, 2012, from http://money.usnews.com/money/blogs/planning-to-retire/2011/08/17/average-retirement-age-grows

Brennan, D. (2008). Coaching in the US: Trends and challenges. *Coaching: An International Journal of Theory, Research & Practice*, 1(2), 186–91.

Brent, C. A. (2011). *Why Wait? The Baby Boomers' Guide to Preparing Emotionally, Financially and Legally for a Parent's Death*. San Ramon, CA: Grandpa's Dream.

Bridges, W. (2004). *Transitions: Making Sense of Life's Changes*. Cambridge, MA: Da Capo Press.

Brint, S. (1998). *Schools and Societies*. Thousand Oaks, CA: Pine Forge Press.

Browning, D. (2010). *Slow Love: How I Lost My Job, Put on My Pajamas and Found Happiness*. New York: Atlas & Co. Publishers.

Buhl, H. M. & Lanz, M. (2007). Emerging adulthood in Europe: Common traits and variability across five European countries. *Journal of Adolescent Research*, 22(5), 439–43.

Burke, P. J. & Cast, A. D. (1997). Stability and change in the gender identities of newly married couples. *Social Psychology Quarterly*, 60(4), 277–90.

Calvo, E., Haverstick, K. & Sass, S. (2007). What makes retirees happier: A gradual or "cold turkey" retirement? (Working Paper No. 2007–18). Chestnut Hill, MA: Center for Retirement Research at Boston College. Retrieved October 21, 2012, from http://www.mrrc.isr.umich.edu/news/events/docs/2007RRC/papers/H4p.pdf

Campbell, J. C. & Campbell, R. (1991). Retirement in Japan. In *Video Letter from Japan II: Choices for Men Approaching Age Sixty*, Asia Society (pp. 7–13). Retrieved October 23, 2012, from: http://www.columbia.edu/cu/weai/exeas/resources/pdf/retirement-japan-campbell.pdf

Candeub, A. & Kuykendall, M. (2011). Modernizing marriage. *University of Michigan Journal of Law Reform*, 44(4), 735–96.

Canfield, J., Hansen, M. V., McAdoo Rehme, C. & Cena Evans, P. (2008). *Chicken Soup for the Soul: Empty Nesters – 101 Stories about Surviving and Thriving When the Kids Leave Home*. Cos Cob, CT: Chicken Soup for the Soul Publishing.

Carr, D. (2008). Social and emotional well-being of single women in contemporary America. In R. M. Bell & V. Yans (eds.), *Women on their Own: Interdisciplinary Approaches* (pp. 58–81). New Brunswick, NJ: Rutgers University Press.

Carroll, J. (2007). Americans: 2.5 is "ideal" family size. Retrieved July 29, 2012, from http://www.gallup.com/poll/27973/americans-25-children-ideal-family-size.aspx

Case, A. & Ardington, C. (2006). The impact of parental death on school outcomes: Longitudinal evidence from South Africa. *Demography*, 43(3), 401–20.

Cassagne, J. & Nisset-Raid, L. (1995). 101 *French Idioms: Understanding French Language and Culture through Popular Phrases.* Chicago, IL: Passport Books.

Cerulo, K. A. (2008). Social relations, core values, and the polyphony of the American experience. *Sociological Forum*, 23(2), 351–62.

Chambers, A. L. & Kravitz, A. (2011). Understanding the disproportionately low marriage rate among African Americans: An amalgam of sociological and psychological constraints. *Family Relations*, 60(5), 648–60.

Chan, K. (2012). Retirement: A personal decision. Message posted on June 28, 2012, to http://web.extension.illinois.edu/cfiv/eb141/category_29.html

Chapman, G. D. (2010). *The 5 Love Languages: The Secret to Love that Lasts.* Chicago, IL: Northfield Publishing.

Chase, K. J. (2010). For some, job loss leads to fulfillment. Retrieved July 16, 2012, from http://www.boston.com/business/articles/2010/07/12/for_some_job_loss_leads_to_fulfillment/

Cherlin, A. J. (2004). The deinstitutionalization of American marriage. *Journal of Marriage & Family*, 66(4), 848–61.

Cherlin, A. J. (2009). The origins of the ambivalent acceptance of divorce. *Journal of Marriage & Family*, 71(2), 226–9.

Chethik, N. (2001). *Father Loss: How Sons of All Ages Come to Terms with the Deaths of Their Dads.* New York: Hyperion Publishing.

Chira, S. (1982). Retirement: Japanese-style. Retrieved October 30, 2012, from http://www.nytimes.com/1982/01/04/style/retirement-japanese-style.html

Chudzikowski, K., Demel, B., Mayrhofer, W., Briscoe, J. P., Unite, J., Milikić, B. B. & Zikic, J. (2009). Career transitions and their causes: A country-comparative perspective. *Journal of Occupational and Organizational Psychology*, 82(4), 825–49.

Cimino, E. (2011). Moving beyond job loss. Retrieved July 11, 2012, from http://www.huffingtonpost.com/estelle-cimino/moving-beyond-job-loss_b_899461.html

Clark, E. J. (1999). The cancer survival toolbox: A breakthrough in self-advocacy. *Illness, Crisis & Loss*, 7(2), 191–4.

Coburn, K. L. & Treeger, M. L. (2009). *Letting Go: A Parents' Guide to Understanding the College Years*. New York: Harper.

Cohen, H. (2011). *The Naked Roommate: And 107 Other Issues You Might Run into in College*. Naperville, IL: Sourcebooks.

Cohn, D., Passel, J. S. & Wang, W. (2011). *New Marriages Down 5% from 2009 to 2010: Barely Half of US Adults are Married – A Record Low*. Washington, DC: Pew Research Center.

Colbert, T. (2009). 3 ways to prevent retirement depression. Retrieved December 11, 2012, from http://www.livestrong.com/article/10662-prevent-retirement-depression/

Coontz, S. (1992). *The Way We Never Were: American Families and the Nostalgia Trap*. New York: Basic Books.

Coontz, S. (2005). *Marriage, a History: From Obedience to Intimacy, Or How Love Conquered Marriage*. New York: Viking.

Copen, C. E., Daniels, K., Vespa, J. & Mosher, W. D. (2012). *First Marriages in the United States: Data from the 2006–2010 National Survey of Family Growth* (National Health Statistics Report, Number 49). Hyattsville, MD: US Department of Health and Human Services – Center for Disease Control and Prevention.

Coreil, J., Corvin, J. A., Nupp, R., Dyer, K. & Noble, C. (2012). Ethnicity and cultural models of recovery from breast cancer. *Ethnicity & Health*, 17(3), 291–307.

Corliss, R., Steptoe, S., Bower, A., Van Dyk, D. & Cole, W. (2004). The marriage savers. *Time*, 163(3), 88–96.

Cove, M. (2010). *Seeking Happily Ever After: Navigating the Ups and Downs of Being Single without Losing Your Mind*. New York: Tarcher.

Cox, K. & McAdams, D. P. (2012). The transforming self: Service narratives and identity change in emerging adulthood. *Journal of Adolescent Research*, 27(1), 18–43.

Crosnoe, R. & Elder Jr., G. H. (2002). Successful adaptation in the later years: A life course approach to aging. *Social Psychology Quarterly*, 65(4), 309–28.

Crow, S. J., Peterson, C. B., Swanson, S. A., Raymond, N. C., Specker, S., Eckert, E. I. D. & Mitchell, J. E. (2009). Increased mortality in bulimia nervosa and other eating disorders. *American Journal of Psychiatry*, 166(12), 1342–6.

Cruickshank, M. (2009). *Learning to Be Old*. Lanham, MD: Rowman & Littlefield.

Cullinane, J. (2012). *The Single Woman's Guide to Retirement*. Somerset, NJ: Wiley.

Cunningham, M. (2008). Changing attitudes toward the male breadwinner, female homemaker family model: Influences of women's employment and education over the lifecourse. *Social Forces*, 87(1), 299–323.

Cutts, S. (2009). *Beating Ana: How to Outsmart Your Eating Disorder and Take Your Life Back*. Deerfield Beach, FL: Health Communications, Inc.

Cytrynbaum, P. (2012). After the divorce: Who takes custody of your friends? Retrieved September 26, 2012, from http://www.psychologytoday.com/blog/because-im-the-mom/201203/after-the-divorce-who-takes-custody-your-friends

Dance, A. (2011). The unemployment crisis. *Monitor on Psychology*, 42(3), 28.

Dannefer, D. & Settersten, R. A. (2010). The study of the life course: Implications for social gerontology. In D. Dannefer & C. Phillipson (eds.), *Handbook of Social Gerontology* (pp. 3–19). Thousand Oaks, CA: Sage.

Davies, C. (2012). Mideast women beat men in education, lose out at work. Retrieved June 16, 2012, from http://www.cnn.com/2012/06/01/world/meast/middle-east-women-education

Davis, L. S. (2009). Everything but the ring. *Time*, 173(20), 57–8.

Day, T. (2012). About retirement care communities. Retrieved December 2, 2012, from http://www.longtermcarelink.net/eldercare/retirement_care_communities.htm

Diamond, J. (2012). Three reasons Japan's economic pain is getting worse. Message posted on April 25, 2012, to http://www.bloomberg.com/news/2012-04-25/three-reasons-japan-s-economic-pain-is-getting-worse.html

Dickler, J. (2011). The rising cost of raising a child. Retrieved June 11, 2012, from http://money.cnn.com/2011/09/21/pf/cost_raising_child/index.htm

Diewald, M. & Mayer, K. U. (2009). The sociology of the life course and life span psychology: Integrated paradigm or complementing pathways? *Advances in Life Course Research*, 14(1–2), 5–14.

Donaldson, C. (2001). *Don't You Dare Get Married Until You Read This!* New York: Three Rivers Press.

Dowd, C. (2011). How baby boomers will change retirement living. Retrieved December 11, 2012, from http://www.foxbusiness.com/personal-finance/2011/06/16/how-baby-boomers-will-change-retirement-living/

Drew, S. (2007). "Having cancer changed my life, and changed my life forever": Survival, illness legacy and service provision following cancer in childhood. *Chronic Illness*, 3(4), 278–95.

Duina, F. (2011). *Winning: Reflections on an American Obsession*. Princeton, NJ: Princeton University Press.

Dye, M. (2010). The advantages of being helpless: Human brains are slow to develop – a secret, perhaps, of our success. Retrieved June 15, 2012, from http://www.scientificamerican.com/article.cfm?id=advantages-of-helpless

Economist (1997). Europe hits a brick wall. *Economist*, 343(8011), 21–3.

Edelman, H. (2006). *Motherless Daughters: The Legacy of Loss*. Cambridge, MA: Da Capo Press.

Eib, L. (2002). *When God and Cancer Meet*. Carol Stream, IL: Tyndale House Publishers.

Elder Jr., G. H. (1994). Time, human agency, and social change: Perspectives on the life course. *Social Psychology Quarterly,* 57(1), 4–15.

Elkins, S. A., Braxton, J. M. & James, G. W. (2000). Tinto's separation stage and its influence on first-semester college student persistence. *Research in Higher Education,* 41(2), 251–68.

Ellis, B. (2012). More Americans delaying retirement until their 80s. Retrieved November 9, 2012, from http://money.cnn.com/2012/10/23/retirement/delaying-retirement/index.html?iid=EL

Eom, J. K., Stone, J. R. & Ghosh, S. K. (2009). Daily activity patterns of university students. *Journal of Urban Planning & Development,* 135(4), 141–9.

Epstein Ojalvo, H. (2012). Why go to college at all? Message posted on February 2, 2012, to http://thechoice.blogs.nytimes.com/2012/02/02/why-go-to-college-at-all/?hp

Essig, L. (2011). Divorce makes you a bad person . . . again. Retrieved September 26, 2012, from http://www.psychologytoday.com/blog/love-inc/201106/divorce-makes-you-bad-person-again

Farrel, C. (2011). Professional women and a secure retirement. Retrieved November 27, 2012, from http://www.businessweek.com/finance/profes sional-women-and-a-secure-retirement-12302011.html

Feuerstein, M. & Findley, P. (2006). *The Cancer Survivor's Guide: The Essential Handbook to Life after Cancer.* New York: Marlowe & Company.

Finer, L. B. (2007). Trends in premarital sex in the United States, 1954–2003. *Public Health Reports,* 122(1), 73–8.

Finkbeiner, A. K. (1996). *After the Death of a Child: Living with Loss through the Years.* New York: Free Press.

Finney, M. I. (2009). *Rebound: A Proven Plan for Starting Over after Job Loss.* Upper Saddle River, NJ: Pearson Education.

Fisher, B. & Alberti, R. (2008). *Rebuilding: When Your Relationship Ends.* Atascadero, CA: Impact.

Fitzgerland, H. (2003). Anticipating a parent's death: Working through grief. Retrieved October 5, 2012, from https://www.americanhospice.org/index. php?option=com_content&task=view&id=21&Itemid=8

Fitzpatrick, D. (2009). *When Your Parent Dies.* Meinrad, IN: One Caring Place.

Fitzpatrick, D. (2011). *Ante la pérdida de nuestros padres.* Madrid: San Pablo Comunicación.

Frank, A. W. (1993). The rhetoric of self-change: Illness experience as narrative. *Sociological Quarterly,* 34(1), 39–52.

Freedman, M. (2011). *The Big Shift: Navigating the New Stage beyond Midlife.* New York: PublicAffairs.

Freeman, S. (2011). Should you consider "reinventing" yourself today for tomorrow's jobs? Message posted on December 23, 2011, to http://jobs. aol.com/articles/2011/12/23/should-you-consider-reinventing-yourself-today-for-tomorrow-s/

Froehls, M. (2011). *The Gift of Job Loss: A Practical Guide to Realizing the Most Rewarding Time of Your Life*. Austin, TX: Peitho Publishing.

Fuscaldo, D. (2012). 10 steps to get you ready for retirement. Retrieved December 19, 2012, from http://www.aarp.org/work/social-security/info-05-2011/10-steps-to-retire-every-day.html

Gabriel, T. (2010). Students, welcome to college: Parents, go home. Retrieved June 5, 2012, from http://www.nytimes.com/2010/08/23/education/23college.html?_r=0

Gadoua, S. P. (2008). *Contemplating Divorce: A Step-by-Step Guide to Deciding Whether to Stay or Go*. Oakland, CA: New Harbinger.

Galbraith, M. E. (2012). What men say about surviving prostate cancer: Complexities represented in a decade of comments. *Clinical Journal of Oncology Nursing*, 16(1), 65–72.

Galland, O. & Oberti, M. (2000). Higher education students in contemporary France. *Journal of Education Policy*, 15(1), 105–16.

Gallia, K. S. & Pines, E. W. (2009). Narrative identity and spirituality of African American churchwomen surviving breast cancer survivors. *Journal of Cultural Diversity*, 16(2), 50–5.

Garrett, W. (n.d.). How to remember a dad after death. Retrieved October 18, 2012, from http://www.ehow.com/how_8190526_remember-dad-after-death.html

Garrity, C. B. & Barris, M. A. (1994). *Caught in the Middle: Protecting the Children of High-Conflict Divorce*. San Francisco, CA: Jossey-Bass.

Geertz, C. (1973). *The Interpretation of Cultures*. New York: Basic Books.

Gergen, M. & Gergen, K. (2005). Positive aging: Reconstructing the life course. In J. Worell & C. D. Goodheart (eds.), *Handbook of Girls' and Women's Psychological Health* (pp. 416–26). New York: Oxford University Press.

Giddens, A. (1991). *Modernity and Self-Identity: Self and Society in the Late Modern Age*. Stanford, CA: Stanford University Press.

Gilbert, A. (2006). *Always Too Soon: Voices of Support for Those Who Have Lost Both Parents*. Emeryville, CA: Seal Press.

Gilbert, A. (2011). *Parentless Parents: How the Loss of Our Mothers and Fathers Impacts the Way We Raise Our Children*. New York: Hyperion.

Gilliam, C. (2005). *Revelations of a Single Woman: Loving the Life I Didn't Expect*. Carol Stream, IL: Tyndale Momentum.

Goldberg, A. E., Downing, J. B. & Moyer, A. M. (2012). Why parenthood, and why now? Gay men's motivations for pursuing parenthood. *Family Relations*, 61(1), 157–74.

Golden, J. (2011). *50 Strategies to Sustain Recovery from Bulimia*. Vienna, VA: Living As You.

Goldman, D. (2009). Worst year for jobs since '45. Retrieved July 6, 2012, from http://money.cnn.com/2009/01/09/news/economy/jobs_december/

Goldwert, L. (2010). Russia has the highest divorce rate in the world; U.S.

has sixth highest rate of marital splits. *New York Daily News*, December 21.

Greenfeld, L. (2005). When the sky is the limit: Busyness in contemporary American society. *Social Research*, 72(2), 315–38.

Greenfeld, L. (2006). *Nationalism and the Mind: Essays on Modern Culture.* Oxford: Oneworld.

Greenhouse, S. (2012). Working late, by choice or not. Retrieved December 20, 2012, from http://www.nytimes.com/2012/05/10/business/retire mentspecial/for-many-reasons-older-americans-remain-at-work.html?page wanted=all

Gregson, J. & Ceynar, M. L. (2009). Finding "Me" again: Women's post-divorce identity shifts. *Journal of Divorce & Remarriage*, 50(8), 564–82.

Grinberg, E. (2012). Caregiving for loved ones the "new normal" for boomers. Retrieved October 5, 2012, from http://www.cnn.com/2012/04/09/living/baby-boomer-caregivers/index.html

Gunn, A. M. (2011). The discursive construction of care when there is no care to be found: Organizational life (re)framed by those on the socio-economic margins facing job loss. *Culture & Organization*, 17(1), 65–85.

Hajer, M. A. (1995). *The Politics of Environmental Discourse: Ecological Modernization and the Policy Process.* New York: Oxford University Press.

Hall, J. A. & Lindholm, C. (1999). *Is America Breaking Apart?* Princeton, NJ: Princeton University Press.

Halvorson-Boyd, G. & Hunter, L. K. (1995). *Living in Limbo: Making Sense of Life after Cancer.* San Francisco, CA: Jossey-Bass.

Hamilton, G. (2011). A people's history of retirement in America. Retrieved December 1, 2012, from http://www.coastaljournal.com/website/index. php?option=com_content&view=article&id=2234:a-peoples-history-of-retirement-in-america&catid=73:analysis&Itemid=100080

Hannon, K. (2012). Ten things to do when you lose your job. Retrieved July 25, 2012, from http://www.forbes.com/sites/kerryhannon/2012/05/18/ten-things-to-do-when-you-lose-your-job/

Hansen, H. P. (2008). Cancer rehabilitation in Denmark: The growth of a new narrative. *Medical Anthropology Quarterly*, 22(4), 360–80.

Harrington, C. L. & Bielby, D. D. (2010). A life course perspective on fandom. *International Journal of Cultural Studies*, 13(5), 429–50.

Harris, J. (2011). A word to husbands (and a few more for wives): 1 Peter 3:1–7. *Journal for Biblical Manhood & Womanhood*, 16(1), 34–9.

Harrison, H. H. (2008). 1001 *Things Every College Student Needs To Know (Like Buying Your Books Before Exams Start).* Nashville, TN: Thomas.

Healy, M. (2008). Adult orphans: When parents die. *Los Angeles Times*, May 5.

Helman, R. & Greenwald, M. (2012). *The 2012 Retirement Confidence Survey: Job Insecurity, Debt Weigh on Retirement Confidence, Savings* (No. 369). Washington, DC: Employee Benefit Research Institute.

Herzog, D. B. & Dorer, D. J. (1999). Recovery and relapse in anorexia and bulimia nervosa: A 7.5-year follow-up study. *Journal of the American Academy of Child & Adolescent Psychiatry*, 38(7), 829–37.

Hewitt, M. E., Ganz, P., Institute of Medicine & National Research Council of the National Academies (eds.) (2006). *From Cancer Patient to Cancer Survivor – Lost in Transition: An American Society of Clinical Oncology and Institute of Medicine Symposium*. Washington, DC: National Academies Press.

Hicks, T. & Heastie, S. (2008). High school to college transition: A profile of the stressors, physical and psychological health issues that affect the first-year on-campus college student. *Journal of Cultural Diversity*, 15(3), 143–7.

Higher Education Research Institute (2007). *First in My Family: A Profile of First-Generation College Students at Four-Year Institutions Since* 1971. University of California, Los Angeles. Retrieved February 2, 2012, from http://www.heri.ucla.edu/pdfs/pubs/briefs/firstgenresearchbrief.pdf

Hollandsworth, S. (2003). Love thy self-help. *Texas Monthly*, 31(9), 120–208.

Hoover, E. & Keller, J. (2011). More students migrate away from home. *Chronicle of Higher Education*, 58(11), A1–A6.

Hutchinson, E. (2011). The psychological well-being of orphans in Malawi: "Forgetting" as a means of recovering from parental death. *Vulnerable Children & Youth Studies*, 6(1), 18–27.

Iacovou, M. & Tavares, L. P. (2011). Yearning, learning, and conceding: Reasons men and women change their childbearing intentions. *Population & Development Review*, 37(1), 89–123.

Idaho Department of Health and Welfare (Producer, Director) (2008). *Surviving colon cancer*. [Video/DVD].

Ingraham, C. (2008). *White Weddings: Romancing Heterosexuality in Popular Culture*. New York: Routledge.

Jackson, K. (2005). Katherine's note. In A. Lombardo & K. Jackson (eds.), *Navigating Your Freshman Year* (pp. xv–xvi). New York: Prentice Hall.

Jacobs, L. F. & Hyman, J. S. (2010). *The Secrets of College Success*. San Francisco, CA: Jossey-Bass.

Jasen, G. (2012). Your first job? Think about retirement. Retrieved December 17, 2012, from http://online.wsj.com/article/SB10001424127887324894104578109171414513996.html

Jay, J. & Kovaric, A. (2007). *Baby on Board: Becoming a Mother without Losing Yourself*. New York: AMACOM.

Jayson, S. (2005). Divorce declining, but so is marriage. Retrieved September 7, 2012, from http://www.usatoday.com/news/nation/2005-07-18-cohabit-divorce_x.htm

Johnson, B. (2011). Economy pushes more college students to live at home. *The Daily Iowan*, January 21. Retrieved from http://www.dailyiowan.com/2011/01/21/Metro/20790.html

Johnson, R. I. (2006). *Better Dads, Stronger Sons: How Fathers Can Guide Boys to Become Men of Character*. Grand Rapids, MI: Fleming H. Revell.

Jones, C. (2002). *She's Leaving Home: Letting Go as My Daughter Goes to College*. Kansas City, MO: Andrews McMeel.

Jones, C. (2011). Hitched: A man's guide to getting and being married. *Esquire*, 155(5), 146–56.

Joseph, L. (2003). *The Job Loss Recovery Guide: A Proven Program for Getting Back to Work – Fast!*. Oakland, CA: New Harbinger Publications.

Joseph, L. (2009). Coping with job loss. Retrieved July 16, 2012, from http://www.washingtonpost.com/wp-dyn/content/discussion/2009/03/19/DI2009031902037.html

Julien, S. (2012a). 5 tips for easing into retirement. Retrieved December 2, 2012, from http://www.aarp.org/work/retirement-planning/info-04-2012/easing-into-retirement.html

Julien, S. (2012b). 9 questions to ask before you relocate. Retrieved October 30, 2012, from http://www.aarp.org/work/retirement-planning/info-08-2012/questions-to-ask-before-moving-retirement.html

Kaiser, K. (2008). The meaning of the survivor identity for women with breast cancer. *Social Science & Medicine*, 67(1), 79–87.

Kamo, Y. (1990). Husbands and wives living in nuclear and stem family households in Japan. *Sociological Perspectives*, 33(3), 397–417.

Karp, D. A. & Holmstrom, L. L. (1998). Leaving home for college: Expectations for selective reconstruction of self. *Symbolic Interaction*, 21(3), 253–76.

Karp, D. A., Holmstrom, L. L. & Gray, P. S. (2004). Of roots and wings: Letting go of the college-bound child. *Symbolic Interaction*, 27(3), 357–82.

Kearl, M. C. (1989). *Endings: A Sociology of Death and Dying*. New York: Oxford University Press.

Kefalas, M. J. (2011). "Marriage is more than being together": The meaning of marriage for young adults. *Journal of Family Issues*, 32(7), 845–75.

Kennedy, K. (2012). Dissent, China's one child policy and Chen Guangcheng. Retrieved June 9, 2012, from http://www.huffingtonpost.com/kerry-kennedy/chinas-one-child-policy_b_1483683.html

Kennedy, S. & Bumpass, L. (2008). Cohabitation and children's living arrangements: New estimates from the United States. *Demographic Research*, 19, 1663–92.

Klinenberg, E. (2012). *Going Solo: The Extraordinary Rise and Surprising Appeal of Living Alone*. New York: Penguin Press.

Kowarski, I. (2010). Newly customized majors suit students with passions all their own. *Chronicle of Higher Education*, 57(3), A18–A19.

Kreider, R. M. & Ellis, R. (2011). *Number, Timing, and Duration of Marriages and Divorces*: 2009 (Current Population Reports P70-125). Washington, DC: US Census Bureau.

Kuchler, B. (2009). *Retirement is a Full-Time Job and You're the Boss*. Minocqua, WI: Willow Creek Press.

Labi, A. (2011). A new notion in Europe: The liberal-arts college. *Chronicle of Higher Education*, 57(36), A24–A26.

LaBrie, J., Lamb, T. & Pedersen, E. (2009). Changes in drinking patterns across the transition to college among first-year college males. *Journal of Child & Adolescent Substance Abuse*, 18(1), 1–15.

Lagier, S. (2010). How to reinvent yourself in retirement. Retrieved December 15, 2012, from http://money.usnews.com/money/blogs/On-Retirement/2010/08/11/how-to-reinvent-yourself-in-retirement

Langdridge, D., Sheeran, P. & Connolly, K. (2005). Understanding the reasons for parenthood. *Journal of Reproductive & Infant Psychology*, 23(2), 121–33.

Lanz, M. & Tagliabue, S. (2007). Do I really need someone in order to become an adult? Romantic relationships during emerging adulthood in Italy. *Journal of Adolescent Research*, 22(5), 531–49.

LaRossa, R. & Sinha, C. B. (2006). Constructing the transition to parenthood. *Sociological Inquiry*, 76(4), 433–57.

LaRowe, M. (2009). *Working Mom's 411: How to Manage Kids, Career and Home*. Ventura, CA: Regal.

Leahy, M. (2004). *1001 Questions to Ask Before You Get Married*. New York: McGraw-Hill.

Leavitt, J. W. (1986). *Brought to Bed: Child-Bearing in America 1750–1950*. New York: Oxford University Press.

Lee, G. R. & Bulanda, J. R. (2005). Change and consistency in the relation of marital status to personal happiness. *Marriage & Family Review*, 38(1), 69–84.

Lee, G. R. & Payne, K. K. (2010). Changing marriage patterns since 1970: What's going on, and why? *Journal of Comparative Family Studies*, 41(4), 537–55.

Lee, L. (2001). *Success without College: Why Your Child May Not Have to Go to College Right Now – And May Not Have to Go At All*. New York: Broadway Books.

Lee-St. John, J. (2008). A fresh new start. *Time*, 172(17), 53–4.

LeMouse, M. (n.d.). Breast cancer: The best way to survive. Retrieved July 14, 2012, from http://www.healthguidance.org/entry/12971/1/Breast-Cancer--The-Best-Way-to-Survive.html

Leonhardt, D. (2009). A decade with no income gains. Retrieved July 6, 2012, from http://economix.blogs.nytimes.com/2009/09/10/a-decade-with-no-income-gain/

Levy, A. (1999). *The Orphaned Adult: Understanding and Coping with Grief and Change after the Death of Our Parents*. New York: Perseus Publishing.

Lieberman, A. F., Compton, N. C., Van Horn, P. & Ippen, C. G. (2003). *Losing a Parent to Death in the Early Years: Guidelines for the Treatment of Traumatic Bereavement in Infancy and Early Childhood*. Washington, DC: Zero to Three Press.

Lieberman, A. F., Compton, N. C., Van Horn, P. & Ippen, C. G. (2007). *Il lutto infantile*. Bologna: Il Mulino.

Lino, M. (2007). *Expenditures on Children by Families, 2006* (No. 1528-2006). Washington, DC: US Department of Agriculture, Center for Nutrition Policy and Promotion.

Lino, M. (2012). *Expenditures on Children by Families, 2011* (No. 1528-2011). Washington, DC: US Department of Agriculture, Center for Nutrition Policy and Promotion.

Livingston, G. & Parker, K. (2011). *A Tale of Two Fathers: More are Active, But More are Absent*. Washington, DC: Pew Research Center.

Lloyd, M. (2009). *Supercharged Retirement: Ditch the Rocking Chair, Trash the Remote, and Do What You Love*. University Place, WA: Hankfritz Press.

Lombardo, A. (2005). Allison's note. In A. Lombardo & K. Jackson (eds.), *Navigating Your Freshman Year* (pp. xiii–xiv). New York: Prentice Hall.

Luecken, L. J. & Roubinov, D. S. (2012). Pathways to lifespan health following childhood parental death. *Social & Personality Psychology Compass*, 6(3), 243–57.

Lupia, A., Krupnikov, Y., Levine, A. S., Piston, S. & Von Hagen-Jamar, A. (2010). Why state constitutions differ in their treatment of same-sex marriage. *Journal of Politics*, 72(4), 1222–35.

Madkour, A. S., Farhat, T., Halpern, C. T., Godeau, E. & Nic Gabhainn, S. (2010). Early adolescent sexual initiation and physical/psychological symptoms: A comparative analysis of five nations. *Journal of Youth & Adolescence*, 39(10), 1211–25.

Manfred, E. (2009). *He's History, You're Not: Surviving Divorce After 40*. Guilford, CT: GPP Lige.

Marks, N. F., Jun, H. & Song, J. (2007). Death of parents and adult psychological and physical well-being: A prospective US national study. *Journal of Family Issues*, 28(12), 1611–38.

Marshall, H. (2004). Midlife loss of parents: The transition from adult child to orphan. *Ageing International*, 29(4), 351–67.

Martinez, G., Daniels, K. & Chandra, A. (2012). *Fertility of Men and Women Aged 15–44 Years in the United States: National Survey of Family Growth* (No. 51). Hyattsville, MD: National Center for Health Statistics.

Mason, K. O. & Yu-Hsia Lu. (1988). Attitudes toward women's familial roles: Changes in the United States, 1977–1985. *Gender & Society*, 2(1), 39–57.

Mason, M. A. (2007). *Mothers on the Fast Track: How a New Generation Can Balance Family and Careers*. New York: Oxford University Press.

Matthews, T. J. & Hamilton, B. E. (2009). Delayed childbearing: More women are having their first child later in life (NCHS Data Brief 21). Retrieved May 1, 2013, from http://www.cdc.gov/nchs/data/databriefs/db21.htm

Matuson, R. C. (2009). Bouncing back after being laid off. Retrieved July 11,

2012, from http://career-advice.monster.com/in-the-office/leaving-a-job/bouncing-back-after-being-laid-off/article.aspx

Mauceri, S. & Valentini, A. (2010). The European delay in transition to parenthood: The Italian case. *International Review of Sociology*, 20(1), 111–42.

Mayle, P. (2000). *Where Did I Come From? A Guide for Children and Parents.* New York: Kensington.

McCabe, R. E., McFarlane, T. L. & Olmsted, M. P. (2003). *The Overcoming Bulimia Workbook: Your Comprehensive Step-by-Step Guide to Recovery.* Oakland, CA: New Harbinger.

McCarren, A. (2009). A laid-off journalist charts a new course via social media. *Nieman Reports*, 63(4), 107–9.

McClain, L. C. (2006). "God's created order," gender complementarity, and the federal marriage amendment. *BYU Journal of Public Law*, 20(2), 313–43.

McEntire, T. (2006). Top 10 benefits of having children. Message posted on September 29, 2006, to http://parenting.families.com/blog/top-10-benefits-of-having-children

McMackin, E. (2010). Education is key to drawing retirees to communities. Message posted on September 9, 2010, to http://businessclimate.com/blog/2010/09/education-is-a-key-to-drawing-retirees-to-communities/

McMillan, B. (2012). Take the 2012 LIVESTRONG cancer survivor survey. Retrieved August 16, 2012, from http://blog.livestrong.org/2012/07/12/take-the-2012-livestrong-cancer-survivor-survey/

McVeigh, B. J. (2002). *Japanese Higher Education as Myth.* Armonk, NY: M.E. Sharpe.

Mead, W. R. (2012). The once & future liberalism. *The American Interest*, 7(4), 5–16.

Meade, R. & Singh, L. (1973). Motives for child-bearing in America and in India. *Journal of Cross-Cultural Psychology*, 4(1), 89–110.

Medina, J. (2010). *Brain Rules for Baby: How to Raise a Smart and Happy Child from Zero to Five.* Seattle, WA: Pear Press.

Melhem, N. M., Porta, G., Shamseddeen, W., Payne, M. W. & Brent, D. A. (2011). Grief in children and adolescents bereaved by sudden parental death. *Archives of General Psychiatry*, 68(9), 911–19.

Mellor, C. (2012). *Fun without Dick and Jane: A Guide to Your Delightfully Empty Nest.* San Francisco, CA: Chronicle Books.

Messina, J. (2007). Helping students cope with homesickness. *University Business*, 10(11), 80.

Meyer, C. (n.d.). What does the term "emotional divorce" mean? Retrieved September 26, 2012, from http://divorcesupport.about.com/od/copingandemotionalissue/f/emotionaldivorc.htm

Meyerhoff, M. (2006). How to adjust to a newborn. Retrieved June 15, 2012, from http://health.howstuffworks.com/pregnancy-and-parenting/pregnancy/postpartum-care/how-to-adjust-to-a-newborn.htm

Millea, H. (2010). Unbreaking my heart: Dealing with the death of a parent. Retrieved August 7, 2012, from http://www.elle.com/beauty/health-fit ness/unbreak-my-heart-dealing-the-death-of-a-parent-455093

Miller, A. J., Sassler, S. & Kusi-Appouh, D. (2011). The specter of divorce: Views from working- and middle-class cohabitors. *Family Relations*, 60(5), 602–16.

Milstead, D. (2012). As two-income family model matures, divorce rate falls. Retrieved September 5, 2012, from http://www.cnbc.com/id/46797203/ As_Two_Income_Family_Model_Matures_Divorce_Rate_Falls

Mitchell, B. A. & Lovegreen, L. D. (2009). The empty nest syndrome in midlife families: A multimethod exploration of parental gender differences and cultural dynamics. *Journal of Family Issues*, 30(12), 1651–70.

Moeller, P. (2011). How to protect yourself from bad break-ups. Retrieved September 14, 2012, from http://money.usnews.com/money/personal-finance/articles/2012/03/27/how-to-protect-yourself-from-bad-break-ups

Montemurro, B. (2003). Sex symbols: The bachelorette party as a window to change in women's sexual expression. *Sexuality & Culture*, 7(2), 3–29.

Montenegro, X. P. (2004). *The Divorce Experience: A Study of Divorce at Midlife and Beyond*. Washington, DC: AARP.

Moon, R. (2010). Be fruitful and multiply? Retrieved May 7, 2012, from http://www.christianitytoday.com/ct/2010/august/3.16.html

Moorjani, A. (2012). *Dying To Be Me: My Journey from Cancer, to Near Death, to True Healing*. Carlsbad, CA: Hay House.

Morrill, M. I., Hines, D. A., Mahmood, S. & Córdova, J. V. (2010). Pathways between marriage and parenting for wives and husbands: The role of coparenting. *Family Process*, 49(1), 59–73.

Most, C. & Wexler, R. (2008). Now what? Re-entering the workforce after divorce. Retrieved September 26, 2012, from http://www.cwmostlaw.com/CM/Articles/Now-What-Re-entering-the-Workforce-after-Divorce.asp

Mowder, B. A. (2005). Parent development theory: Understanding parents, parenting perceptions and parenting behaviors. *Journal of Early Childhood and Infant Psychology*, 1, 46–64.

Mrosko, T. (2010). Turn a job loss into an opportunity. Retrieved July 12, 2012, from http://www.cleveland.com/employment/plaindealer/index. ssf/2010/05/turn_a_job_loss_into_an_opportunity.html

Murphy, R. (n.d.). Top 10: Hidden benefits of having children. Retrieved May 15, 2012, from http://www.askmen.com/top_10/entertainment/top-10-hidden-benefits-of-having-children_1.html

Myers, E. (1997). *When Parents Die: A Guide for Adults*. New York: Penguin.

Myers, L. & Austin, M. (2010). Edwards admits fathering child with mistress. Retrieved September 24, 2010, from http://today.msnbc.msn.com/ id/34963767/ns/today-today_news/t/edwards-admits-fathering-child-mis tress/#.UGBt4rJlQf4

Myles, R. C. (2007). *The Next Generation of Dads: A Book about Fathers, Mentors and Male Role Models*. Parker, CO: Thornton Publishing.

Nelson, J. & Bolles, R. (2007). *What Color is Your Parachute? Planning Now for the Life You Want*. Berkeley, CA: Ten Speed Press.

New Oxford Review (2012). The future of marriage in America. *New Oxford Review*, 79(3), 12–14.

Newbold, S. P. (2010). An extraordinary administrative legacy: Thomas Jefferson's role in transforming higher education curriculum in the United States. *Public Voices*, 11(2), 15–25.

Newman, J. (2012). The unbridled shower: Celebrating divorce. Retrieved November 13, 2012, from http://www.nytimes.com/2012/09/16/fashion/the-unbridled-shower-celebrating-divorce-not-with-a-whimper-but-a-bang.html?pagewanted=all&_r=0

Newman, K. S. (1999). *Falling from Grace: Downward Mobility in the Age of Affluence*. Berkeley, CA: University of California Press.

Newman, K. S. (2009). What to do when you lose your job: Stop blaming yourself. Retrieved June 29, 2012, from http://roomfordebate.blogs.nytimes.com/2009/03/05/what-to-do-when-you-lose-your-job/

Newton, C. R., Hearn, M. T., Yuzpe, A. A. & Houle, M. (1992). Motives for parenthood and response to failed *in vitro* fertilization. *Journal of Assisted Reproduction & Genetics*, 9(1), 24–31.

Norris, F. (2010). When being out of work becomes a chronic condition. Retrieved July 14, 2012, from http://www.nytimes.com/2010/07/17/business/17charts.html

Northrup, C. (2012). *The Wisdom of Menopause: Creating Physical and Emotional Health during the Change*. New York: Random House.

O'Brien, J. (2011). *Choose to Live: Our Journey from Late Stage Cancers to Vibrant Health*. New York: Expert Academy Press.

O'Connell, M. & Feliz, S. (2011). *Same-Sex Couple Household Statistics from the 2010 Census* (SEHSB Working Paper No. 2001–26). Unpublished manuscript.

O'Donnell, J. T. (2012). Layoff advice: 4 steps to take right after the axe falls. Retrieved July 9, 2012, from http://jobs.aol.com/articles/2012/06/01/4-immediate-steps-for-layoff-victims/

Olds, J. & Schwartz, R. (2009). *The Lonely American: Drifting Apart in the Twenty-First Century*. Boston, MA: Beacon Press.

Olmstead, S. B., Futris, T. G. & Pasley, K. (2009). An exploration of married and divorced, nonresident men's perceptions and organization of their father role identity. *Fathering*, 7(3), 249–68.

Orenstein, P. (2000). *Flux: Women on Sex, Work, Kids, Love and Life in a Half-Changed World*. New York: Doubleday.

Organization for Economic Co-operation and Development (2011). *OECD Factbook* 2011. Paris: Organization for Economic Co-operation and Development.

Osteen, J. (2011). Valuing each child. Retrieved May 7, 2012, from http://www.joelosteen.com/HopeForToday/ThoughtsOn/Family/ValuingEachChild/Pages/ValuingEachChild.aspx

Oswald, R. F. (2000). A member of the wedding? Heterosexism and family ritual. *Journal of Social & Personal Relationships,* 17(3), 349–68.

Page, S. (2002). *If I Am So Wonderful, Why Am I Still Single?* New York: Three Rivers Press.

Parade, S. H., Leerkes, E. M. & Blankson, A. N. (2010). Attachment to parents, social anxiety, and close relationships of female students over the transition to college. *Journal of Youth & Adolescence,* 39(2), 127–37.

Parent, L. (2011). When job loss leads to depression. Retrieved July 15, 2012, from   http://www.everydayhealth.com/depression/job-loss-and-depression.aspx

Park, K. (2002). Stigma management among the voluntary childless. *Sociological Perspectives,* 45(1), 21–45.

Paul, M. (2011). Parents, what kind of role model are you? Message posted on July 18, 2011, to http://www.huffingtonpost.com/margaret-paul-phd/parents-what-kind-of-role_b_901672.html

Paul, P. (2008). Million-dollar babies. Retrieved July 12, 2012, from http://www.time.com/time/nation/article/0,8599,1726386,00.html

Payne, J. W. (2006). Forever pregnant. Retrieved June 1, 2012, from http://www.washingtonpost.com/wp-dyn/content/article/2006/05/15/AR2006051500875.html

Pearcey, M. (2005). Gay and bisexual married men's attitudes and experiences: Homophobia, reasons for marriage, and self-identity. *Journal of GLBT Family Studies,* 1(4), 21–42.

Pecorino, L. (2011). *Why Millions Survive Cancer: The Successes of Science.* New York: Oxford University Press.

Pew Research Center (2010). *The Decline of Marriage and Rise of New Families.* Washington, DC: Pew Research Center.

Pierson, R. H. (1985). *Guide to Spanish Idioms: A Practical Guide to 2500 Spanish Idioms.* Lincolnwood, IL: Passport Books.

Pinsky, C. (2012). Deal with the emotions of job loss before new-job hunt. *Northern Colorado Business Report,* 17(19), 11–17.

Pope, A. (2005). Personal transformation in midlife orphanhood: An empirical phenomenological study. *Omega: Journal of Death & Dying,* 51(2), 107–23.

Potter, J. (2003). Discourse analysis. In M. Hardy & A. Bryman (eds.), *Handbook of Data Analysis* (pp. 607–24). London: Sage.

Quadagno, J., MacPherson, D., Keene, J. R. & Parham, L. (2001). Downsizing and the life course consequences of job loss: The effect of age and gender on employment and income security. In V. W. Marshall, W. R. Heinz, H. Krüger & A. Verma (eds.), *Restructuring Work and the Life Course* (pp. 303–18). Toronto: University of Toronto Press.

Rainey, B. & Yates, S. (2008). *Barbara & Susan's Guide to the Empty Nest: Discovering New Purpose, Passion & Your Next Great Adventure*. Little Rock, AR: Family Life.

Rando, T. A. (1991). *How to Go On Living When Someone You Love Dies*. New York: Bantam Books.

Ratnarajah, D. & Schofield, M. J. (2007). Parental suicide and its aftermath: A review. *Journal of Family Studies*, 13(1), 78–93.

Rechis, R. & Boerner, L. (2010). *How Cancer Has Affected Post-Treatment Survivors: A Livestrong Report*. LIVESTRONG. Retrieved May 12, 2013, from http://livestrong.org/pdfs/3-0/LSSurvivorSurveyReport

Rhodes, K. (2011). Where change begins: Wake-up call (part 2). Retrieved July 12, 2012, from http://cbaclelegalconnection.com/2011/12/where-change-begins-wake-up-call-part-2/

Rich, P., Copans, S. & Copans, K. G. (1999). *The Healing Journey through Job Loss: Your Journal for Reflection and Revitalization*. New York: John Wiley & Sons.

Riley, D. (2001). Fathers caring for their children. *Child Care Connections*, 10(1), 1–2.

Riley, G. (1991). *Divorce: An American Tradition*. New York: Oxford University Press.

Ritzer, G. (1996). *The McDonaldization of Society: An Investigation into the Changing Character of Contemporary Social Life*. Thousand Oaks, CA: Pine Forge Press.

Rosenblatt, C. L. (2010). *The Boomer's Guide to Aging Parents: The Complete Guide*. San Rafael, CA: AgingParents.com.

Rosenblatt, P. C. & Barner, J. R. (2006). The dance of closeness-distance in couple relationships after the death of a parent. *Omega: Journal of Death & Dying*, 53(4), 277–93.

Rosenthal, C. J. & Marshall, V. W. (1988). Generational transmission of family ritual. *American Behavioral Scientist*, 31(6), 669–84.

Ross, J., Godeau, E. & Dias, S. (2004). Sexual health. In C. Currie, C. Roberts, A. Morgan, R. Smith, W. Settertobulte, O. Samdal & V. B. Ramsussen (eds.), *Health Behaviour in School-Aged Children (HBSC) Study: International Report from the 2001/2002 Survey* (pp. 153–60). Copenhagen, Denmark: World Health Organization.

Rostila, M. & Saarela, J. M. (2011). Time does not heal all wounds: Mortality following the death of a parent. *Journal of Marriage & Family*, 73(1), 236–49.

Rumberger, R. W., Ghatak, R., Poulos, G., Ritter, P. L. & Dornbusch, S. M. (1990). Family influences on dropout behavior in one California high school. *Sociology of Education*, 63(4), 283–99.

Russell, J. C. (2011). The use of narratives to contextualize the experiences and needs of unemployed, underemployed, and displaced workers. *Journal of Employment Counseling*, 48(2), 50–62.

Rutherford, B. (2007). *Phased Retirement: Transitioning from Employment to Retirement*. Amazon Kindle.

Safer, J. (2008). *Death Benefits: How Losing a Parent Can Change an Adult's Life – For the Better*. New York: Basic Books.

Saint-Paul, G. (1997). The rise and persistence of rigidities. *American Economic Review*, 87(2), 290–4.

Salpeter, M. (2011). *Social Networking for Career Success: Using Online Tools to Create a Personal Brand*. New York: LearningExpress.

Sandfield, A. (2006). Talking divorce: The role of divorce in women's constructions of relationship status. *Feminism & Psychology*, 16(2), 155–73.

Savage, M. (2003). *You're On Your Own (But I'm Here If You Need Me): Mentoring Your Child during the College Years*. New York: Fireside.

Schaefer, J. (2009). *Goodbye Ed, Hello Me: Recover from Your Eating Disorder and Fall in Love with Life*. New York: McGraw-Hill.

Schafer, M. H. (2009). Parental death and subjective age: Indelible imprints from early in the life course? *Sociological Inquiry*, 79(1), 75–97.

Scherger, S. (2009). Social change and the timing of family transitions in West Germany: Evidence from cohort comparisons. *Time & Society*, 18(1), 106–29.

Scheuble, L. & Johnson, D. (2005). Married women's situational use of last names: An empirical study. *Sex Roles*, 53(1), 143–51.

Schlessinger, L. (2009). *In Praise of Stay-At-Home Moms*. New York: HarperCollins.

Schlossberg, N. (2003). *Retire Smart, Retire Happy: Finding Your True Path in Life*. Amazon Kindle: American Psychological Association.

Schlozman, S. C. (2003). The pain of losing a parent. *Educational Leadership*, 60, 91–2.

Schneider, D. (2011). Wealth and the marital divide. *American Journal of Sociology*, 117(2), 627–67.

Schooling, C. M., Jiang, C., Lam, T. H., Zhang, W., Cheng, K. K. & Leung, G. M. (2011). Parental death during childhood and adult cardiovascular risk in a developing country: The Guangzhou biobank cohort study. *PLOS ONE*, 6(5), 1–8.

Schreiber, L. A. (2004). When a parent dies. Retrieved May 12, 2013, from http://www.oprah.com/spirit/When-a-Parent-Dies-Dealing-with-the-Death-of-a-Parent/8

Schuurman, D. (2003). *Never the Same: Coming to Terms with the Death of a Parent*. New York: St. Martin's Press.

Schwartz, P. (1995). *Love between Equals: How Peer Marriage Really Works*. New York: Free Press.

Scott, E. K., London, A. S. & Gross, G. (2007). "I try not to depend on anyone but me": Welfare-reliant women's perspectives on self-sufficiency, work, and marriage. *Sociological Inquiry*, 77(4), 601–25.

Sears, R. W. & Sears, J. M. (2006). *Father's First Steps: 25 Things Every Dad Should Know.* Boston, MA: The Harvard Common Press.

Sekse, R. J. T., Raaheim, M., Blaaka, G. & Gjengedal, E. (2009). Cancer as a life-changing process: Women's experiences five years after treatment for gynaecological cancer. *International Journal of Qualitative Studies on Health & Well-being,* 4(4), 288–98.

Sellers, B. (2010). I lost my job last Friday. Message posted on December 7, 2010, to http://www.huffingtonpost.com/bob-sellers/i-lost-my-job-last-friday_b_793552.html

Settersten, R. A. & Cancel-Tirado, D. (2010). Fatherhood as a hidden variable in men's development and life courses. *Research in Human Development,* 7(2), 83–102.

Settersten, R. A. & Trauten, M. E. (2009). The new terrain of old age: Hallmarks, freedoms, and risks. In V. L. Bengtson, D. Gans, N. Putney & M. Silverstein (eds.), *Handbook of Theories of Aging* (pp. 455–69). New York: Springer.

Shahid, S. & Thompson, S. C. (2009). An overview of cancer and beliefs about the disease in indigenous people of Australia, Canada, New Zealand and the US. *Australian & New Zealand Journal of Public Health,* 33(2), 109–18.

Shaiken, H. (2009). What to do when you lose your job: Get the government to help. Retrieved June 29, 2012, from http://roomfordebate.blogs.nytimes.com/2009/03/05/what-to-do-when-you-lose-your-job/

Sherman, E. A. (1987). *Meaning in Mid-Life Transitions.* Albany, NY: State University of New York Press.

Shira, D. (2012). Jay-Z: Blue Ivy Carter will probably be the "worst, spoiled little kid ever." Retrieved May 9, 2012, from http://www.people.com/people/article/0,,20593271,00.html

Shrestha, L. (2006). *Life Expectancy in the United States* (CRS Report for Congress No. RL32792).

Shukert, R. (2008). When did "married without children" become gauche? Retrieved May 17, 2012, from http://www.thedailybeast.com/articles/2008/11/15/to-hell-with-junior.html

Sidner, S. (2012). Indian father accused of killing baby "for being a girl." Retrieved June 21, 2012, from http://www.cnn.com/2012/06/14/world/asia/india-female-infanticide/index.html

Silver, J. K. (2006). *After Cancer Treatment: Heal Faster, Better, Stronger.* Baltimore, MD: Johns Hopkins University Press.

Silver, N. (2012). *The Signal and the Noise: Why So Many Predictions Fail – But Some Don't.* New York: Penguin.

Silverman, P. R. (2010). Raising grieving children: How children can survive the death of a loved one. Retrieved October 18, 2012, from http://www.psychologytoday.com/blog/raising-grieving-children/201008/what-is-lost-when-parent-dies

Simons, R. L., Beaman, J., Conger, R. D. & Chao, W. (1993). Childhood experience, conceptions of parenting, and attitudes of spouse as determinants of parental behavior. *Journal of Marriage and the Family*, 55(1), 91–106.

Simring, S. & Simring, S. K. (2001). *Making Marriage Work for Dummies*. New York: Hungry Minds.

Singer, A. (2011). *Creating Your Perfect Family Size: How to Make an Informed Decision about Having a Baby*. San Francisco, CA: Jossey-Bass.

Slaughter, A. (2012). Why women still can't have it all. Retrieved August 11, 2012, from http://www.theatlantic.com/magazine/archive/2012/07/why-women-still-cant-have-it-all/309020/

Smith, A. (2009). Layoffs in Europe: Deal or no deal? *HR Magazine*, 54(1), 71–3.

Smith, M. B. (2000). *Should I Get Married?* Downers Grove, IL: InterVarsity Press.

Smith, W. L. & Zhang, P. (2008). Perceived factors facilitating students' transition from high school to college. *Michigan Sociological Review*, 22, 19–40.

Snyder, K. A. & Pearse, W. (2010). Crisis, social support, and the family response: Exploring the narratives of young breast cancer survivors. *Journal of Psychosocial Oncology*, 28(4), 413–31.

Spearman, J. & Murphy, J. (2007). Most unwanted pregnancies occur to women age 20–29: National campaign announces expanded mission to tackle this problem. Retrieved May 4, 2012, from http://www.thenational-campaign.org/press/press-release.aspx?releaseID=8

Springer, S. H. (2012). *Marriage, for Equals: The Successful Joint (Ad)Ventures of Well-Educated Couples*. Indianapolis, IN: Dog Ear Publishing.

Srivastava, S., Tamir, M., McGonigal, K. M., John, O. P. & Gross, J. J. (2009). The social costs of emotional suppression: A prospective study of the transition to college. *Journal of Personality & Social Psychology*, 96(4), 883–97.

Stamm, J. (2008). *Bright from the Start: The Simple, Science-Backed Way to Nurture Your Child's Developing Mind from Birth to Age 3*. New York: Penguin.

Stamp, G. H. & Banski, M. A. (1992). The communicative management of constrained autonomy during the transition to parenthood. *Western Journal of Communication*, 56(3), 281–300.

Stelter, B. (2009). In 2009, layoffs is the business to be in. Retrieved July 9, 2012, from http://www.nytimes.com/2009/01/21/business/21layoffs.html?_r=1

Stewart, W. (2004). The role of perceived loneliness and isolation in the relapse from recovery in patients with anorexia and bulimia nervosa. *Clinical Social Work Journal*, 32(2), 185–96.

Straits, D. (2009). Emotional stages of a job loss. Retrieved July 14, 2012, from http://www.theladders.com/career-advice/emotional-stages-job-loss

Stroebe, M. S., Hansson, R. O., Stroebe, W. & Schut, H. (eds.) (2001).

Handbook of Bereavement Research: Consequences, Coping, and Care. Washington, DC: American Psychological Association.

Swidler, A. (2001). *Talk of Love: How Culture Matters.* Chicago, IL: University of Chicago Press.

Syed, M. & Azmitia, M. (2009). Longitudinal trajectories of ethnic identity during the college years. *Journal of Research on Adolescence,* 19(4), 601–24.

Syrtash, A. (Ed.). (2006). *How to Survive the Real World: Life after College Graduation.* Atlanta, GA: Hundreds of Heads Books.

Takagi, E. & Silverstein, M. (2008). Intergenerational coresidence of older adults and married children in Japan: Accommodations of needs, culture, and power. Conference Paper – American Sociological Association, Boston, MA.

Taylor, P. (2011). 5 common retirement misconceptions. Retrieved December 10, 2012, from http://money.usnews.com/money/blogs/On-Retirement/2011/12/30/5-common-retirement-misconceptions

Taylor, P., Funk, C. & Clark, A. (2007). *Generation Gap in Values, Behaviors: As Marriage and Parenthood Drift Apart, Public is Concerned about Social Impact.* Washington, DC: Pew Research Center.

Taylor, P., Parker, K., Fry, R., Cohn, D., Wang, W., Velasco, G. & Dockterman, D. (2011). *Is College Worth It? College Presidents, Public Assess Value, Quality and Mission of Higher Education.* Washington, DC: Pew Research Center.

Teeley, P. & Bashe, P. (2005). *The Complete Cancer Survival Guide: Everything You Must Know and Where to Go for State-of-the-Art Treatment of the 25 Most Common Forms of Cancer.* New York: Broadway Books.

Testa, M. R. (2006). *Childbearing Preferences and Family Issues in Europe.* Vienna Institute of Demography, Austrian Academy of Sciences: Eurobarometer.

The National Cancer Institute (2010). *Facing Forward: Life after Cancer Treatment* (No. 10). Bethesda, MD: National Cancer Institute.

The Transition Network, Rentsch, G. & Sherr, L. (2008). *Smart Women Don't Retire – They Break Free: From Working Full-Time to Living Full-Time.* New York: Springboard Press.

Time (2007). The state of divorce: You may be surprised. *Time,* 169, 16.

Tinto, V. (1987). *Leaving College: Rethinking the Causes and Cures of Student Attrition.* Chicago, IL: University of Chicago Press.

Tinto, V. (1988). Stages of student departure: Reflections on the longitudinal character of student leaving. *Journal of Higher Education,* 59(4), 438–55.

Tocqueville, A. de (2010). In Heffner R. D. & Gregorian V. (eds.), *Democracy in America.* New York: Signet Classics.

Tognoli, J. (2003). Leaving home: Homesickness, place attachment, and transition among residential college students. *Journal of College Student Psychotherapy,* 18(1), 35–48.

Torr, B. M. (2011). The changing relationship between education and marriage in the United States, 1940–2000. *Journal of Family History,* 36(4), 483–503.

Trail, T. E. & Karney, B. R. (2012). What's (not) wrong with low-income marriages. *Journal of Marriage & Family,* 74(3), 413–27.

Tugend, A. (2011). Fears, and opportunities, on the road to retirement. Retrieved November 27, 2012, from http://www.nytimes.com/2011/06/04/ your-money/04shortcuts.html?pagewanted=all&_r=1&

Turley, R. (2006). When parents want children to stay home for college. *Research in Higher Education,* 47(7), 823–46.

Uchitelle, L. & Leonhardt, D. (2006). Men not working, and not wanting just any job. Retrieved July 9, 2012, from http://www.nytimes.com/2006/07/31/ business/31men.html?_r=1&pagewanted=1&ei=5088&en=08d251c4a143 ae84&ex=1311998400&partner=rssnyt&emc=rss

Umberson, D. (2003). *Death of a Parent: Transition to a New Adult Identity.* New York: Cambridge University Press.

United Nations (2010). *The World's Women* 2010: *Trends and Statistics.* New York: United Nations.

Valeo, T. (2012). On the death of my father: How one son coped with his father's illness and death. Retrieved October 13, 2012, from http://men. webmd.com/features/death-my-father

Van der Wende, M. (2011). The emergence of liberal arts and sciences education in Europe: A comparative perspective. *Higher Education Policy,* 24(2), 233–53.

Van Schalkwyk, G. (2005). Explorations of post-divorce experiences: Women's reconstructions of self. *Australian & New Zealand Journal of Family Therapy,* 26(2), 90–7.

Van Wyden, G. (n.d.). What to do after a parent's death. Retrieved October 18, 2012, from http://www.ehow.com/way_5501797_do-after-parents-death.html

Vedder, R. (2010). Why did 17 million Americans go to college? Message posted on October 20, 2010, to http://chronicle.com/blogs/innovations/ why-did-17-million-students-go-to-college/27634

Ventura, S. J. (2009). *Changing Patterns of Nonmarital Childbearing in the United States* (No. 18). Hyattsville, MD: National Center for Health Statistics.

Villar, E. & Albertin, P. (2010). "It is who knows you". The positions of university students regarding intentional investment in social capital. *Studies in Higher Education,* 35(2), 137–54.

Waehler, C. A. (1996). *Bachelors: The Psychology of Men who Haven't Married.* Westport, CT: Praeger.

Waite, L. J. (2000). The family as a social organization: Key ideas for the twenty-first century. *Contemporary Sociology,* 29(3), 463–9.

Waite, L. J. & Gallagher, M. (2001). *The Case for Marriage: Why Married*

People are Happier, Healthier, and Better Off Financially. New York: Broadway Books.

Waldrop, S. (2007). Pursuing lifetime dreams in retirement. Retrieved November 28, 2012, from http://www.bankrate.com/finance/retirement/pursuing-lifetime-dreams-in-retirement-2.aspx

Wallace, C. (2004). *All Dressed in White: The Irresistible Rise of the American Wedding*. New York: Penguin Books.

Wallerstein, J. S. & Blakeslee, S. (1994). *Second Chances: Men, Women, and Children a Decade after Divorce*. New York: Houghton Mifflin.

Wallerstein, J. S., Lewis, J. & Blakeslee, S. (2000). *The Unexpected Legacy of Divorce: A 25 Year Landmark Study*. New York: Hyperion.

Wang, W. (2012). *The Rise of Intermarriage: Rates, Characteristics Vary by Race and Gender*. Washington, DC: Pew Research Center.

Warburg, M. (2008). Dannebrog: Waving in and out of Danish civil religion. *Nordic Journal of Religion and Society*, 21(2), 165–84.

Waxman, B. (2010). *How to Love Your Retirement: The Guide to the Best of Your Life*. Atlanta, GA: Hundreds of Heads Books.

Weber, M. (1978). *Economy and Society: An Outline of Interpretive Sociology*. Berkeley, CA: University of California Press.

Wegscheider-Cruse, S. (1993). *Life after Divorce: Create a New Beginning*. Deerfield Beach, FL: Health Communications.

Weitzman, L. J. (1985). *The Divorce Revolution: The Unexpected Social and Economic Consequences for Women and Children in America*. New York: Free Press.

Whelan, C. B. (2008). Marrying tradition and modernity. *Wall Street Journal – Eastern Edition*, 251(43), W11.

Whitehead, B. D. (1996). *The Divorce Culture*. New York: Alfred Knopf.

Wilcox, W. B. & Marquardt, E. (2011). *The State of Our Unions: When Baby Makes Three – How Parenthood Makes Life Meaningful and How Marriage Makes Parenthood Bearable*. Charlottesville, VA: The National Marriage Project.

Williams, J. (2012). What will your identity be when you retire? Message posted on April 10, 2012, to http://blog.welcomingretirement.com/identity-retire/

Winerip, M. (2011). Teacher, my dad lost his job. Do we have to move? Retrieved July 17, 2012, from http://www.nytimes.com/2011/01/31/education/31winerip.html?_r=1&pagewanted=all

Wisenberg, D. (2012). US retirement trails other nations. Retrieved December 4, 2012, from http://money.msn.com/retirement-plan/us-retirement-trails-other-nations-cnbc.aspx

Wolfelt, A. & Duvall, K. J. (2010). *Healing after Job Loss: 100 Practical Ideas*. Fort Collins, CO: Companion Press.

Wright, H. N. (2004). *101 Questions to Ask Before You Get Engaged*. Eugene, OR: Harvest House.

Wright, S. (2008). Child-free couples: Thriving without kids. Retrieved May 17, 2012, from http://www.webmd.com/sex-relationships/features/child-free-couples-thriving-without-kids

Xiao, H. F. (2010). "Love is a capacity": The narrative of gendered self-development in Chinese-style divorce. *Journal of Contemporary China*, 19(66), 735–53.

Zakaria, F. (2009). The rise of the right. *Newsweek*, 154(20), 20.

Zappert, L. (2001). *Getting it Right: How Working Mothers Successfully Take Up the Challenge of Life, Family, and Career.* New York: Touchstone.

Zaslow, J. (2010). Families with a missing piece: A new look at how parent's early death can reverberate decades later. Retrieved August 7, 2012, from http://online.wsj.com/article/SB10001424052748704875604575280400596257236.html.html

Zawodny, K. (2012). Phased retirement. Message posted on September 25, 2012, to http://www.opm.gov/Blogs/Retire/2012/9/25/Phased-Retirement/

Zelinski, E. (2009). *How to Retire Happy, Wild, and Free: Retirement Wisdom that You Won't Get from Your Financial Advisor.* Lanham, MD: Visions International Publishing.

Zhao, E. (2010). Fewer Americans see college as good investment. Message posted on July 23, 2010, to http://blogs.wsj.com/economics/2010/07/23/fewer-americans-see-college-as-good-investment/

Zinser, L. (2010). Woods divorce becomes final. Retrieved July 22, 2012, from http://www.nytimes.com/2010/08/24/sports/golf/24woods.html

Zuckerman, M. (2011). Why the jobs situation is worse than it looks. Retrieved June 6, 2012, from http://www.usnews.com/opinion/mzuckerman/articles/2011/06/20/why-the-jobs-situation-is-worse-than-it-looks

Index